Relevance of Ambedkarism in India

Relevance of Ambedkarism in India

SECOND EDITION

Edited by
K.S. Chalam

RAWAT PUBLICATIONS
Jaipur • New Delhi • Bangalore • Guwahati • Kolkata

ISBN 978-81-316-0956-9

First edition, 1993
Second edition, 2018

Published by
Prem Rawat for **Rawat Publications**
Satyam Apts., Sector 3, Jawahar Nagar, Jaipur 302 004 (India)
Phone: 0141 265 1748 / 7006 Fax: 0141 265 1748
E-mail: info@rawatbooks.com
Website: www.rawatbooks.com

New Delhi Office
4858/24, Ansari Road, Daryaganj, New Delhi 110 002
Phone: 011-23263290

Also at *Bangalore, Guwahati* and *Kolkata*

Typeset by Rawat Computers, Jaipur
Printed at Chaman Enterprises, New Delhi

Contents

Preface to the Second Edition 9

Acknowledgements 11

The Contributors 13

Introduction 15

1 The Relevance of Ambedkarism in India Today 21
M. Gopala Krishna Reddy

Part I
Ambedkar as Philosopher and Theoretician

2 Philosophy of Ambedkar: Some Observations 27
S.G. Kulkarni

3 Ambedkar as a Philosopher and a Theoretician: An Evaluation 35
A.M. Rajasekhariah

4 The Post-Ambedkar Indian Experience 46
K. Wilson

5 Ambedkar and Marxism: A Critical Examination of the Case for Synthesis 51
Sharad Patil

6 The Buddhist Ambedkar 66
B.V.S. Bhanusree

7 Buddhism, Secularism and Ambedkar 75
K.N. Kadam

8 Democratisation of Higher Education in India: Ambedkar's Vision 90
K.S. Chalam

9 Educational Philosophy of Ambedkar 109
K.P. Subba Rao

10 Ambedkar's Life: A Search for Social Justice 114
P. George Victor

11 The Socio-Political Philosophy of Ambedkar 122
T. Krishna Kanth

12 Ambedkar as a Theoretician and Policy-Maker 128
G. Saibaba

Part II
Socio-Economic Ideas of Ambedkar and their Relevance

13 Development Philosophy of Dr B.R. Ambedkar 137
K.S. Chalam

14 Socio-Economic Ideas of Ambedkar and their Relevance 150
S.K. Sarkar

15 Ambedkar on Economic Development and Social Justice 161
G. Nancharaiah

16 Ambedkar's Views on Small Holdings in India 170
C. Sivarama Krishna Rao

17 Ambedkar and Democratic Socialism in India 175
K.S. Chalam

18 Caste and Patriarchy: Ambedkar's Insight into the Status of Indian Women 181
M. Nalini

19 Ambedkar's Views on the Indian Caste System 191
V. Subrahamanyam

Part III
Ambedkar as Constitution-maker and Institutions Breaker

20 Ambedkar: A Creative Iconoclast — 199
V.R. Krishna Iyer

21 Ambedkar: An Architect of Indian Constitution — 209
Rega Jaganmohana Rao

22 Sixty-Five Years of Indian Constitution: A Prolegomenon of Social Justice — 222
K.S. Chalam

23 Ambedkar's Contribution to the Demolition of Tradition in India — 232
K.S. Chalam

24 Practicability of Ambedkar's Views on Annihilation of Caste — 239
K.E. Rajpramukh

25 Sudras in the *Vedas*: A Critical Exposition by Ambedkar — 245
R.K. Chauhan

Part IV
Perspectives of Research on Ambedkar

26 Perspectives of Research on Ambedkar's Socio-Economic Philosophy — 255
A. Somasekhar

27 Post-Ambedkar Scheduled Castes Agitations in Andhra Pradesh: A Critical Evaluation — 265
K.S. Chalam

Bibliography — 280

Index — 287

Preface to the Second Edition

It is heartening to note that the second edition of the book is now in your hands. The book was an outcome of a seminar that I had organised in 1992 at Andhra University, Visakhapatnam, on the occasion of Babasaheb Ambedkar's centenary. The book was received by the public with great enthusiasm as no title under 'Ambedkarism' was available at that time. It was even considered as one of the 100 bestselling books. There has been a demand for a second edition of the book for quite some time. Apart from running out of stock with the publisher, the contents of the book are considered as more relevant today than before. While making a proposal for the seminar, I had posed the question, what constitutes Ambedkarism? The contributors to the volume, who had participated in person and made presentations in the deliberations, (except one or two) revised their papers based on the discussions. They have answered the above question enabling us to establish what 'Ambedkarism' stands for.

The major part of the book consists of the papers that have tried to establish Ambedkar as a philosopher and a theoretician. The authors, some of them reputed scholars, have established that Ambedkar as an ideologue had tried to answer and accommodate established ideologies like Marxism, Buddhism, Socialism, etc. in his crusade against fundamentalism. Sharad Patil, Krishna Iyer, Rajasekhariah, K.S. Chalam, S.K. Sarkar, K.N. Kadam, S.G. Kulkarni and others have addressed issues like, whether Ambedkar can be considered as a secularist? What are the important elements in Ambedkarism that constitute the Dalit enlightenment project? Whether Ambedkar is relevant today as a creative iconoclast? What are the Hindu institutions that Ambedkar wanted to demolish? What is the significance of Ambedkar's faith in parliamentary democracy in the post-cold war era? What is the impact of Ambedkarism on post-Ambedkar social movements? Some of these questions are answered by the writers in their respective papers making the book unique. There are several scholarly writings in the post-Ambedkar centenary years, mostly written by western scholars. It is observed in these writings that the scholars have tried to establish Ambedkar as a Dalit idol and relate it with the Dalit identity struggles for upliftment. Some of the studies analysed the Dalit movements with backdrop of Ambedkar as a leader. But, Ambedkar is increasingly going beyond this image as events in India and abroad are unfolding one after the other. The fall of Soviet Union, the death of ideology in the people's movements, the increasing reliance on democratic values, the unrest that engulfs human beings despite increase in the rates of economic growth etc. are making Ambedkar a universal icon. For, he has addressed these very issues in his writings as an intellectual of the 20th century. The papers in the book have addressed some of these important questions that are re-emerging in recent times making his vision as a theoretician and pragmatist to riposte. Perhaps that makes the book relevant once again after a gap of around 25 years. Some of the contributors left the mortal world. Therefore, we have not attempted to get the papers revised instead added some of my papers that specifies Ambedkar's development vision. I have also added a published research paper to provide a clue that how Ambedkarism remains relevant for scholars to reflect in social sciences research.

I am grateful to the innumerable admirers and followers of Ambedkar who have been encouraging us in all these years. Pranit Rawat has come forward to get the second edition published at a short notice.

Hyderabad **K.S. Chalam**

Acknowledgements

The anthology on 'The Relevance of Ambedkarism in India Today' is a selection of papers submitted at the seminar held at Academic Staff College, Andhra University, Visakhapatnam, during 26–27 September 1992. The seminar was sponsored by the Social Welfare Department, Government of Andhra Pradesh, Hyderabad. A number of academicians have participated in the deliberations of the seminar, making it a serious exercise. Prof. K. Venkateswarlu, Department of Politics and Public Administration, Andhra University; Prof. S.K. Sarkar, former Vice-Chancellor, Kalyani University; and Prof. R. Jaganmohana Rao, Principal, College of Law, Andhra University, have acted as section presidents of the seminar. Prof. Gopal Guru, Sri Sharad Patil, Dr Kancha Ilaiah, Dr K. Srinivasulu, Dr A. Bobbili, Dr G. Anjaneyulu, and Sri A.C. Das, M.P., have extended their support in making the seminar a memorable event.

I am grateful to the following who have provided me with necessary help in conducting the seminar: Sri K. Madhavara Rao, Principal Secretary, Finance & Planning, Government of Andhra Pradesh; Sri P. Kamaleswara Rao, Commissioner of Social Welfare, Government of Andhra Pradesh; and Sri K. Pradeep Chandra, District Collector, Visakhapatnam.

My colleagues Dr M. Ramesh Babu, Dr D. Pulla Rao and our office staff R. Dayanand, Ch. V.S. Patrudu, N.V.N. Sarma and D. Viswanadham have worked hard in the preparation of the final draft of the book for print. I am grateful to all of them.

K.S. Chalam

The Contributors

A. Somasekhar, former Director, Department of Social Welfare, Government of Andhra Pradesh, Hyderabad.

A.M. Rajasekhariah, former Professor of Political Science, Karnataka University, Dharwad.

B.V.S. Bhanusree, former Professor, Department of Philosophy, Andhra University, Visakhapatnam.

C. Sivarama Krishna Rao, former Professor of Economics, Kakatiya University, Warangal.

G. Nancharaiah, former Professor of Economics, University of Hyderabad.

G. Saibaba, former Professor of Economics, S.V. University P.G. Centre, Kurnool.

K. Wilson, former Professor of Philosophy, Osmania University, Hyderabad.

K.E. Rajpramukh, former Professor of Anthropology, Andhra University, Visakhapatnam.

K.N. Kadam, author on Babasaheb Ambedkar, comes from Pune and his family was closely associated with Dr B.R. Ambedkar.

K.P. Subba Rao, former Professor of Education, Andhra University, Visakhapatnam.

K.S. Chalam, former Vice-Chancellor, Dravidian University, Kuppam; Director, Academic Staff College, Andhra University, Visakhapatnam; Ex-member, UPSC.

M. Gopala Krishna Reddy, former Vice-Chancellor, Andhra University, Visakhapatnam.

M. Nalini, Professor of Political Science, Andhra University, Visakhapatnam.

P. George Victor, former Professor of Philosophy, Andhra University, Visakhapatnam.

R.K. Chauhan, former Secretary, University Grants Commission, New Delhi.

Rega Jaganmohana Rao, former Principal, Dr B.R. Ambedkar Law College, Andhra University, Visakhapatnam.

S.G. Kulkarni, former Professor of Philosophy, University of Hyderabad, Hyderabad.

S.K. Sarkar, former Professor of Physics, Calcutta University and former Vice-Chancellor, Kalyani University, Calcutta.

Sharad Patil, Founder President of Satya Sodhak Communist Party, Dhule, Maharashtra.

T. Krishna Kanth, former Professor of Political Science, Kakatiya University, Warangal.

V. Subrahamanyam, former Professor of Anthropology, Andhra University, Visakhapatnam.

V.R. Krishna Iyer, formerly Judge, Supreme Court of India.

Introduction

The extended birth centenary of Babasaheb Dr B.R. Ambedkar has evoked interest not only among his followers, but also among the intellectual community in the country. But, the ritualistic way in which the centenary had been celebrated did not help in any meaningful way to consolidate or to strengthen the ideology, which Ambedkar had developed during his life time. A number of seminars and public meetings have been organised throughout the country either to please the followers or to satisfy the egos of the organisers. Those who have attended such seminars are of the opinion that the paper readers have neither read his published works carefully nor attempted to look into the Maharashtra government's colossus publications. An attempt is also being made to interpret him as a saviour of democracy built on capitalist principles. His writings are misinterpreted and new ideas are read in his radical and quite often traditional values of the Buddhist era. This does not mean that Ambedkar is without flaws. There are a number of contradictions that can be found in his writings and also in his personality. But those contradictions and flaws need to be understood in the context and also in the backdrop of the historical significance of his movement in this country. In fact,

Ambedkar has firmly believed in Buddhist dictum that nothing is permanent in the world, everything is in the process of change.

Ambedkar has a many-sided personality unlike most of his contemporaries. He is a well educated and cultured intellectual of high standards who has not only reflected on theoretical issues but also participated in mass movements and lead an onslaught against the inegalitarian society. He has accumulated unimaginable depths of knowledge in all fields of human society to become a real founder of an ideology. He has witnessed the greatest changes in human history during his lifetime and was a harbinger of that change in India. Though trained as a social scientist, he became a philosopher and a statesman by practice and vocation. Later in his life, he resigned himself to deep study and reflection, thereby producing priceless literature which is to be interpreted (now available as unpublished works) and analysed in the changed circumstances of our times.

A number of attempts are being made now by communal forces to deify him and ultimately make his ideology which he has assiduously built for the use of posterity as useless and irrelevant. This needs to be halted. An honest attempt is to be made to interpret him what he is and what he ought to have been in this country.

The major thrust of the papers is not on Ambedkar, but on Ambedkarism. Like many ideologies, Ambedkarism is also an ideology. Interestingly, the founder of the ideology is not Ambedkar but his guru Mahatma Jyoti Rao Phuley. Dr Ambedkar has developed this ideology to its logical perspective and has created an awareness among the masses and the intellectuals, that the caste and casteism are the real enemies of the people. When we are referring to Ambedkarism as an ideology, we must remember that it should possess a system of political, legal, cultural, social, and philosophical views and ideas that influence a whole group or national culture. In this context, the ideas of Phuley and Ambedkar, particularly the advanced and analytical ideas developed by Ambedkar through his writings and speeches do qualify for the term 'Ambedkarism'. The attributes of Ambedkarism are many, but the principle attribute is that it is an ideology that fights against hierarchically based socio-economic order. We have drawn these tentative attributes as a paradigm and invited serious deliberations at the seminar. Out of several themes that came to our mind, we found that the following three themes are important to establish a scientific ideology. These are: (1) Ambedkar as a philosopher and theoretician, (2) the socio-economic ideas of Ambedkar and their relevance, and (3) Ambedkar as the Constitution-maker and institutions breaker. We have selected these themes with a purpose. Unless Ambedkar is established as a philosopher and theoretician, it is difficult to sustain his ideology. Dr Ambedkar has written perhaps on all questions that were found relevant not only to his times but also to posterity. Therefore, he has extensively written on philosophical issues which have been later published as unpublished writings. As Dr Ambedkar himself has said that 'philosophy' is not a purely theoretic matter. It has practical potentialities. Philosophy has its roots in the problem of life and whatever theories philosophy propounds must return to society as instruments of re-constructing society. It is not enough to know. Those who know must endeavour to fulfil. This dialectical and pragmatic approach of Dr Ambedkar would definitely establish him as a theoretician.

The most important contribution of Dr Ambedkar to this ideology is his consistent and relentless struggle against the institution of caste. Several people have written on caste in India and abroad. But none of them has used it as a political weapon to fight against it. As a 'creative iconoclast', to use Justice Krishna Iyer's phrase, Dr Ambedkar has used some of his writings on caste as political weapons. Therefore, one need not to consider all his writings on caste as serious pieces of academic research. But, one very important service that Dr Ambedkar did to Indian society is his writings, speeches and also his struggles against the ideology of caste and thus saved the people who have been following the unilinear approach through the category of class. Had he not raised the issue at an intellectual and also at the level of practice, it might have dominated the oppressed classes fight against 'oppression' as an obscure movement without a solution or salvation.

Now Ambedkarism is being studied as a relevant ideology not only by his followers but even by his critics and Marxists to understand the real India. A number of new issues like nation, gender, race, tribe, caste and class are now being raised as contemporary problems. Further, caste is not a universal category of stratification in all regions of the country, it is to be considered in its economic context as caste has been considered by Hindus as property. It may not be out of place to cite Marx here who has made a distinction between property and possession to make out a clear difference between the western concept of property and oriental concept of possession or community ownership. In this context, caste is to be understood as property possessed by each caste group to further capitalise the property with opportunities of education, power, etc. which are now available to few castes. This is how one should look at the caste so as to overcome the vexed dichotomy of base and superstructure. Research in the area of stratification and differentiation in this country have struck around this dichotomy for over half a century as Marxist scholars were not willing to understand this reality. We kept this hypothesis here for discussion to analyse and resolve this problem in the context of Ambedkarism.

The economic ideas of Dr Ambedkar, particularly his writings on productivity of agriculture, modified version of state socialism, centre-state financial relations, etc. need to be examined in the light of his political and philosophical commitments to democracy.

Dr Ambedkar is now being popularised as the Constitution-maker but he is the one who has vociferously declared in the Constituent Assembly in 1948 that if the Constitution does not solve the contradictions in our socio-economic structure, those who suffer from inequality will blow up the structure of political democracy. At the same time, he is the one who has built educational institutions as a movement, used his position as chairman of the drafting committee of the Constitution to incorporate democratic and secular ideas and fought against the traditional institutions like caste. Therefore, it is a task before the academia now to analyse Dr Ambedkar and find out how he can be described as a creative destructor. Dr Ambedkar, as many people tend to believe, did not fight against untouchability. Thanks to Arjun Dangle, Dr Ambedkar in his historic 1927 Mahad speech which is now available in English, said that 'if we leave the caste system alone and adopt only the removal of untouchability as our policy, people will say that we have chosen a low aim … . If untouchability alone is removed, we may change from Ati-Sudras to Sudras; but can we say that this radically removes untouchability? ... If we want to remove untouchability in the home as well as outside, we must break down the prohibition against inter-marriage'.

There are several other issues like minority question, linguistic states, labour problems, industrial development, Hindu Code Bill, etc. which need to be examined in the light of the ideology of Ambedkarism to establish 'the two principles of one caste only and of equality'.

Apart from the objective of creating an intellectual forum, the following were the main objectives for which the seminar was organised:

1. To request specialists and scholars in different fields of study to work on a particular theme and present their views on Ambedkarism.
2. To project Ambedkar as a philosopher, theoretician and a social revolutionary by interpreting his writings and speeches in their totality.
3. To understand the relevance of his ideas in the contemporary society in general and with reference to the Indian situation in particular.
4. To identify issues for further study and continuous dialogue by building an intellectual task force on Ambedkarism.

The seminar which was organised at Andhra University, Visakhapatnam, from 26 to 27 September 1992, was attended by around 70 participants drawn from various parts of the country. There were 25 scholars and activists who have made their presentations in the broad themes identified above. I have added some of my recent papers to provide the current thinking on the subject. There are eleven papers in Section I, consisting of the philosophical and theoretical contributions of Ambedkar. It is well established that Ambedkar is a philosopher of par excellence and a socio-economic theory builder of indigenous nature. In Section II, the socio-economic ideas of Ambedkar and their practical significance are presented. The development philosophy of Ambedkar based on recent studies is included here. The relevance of these ideas are critically evaluated in the papers presented in this section. Apart from his philosophical and theoretical exercises, Dr Ambedkar had made historical contributions in the form of drafting the Indian Constitution. However, Dr Ambedkar did not spare any institution or tradition which was found to be an obstacle for the development of the Indian polity and society. Therefore, he was also discussed as the Constitution-maker and also as institutions breaker. In Section III, six papers relating to this area have been presented. The last section is on the identification of some issues and areas in Ambedkarism that examined the post-Ambedkar agitations and the possible areas of study in future.

On the whole, a comprehensive analysis on the contributions of Ambedkar to the socio-economic development of the country and the relevance of these ideas in the form of an ideology (Ambedkarism) has been made available in this book.

The present edition of the book with new material on the development vision of Dr B.R. Ambedkar, it is hoped, would throw open new areas of researches.

1

The Relevance of Ambedkarism in India Today

M. Gopala Krishna Reddy

I am very happy to associate myself with the national seminar on 'The Relevance of Ambedkarism in India Today' being organised by our Academic Staff College. We have celebrated the birth centenary of Babasaheb Ambedkar in our university in a befitting manner by renaming our Law College and also our P.G. Centre at Srikkakulam after his name. But the present seminar on Ambedkarism is a very important academic exercise which will bring out the real contributions of Ambedkar to emancipate the humanity in general and the depressed sections of society in particular.

The seminar is rightly called as the relevance of Ambedkarism because Ambedkarism as a movement has already taken roots in this country. But I do not claim any expertise in Ambedkarism as I am slowly acquainting myself with his writings now. As a student of economics, I learnt about Ambedkar as an economist who has done extensive work in public finance and particularly on the evolution of provincial finance in British India.

Extracts of presidential address delivered at the seminar.

Dr Ambedkar is the only Indian economist of the first quarter of this century who had obtained two PhD degrees in economics from two premier universities of the world. However, I am attracted by his philosophical writings. Dr Chalam has rightly chosen one theme in the seminar on Ambedkar as a philosopher and theoretician. Dr Ambedkar had gone through all the religious scriptures of our country and had ultimately come to the conclusion that Buddhism is the only religion which can bring salvation to humanity. He had also looked at the democratic principles of Buddhism and embraced it during his last days of his sojournity on earth. Among the many things which Dr Ambedkar claimed in favour of Buddhism is the one that it is an indigenous religion. I am told that a number of scholars are now working on his unpublished writings. More light is now found on his unpublished writings than the heat and dust that is created out of his published writings. Therefore, the seminar is really a fitting tribute to that great leader arranged at an appropriate time when all his writings are available now.

I am really attracted by his scholarship and perseverance with which he has examined the corpus of Hindu scriptures. I am of the opinion that Dr Ambedkar has critically examined Hindu religion to find out how deep is our religion and how sublime are our principles of life. In his 'Riddles in Hinduism', one can find his scholarship and erudition. He has almost gone through all the *Vedas*, *Smritis* and *Upanishads* ultimately to find out why the Hindu's social life is devoid of change. I have learnt for the first time that the Hindu way of life consists of two *dharmas*, namely, the *vamadharma* and the *ashramadharma* from his writings. The *vamadharma* is a theory of the organisation of the society while the *ashramadharma* is a theory of regulating the life of an individual. In other words, Dr Ambedkar found that the Hindu religion has been regulating both the individual growth as well as the growth of the society. He has given a comparative analysis of the codes prescribed for each *ashrama*. Dr Ambedkar pointed out that the theory of stages is not known in *Vedas* except that of *brahmacharya*. Comparing the *vanaprastha* with *Sanyas* and *Grihasta* with *Vanaprastha*, Dr Ambedkar says that there are striking resemblances between them. Comparing *vanaprastha* with *sanyas*, there are only a few differences in the modes of life prescribed for them. First, a *vanaprastha* does not abandon his wife or his right over his property. But a *sanyasi* must abandon both. Secondly, a *vanaprastha* is not expressly placed under such a disability. Dr Ambedkar has analysed this *ashram* to make the institution of marriage compulsory. Later, Dr Ambedkar related this institution of marriage as a strategy of Manu to fight Buddhism. I have illustrated this point to show the power of logic and scholarship of Dr Ambedkar to drive at a point which he wanted to prove.

Another very interesting principle to which Dr Ambedkar was so attached is the principle of democracy. As a patriot, he has argued that 'western students of democracy have spread the belief that democracy has stemmed either from Christianity or from Plato and that there is no other source of inspiration for democracy. If they had known that India too had developed the doctrine of Brahmaism, which furnishes a better foundation for Democracy, they would not have been so dogmatic. India too must be admitted to have a contribution towards a theoretical foundation for democracy.' Here, Dr Ambedkar made a distinction between Brahmaism and Brahmanism. According to him, Brahmaism consists of the three *mahavakyas*: (1) *Sarvam Khalvidam Brahma*—All this is Brahma, (2) *Aham Brahmasmi Atma*—self is the same as Brahma. Therefore, I am Brahma, and (3) *Tatvamasi-Atman*—self is the same as Brahma. Therefore, though art also Brahma. He has criticised the Hindus that they could not distinguish between Brahmaism and Vedanta. The fundamental difference between the two is that Brahmaism does not treat the world as unreal, whereas Vedanta does. The essence of Brahmaism is that the world is real and the reality behind the world is Brahma. Everything, therefore, is of the essence of Brahma. Democracy demands that each individual shall have every opportunity for realising its worth. It also requires that each individual shall know that he is as good as everybody else. Those who sneer at *Aham Brahmasmi* (I am Brahma) as an imprudent utterance forget that the other part of the *mahavakya*, namely *Tatvamasi* (Though art also Brahma). If *Aham Brahmasmi* says, Dr Ambedkar has stood along without the conjunct of *Tatvamasi*, it may not have been possible to sneer at it. But, with the conjunct of *Tatvamasi*, the charge of selfish arrogance cannot stand against Brahmaism. This theory of Brahmaism, Dr Ambedkar says, has certain social implications which have a tremendous value as a foundation for democracy. If all persons are parts of Brahma, then all are equal and all must enjoy the same liberty which is what democracy means. This interpretation of the *mahavakyas* by Dr Ambedkar would put him definitely one of the greatest philosophers of India. As a pragmatist, however, Dr Ambedkar worked beyond this interpretation and questioned why this doctrine failed to generate equality in India. He has lamented that it was not made the basis of Hindu *dharma*. Therefore, he sought after a religion which had provided him the answer. Dr Ambedkar ultimately found it in Buddhism and became a modem Buddha. Friends, I have made some observations on the basis of my love for philosophy and found Dr Ambedkar as a refreshing philosopher. Like Dr Ambedkar, I started as an economics teacher and now dabbling with philosophy. Incidentally, the chief guest Mr Kamaleswara Rao was a student of economics and the director of the seminar Dr Chalam is also from the same discipline. Therefore, I am sure that the seminar will seriously deliberate upon the ideas of Dr Ambedkar and find out the ideas that are most relevant to our society which is at crossroads now.

Part I

Ambedkar as Philosopher and Theoretician

2

Philosophy of Ambedkar

Some Observations

S.G. Kulkarni

A serious study of Ambedkar's philosophical thoughts has been necessitated due to three following reasons:

1. Academic philosophy in this country is guilty of deliberately neglecting his ideas and insights. Thus, contemporary Indian philosophy under its rubric includes the thoughts of such eminent thinkers as Aurobindo, Gandhi, I.C. Bhattacharya, etc. However, precisely because Ambedkar, unlike these thinkers, adopted towards the whole of Indian tradition a stance which was uniquely critical, every attempt is made to black out his philosophical thinking. Though his critique of Hindu tradition is as powerful and devastating as Gandhi's critique of western civilisation in *Hind Swaraj*, it was not accorded the equal amount of academic respect perhaps due to our narcissism and refusal to face bitter truths about ourselves. Hence, academic integrity demands a serious study of Ambedkar's philosophy. The lame excuse that his philosophical writings like *The Philosophy of Hinduism and Riddles in Hinduism* were not available to us till now cannot be given any more.
2. In the post-Independence India, four movements have called into question in a fundamental way our perception of

ourselves and our paradigms of social reconstruction. They are peasant movement, women's movement, environmental movement and Dalit movement. All these seminal movements can fructify only if they are based on rich and profound philosophical ideas. It is only Ambedkar who in a self-conscious and sustained manner seeks to develop a philosophy for Dalit movement. It is his philosophy that we find a critique of tradition without abdicating the responsibility towards the construction of an alternative. The critique of the tradition is accompanied in Ambedkar by a refusal to accept readymade alternatives manufactured in the West.

3. Even when Ambedkar is recognised as a thinker, the educated Indians have a naive and simplified image of him. They cast him in the categories into which most of them fit. He is, thus, treated as a liberal in politics, individualist in social theory and humanist in ethics. In short, he is portrayed as a westernised intellectual seeking his source of inspiration and intellectual moorings in European philosophical stream. As we shall see, this is a gross distortion of Ambedkar's basic orientation of thought. A serious study is called for in order to do justice to the originality of his philosophical thinking and intellectual convictions.

Though all the three reasons propelled my attempt to reflect on Ambedkar's philosophy, it is the last which has been the immediate one. My observations centre around the belief that Ambedkar stands far from, and in fact in direct contradiction to, the basic thrust of modern western thought, both in form and in content.

Two of the most important concepts of Ambedkar's philosophy are the concepts of the ethical and the religious. The primacy of these concepts in the scheme of his thought mark his departure from the contemporary western philosophy which has only a nominal importance for these concepts. One can take in this connection his attack on Marxism. Marxism has been attacked by its critics on the basis of the supposed untenability of its conception of science or its inability to understand human nature. A thinker like Lohia accuses it of subsuming the dynamics of the eastern society under a scheme which is physically extracted out of

European experience and hence of being the last bullwark of cultural imperialism. Marxism is also criticised for its inability to come to terms with a phenomenon like caste system—a criticism justified by the fact that Marxists tend to treat caste more as a puzzle than as a problem and thus seek to push it under the carpet. None of these criticisms satisfy Ambedkar. His attack on Marxism is ethical and he questions the basic tenets of end justifying the means and religions the opium of the people. The superiority of Buddhism over Marxism is construed by him not in terms of scientificity but ethicality, not in terms of rationality but religiosity. The centrality of the ethical and the religious in Ambedkar is reinforced in his attack on Hinduism. The Hindu society is criticised by him not because it is indifferent to the scientific mode of understanding the world, nor because it is inimical to economic prosperity due to its obsession with spiritual liberation or social equilibrium. It is, according to him, anti-ethical in the sense that it has negated the very idea of moral reflection as is evidenced by the fact that Hindu ethics remain at the level of customs and its idea of virtue and sin does not go beyond observance and violation of scriptural injunctions pertaining to rituals and caste practices.[1] It has never occurred to it that morality concerns inner life. Hindu ethics, therefore, remains imbecile. It is no ethics at all. Thus, the major plank of his attack on Hinduism is ethics. Similarly, another major plank of attack is religion. The last two sentences of his devastating attack on Hinduism in his *Philosophy of Hinduism* are: 'It is a misnomer to call it religion. Its philosophy is opposed to very thing for which religion stands'.[2] Hence, Hinduism is anti-religious, not merely a delinquent religion.

The central place of religion in Ambedkar's philosophy is brought out again by his characterisation of philosophy and religion. He says: 'Philosophy is static because it is concerned only with knowing truth. Religion is dynamic because it is concerned with love of truth'.[3] Thus, according to him, all genuine and complete philosophy is ultimately religious. The litmus test of a philosophy is whether it organically relates itself to real life process via a religion which nurtures and ennobles the community life of a people. Seen in this light, the philosophy of *Upanishads* is, according to him, a grand failure; its 'truth' had no hearing on the real life of our people which remained in the thraldom of debasement—a debasement justified by Brahminical ideologies in general and Manu in particular. In other words, Upanishadic philosophy was condemned to be ineffective because it grew in the anti-religious soil of Hindu social order.

One of the central tenets of modern western philosophy is 'utilitarianism'. Utilitarianism, according to which the ethical criterion of an action is the maximum happiness of maximum number of people, is the ethical component liberal political theory. Is Ambedkar a utilitarian? Does he give primacy to utility in his philosophical analysis? Looking at his analysis of religion, one finds that utility, according to him, is only a secondary criterion for judging right and wrong. It is secondary because it is the norm in a society of antique religion which is only the first phase of the revolutionary transformation that religion has undergone. The primary criterion is justice because it is the norm for judging right and wrong in the society of modern religion. In other words, justice and not utility alone can be the norm because justice is the norm of judging in a society which is religiously speaking, more evolved. The transition from utility to justice, according to Ambedkar is so important that primacy of justice over utility is axiomatic. Denial of this axiom is the denial of the great revolution in the history of religion which 'was not ... a revolution in the religious organisation of society resulting in the shifting of the centre—from society to the individual—it was a revolution in the norms'.[4] By subordinating utility to justice in his analytical scheme Ambedkar departs from the very first tenet of utilitarian ethics in particular, and liberal philosophy in general.

Is Ambedkar an individualist in his social and political philosophy? Does he, following the liberal thought, hold individual to be ultimate fact to which societal totality can be reduced? Going by his stance in constitutional assembly debates that it is the individual and not village that should be the unit, it appears that he is an individualist. Also, the expression 'individual' seems to figure heavily whenever he speaks of a genuine and evolved ethics. But Ambedkar's conception of individual and his essence has nothing to do with and is in fact antithetical to the modern western conception of an individual. The liberal thought maintains that essence of an individual is economic satisfaction, that is, consumption. For western radicalism, an individual is essentially a producer, and since production is essentially social, the individual evaporates in the realm of the social. For Ambedkar, an individual is neither consumer nor producer essentially but a moral agent. In other words, what distinguishes a human individual from an animal is the capacity for moral responsibility. Since the moral responsibility is, by definition, towards the 'other', the 'other' is the pre-condition and therefore not extraneous to one's individuality. In other words, in Ambedkar's scheme, the individual's essence consists in his ability to transcend one's individuality. The possessive individualism is, therefore, a false consciousness. It is in this way Ambedkar, while celebrating the individual, transcends the bounds within which modern individualism holds the individual captive. Whereas for modern individualism the best ethical ideals is 'enlightened self-interest', for Ambedkar, it is transcending one's individuality through the exercise of one's capacity for moral responsibility.

More importantly, the locus of the moral responsibility is the recognition of an objectively existing moral law or *dharma*—an idea which Ambedkar considers central to his own religion—Buddhism. Hence, the individual for his essence depends upon something beyond himself, something without which he ceases to be himself. This idea of individual as ontologically dependent on moral law that should make it evident that Ambedkar refuses to adopt the individualist philosophy so germane to modern western thought whose two pillars are: (1) the idea of a de-valued objective world, and (2) the idea of man as self-defining subject. According to Ambedkar, objective world is not devalued since *dharma* itself is objective and man is not self-defining since he is defined by *dharma* in the sense that valuation of human actions has to be in accordance with *dharma* and not our self-interest, 'enlightened' or 'otherwise'. Hence, Ambedkar could maintain individualism and yet accept Buddhism which denies, at a metaphysical plane, the very idea of individual self as a substantive entity.

In other words, the philosophical achievement of Ambedkar consists in working out a conception of individual without being an individualist of modern western brand, a conception of individual which is not in conflict with Nairatmyavada, Ambedkar goes even beyond this. By his construal of individual in terms of moral responsibility and therefore moral law or *dharma* and identifying that as the regulative principle of Buddhism, Ambedkar brings back Buddhism in trying to meet the theoretical challenges of Brahminical philosophy, fell into the trap of over-intellectualism. The ethical aspect was eclipsed by abstruse discussion of logical issues. Ambedkar gave Buddhism a new existential grounding by renewing its practical sense of purpose, the sole of its founder. On the other hand, he made available a vibrant worldview and way of life to a whole people who were systematically denied any opportunity for engaging in philosophy and religion. After all untouchability is not a mere physical act, not even mere social practice, but a symbol of cultural alienation. Further, Ambedkar's conversion to Buddhism, the most significant philosophical episode in our history, constitutes a bold attempt by a towering Indian thinker to transcend the tradition-modernity dichotomy which has a seductive grip on the colonial mind. He thus created an alternative to a society which cannot be moved by the metropole ideology of secularism and finds its traditional religion morally reprehensible. This is the relevance of Ambedkar's philosophy in India today.

I now raise some points concerning the relation between the thoughts of Ambedkar and Gandhi. I believe that once we delink Ambedkar's basic orientation of thought from the ethos of western liberalism, his ideas do not appear to be as antithetical to Gandhi's thought as they are made out to be. It is true that Gandhi criticised[5] the dominant view in the constituent assembly spiritedly championed by Ambedkar that it is the individual and not village that should be the political unit.[6] Against this view, Gandhi argued for the centrality of village for Indian polity. Ambedkar scathingly attacked Indian village whose cause Gandhi espoused. But it must not be forgotten that just as Ambedkar did not mean by 'individual'. The individual given to us by western liberalism and capitalist system, but a spiritualised one, so Gandhi did not mean by village what existed or exists, but an idealised one.

However, one might really feel that Gandhism and Ambedkarism cannot be reconciled because of their diametrically opposite positions on the question of caste. We all know that Ambedkar rightly made caste a special or even single target of attack whereas Gandhi even went to the extent of giving caste system the credit of saving whatever that could be saved from the colonial onslaught; or, at least, Gandhi considered traditional caste system to be much less harmful than modem class system. So, it might appear that Ambedkar with his explicit anticasteism and Gandhi with his implicit procasteism are irreconcilable. But this view, I think, is highly questionable. It is unfair to attribute to Gandhi the ideas which were central to the ethos of traditional caste system. Rather, while not speaking against caste system, Gandhi was in an important way undermining it. This point has been very well brought out by Ashis Nandy when he says: 'Coomaraswamy defended premodern caste system because he found it more humane than the modern class system. Gandhi also did so, but went further, i.e. sought to reorder the hierarchy of skills to relegitimise the manual and the unclean and delegitimate the Brahminic and clean. (I remember anthropologist Surjit Sinha once saying that while Rabindra Nath Tagore wanted to turn all Indians into Brahmins, Gandhi sought to turn them into Sudras ...)'.[7]

In fact, whatever little sympathy Gandhi had for caste system and whatever faith he had in reforming it, he lost it in the last years of his life. Ram Manohar Lohia, his close but critical associate and one of the leading lights of anti-caste movement of post-Independence India, very illuminatingly says: 'Gandhiji does not seem to have been aware of the full implications of the caste system right up to few years before his death. He started with some kind of romantic idealisation of it. He tried to shear it of its evils, as though the thing was not evil in itself. It was only some time around the last great struggle for freedom, the open rebellion of 1942, that he recognised the inherent evil of the caste system. It is true that he had all along tried to remove untouchability. That was a reformer's act, not revolutionary's. He had for a long time wanted to maintain the caste system, but reform it of its dross. He changed his position only a few years before his death, when he became a revolutionary also in respect of caste. It was too late then. The weakness of his earlier position had already caused a basic anemia in the nationalist movement.'[8]

It is necessary to cleanse Gandhi's thought of 'the weakness of his earlier position' in order to make it a powerful means of social transformation. By doing so, we will be able to work out what can be called critical Gandhism. Ambedkar's ideas can be of immense value in doing so. In other words, Gandhi's critical traditionalism and Ambedkar's critical modernism can together give rise to critical Gandhism. Since, of the four great movements of our times which I mentioned earlier, the Dalit movement is inspired by Ambedkar and the others are wholly or partly inspired by Gandhi and since all these four movements must converge at one point which constitutes the focal point or our national consciousness, the proximity between Gandhi and Ambedkar is our only hope and need. When all the imported ideologies have exposed themselves as hollow both here and in their place of birth, Gandhi's vision and Ambedkar's thought constitute two pillars on which we can build what may called 'the Sudra consciousness' which can challenge the Brahminical ideology of both varieties—traditional and modern.

Notes

1. Moon, Vasant (Ed.), 'Annihilation of Caste', in *Dr. Babasaheb Ambedkar: Writings and Speeches*, Vol. 1, Education Department, Government of Maharashtra, Bombay, 1989, pp. 82–83.
2. Ibid., p. 92.
3. Ibid., p. 86.
4. Ibid., p. 22.
5. *Harijan*, 21 December 1947.
6. *Panchayati Raj as the Basis of Indian Polity: An Exploration into the Proceedings of the Constituent Assembly*, Association of Voluntary Agencies for Rural Development, New Delhi, pp. 24–25.
7. Nandy, Ashis, 'Cultural Frames for a Social Transformation: A Credo', *Alternatives*, Vol. XVI, 1987, p. 115.
8. Lohia, Ram Manohar, *Guilty Men of India's Partition*, Bombay: Sindhu Publications Ltd., 1990 (first published in 1960), p. 65.

3

Ambedkar as a Philosopher and a Theoretician

An Evaluation

A.M. Rajasekhariah

Ambedkar has been widely acknowledged as the leader of the depressed classes, the champion of the dumb and the downtrodden millions of this country and above all as the chief architect of the Indian Constitution. Yet this is a very limited and restricted view of his role and personality. This description does not exhaust his contribution. He was, in fact, the architect of modern Indian state and society. While acknowledging his greatness as a leader, it should not be forgotten that he was an outstanding thinker and a scholar of great eminence. He was an academician and writer who thought systematically and presented his research findings of a fundamental nature in the course of his writings on problems social, economic, political, legal and constitutional. The sheer output of his writings entitles him to be ranked as a great writer of our times. Ambedkar might not have written poems, plays or fiction. But he wrote remarkable prose in both Marathi and English in a style that is lucid, logical, highly expressive and thought provoking. The entire body of his writings can very well be classified as 'literature of thought'.

A Multi-Faceted Personality

Ambedkar was a multi-faceted and multi-dimensional personality. But he had set for himself the main task and chief goal of uplifting and emancipating the millions of his Untouchable brethren from the squalor of poverty, ignorance, slavery and humiliation. In whatever he wrote, he expressed not only his deep concern for them, but presented his thoughts and action plan based on deep research into their problems. In his writings he dives deep into the social, economic and political history of India and has contributed a good deal to the understanding of the Indian society and polity. He was one of our most prominent social thinkers whose ideas on various socio-political history of India has contributed a good deal to the understanding of the Indian society and polity. He was one of our most prominent social thinkers whose ideas on various socio-political and economic problems such as the caste system, the origins of the pernicious practice of untouchability, the dismal poverty of India, the emancipation of the downtrodden through political action etc. are original and characteristically his own. They open up new vistas and horizons to the present day public policy and policy-makers. His findings and suggestions are relevant today and they speak volumes for his profound scholarship and intellectual capacities. He has thrown a flood of light on Indian society, particularly its drawbacks and the unseemly side, its development and its socio-political and economic ramifications. According to him, the Indian society, or to be more specific the Hindu society, is one of graded inequalities. To him, the Indian social and political history is nothing but a 'glorification of upper castes and degradation of the lower castes'. He considered all Hindu social institutions such as the caste system, untouchability etc. as an artificial creation of the vested interests and their philosophers who rationalised these pernicious institutions. The unfortunate outcome of all this conspiracy was the artificial division of society into the 'privileged' and the 'slavish' and the 'sluggish' sections, consisting of the 'upper castes' and the 'lower castes' respectively. Ambedkar's main concern all along his life was to fight this injustice and inhumanity by all possible and necessary means and usher in a just and egalitarian society. It is very appropriate that as part of his birth centenary celebrations, a systematic and scientific evaluation of his valuable ideas and thought process is made to enable us to appreciate his precious contribution to the Indian society and polity. It is also to be recognised that he contributed immensely to the building up of a body of thought on the problems of Indian society. An understanding of this body of thought and its application to cure the ills of our society is indispensable if we are to move towards modernisation of our society. In other words, Ambedkar was not merely a leader of men but also a leader of thought. Hence, his entitlement to be characterised as a thinker and a philosopher.

Ambedkar was not a philosopher in the generally accepted sense. He did not develop consciously a philosophy for the sake of it. He may not have been a theoretician because mere theory building was not his objective, nor was it his concern. But as a researcher, thinker and writer, he undoubtedly belonged to the realm of thought. He formed and developed his own ideas and view of man, society and their inter-relationship. So much so he had all the ingredients of a thinker and a philosopher. If philosophy is a 'persistent attempt to think things through', he was second to none in this respect. If philosophy 'grows out of the need of each thinking person to find an intelligible order in his life, so that he can think and feel that things make sense', Ambedkar's claim to be ranked as a philosopher is incontrovertible. Generally speaking, philosophy has to be an integral whole. It is a system of inter-relations between different aspects of a problem. It has to take into account all aspects of human life, activity and thought. Ambedkar was fully conscious of this ingredient of thought if it is to develop into a philosophy, and he developed it fully.

Once we categorise Ambedkar as a thinker and philosopher, it remains to be seen whether he was interested in an abstract or obscurantist body of thought or whether he was motivated by a purposeful action-oriented philosophy. The social milieu in which he lived was a very important consideration and it was basic to the development of his thought process and personality. The constraints of an unjust social order led him into the realm of action as he was not only a thinker but a determined and committed social engineer and a reformer. He was not interested in armchair philosophy. Naturally he was indifferent to epistemology in a way. His philosophy was not abstract and obscurantist. It was more of a practical nature and realistic in its approach. Nor was it purely normative, let alone dogmatic. Dogma had no place at all in his schema. His philosophy was in fact pragmatic and programmatic. He always lived in the world of action. In his search for meaning to life, he tried to bring together the ideals of his thought and the realities of life. So he did not indulge in developing a metaphysical body of thought.

Though not a philosopher in the traditional sense like Plato or Aristotle, he nevertheless developed his own social and political ideas and ideals. There emerged out of these a clash between idealism and realism, empiricism and rationalism, naturalism and humanism, individualism and socialism, nationalism and inter-nationalism.[1] His philosophy was not just speculative or idealistic, or ethical. According to him, philosophy has to be essentially related to real human problems and issues, because social environment and philosophy are complimentary. In a sense, it is to be an expression of vital human affairs and is a sincere attempt to bridge the gulf between theory and practice, materialism and spiritualism. He had no sympathy and interest in a philosophy which did not study the actual human problems. His thought process arose out of his dejection with the inhuman treatment meted out to his community by the caste Hindus. The servile class consisting of the Untouchables and the Sudras were forever condemned to a life of poverty, ignorance, ignominy, hatred and contempt. His main concern was the total emancipation of the servile class from the clutches of the privileged and the arrogant caste Hindus. In whatever he said and whatever he did, this was uppermost in his mind. Hence, 'he was in total engagement throughout his life with this social phenomenon, as a humanist who charitably looked for what made true humanity. These were later to figure in all his endeavours.'[2] In other words, Dr Ambedkar had a 'mission' in his life and that was one of 'man-making'. In everything he did this was the goal and this was his philosophy.

When we speak of a body of thought called philosophy, it is customary to classify it into certain categories such as political, social, ethical, etc. But it is rather difficult to separate and compartmentalise philosophy into social, political, etc. because philosophy is an integral whole as we have already noted. Therefore, it may be difficult to classify Ambedkar's philosophy. Even then as he was concerned with different aspects of human life and their inter-relationships, the ideas he formulated and expressed on different aspects of life could be classified accordingly.

His Economic Ideas

As we know, Ambedkar was an academician and an economist by training. He was basically a social scientist. His life was a saga of great scholastic attainments. It was his rare privilege to get highest recognition in the academic field, even though learning was forbidden to him under the most irrational *chaturvama* dispensation. As a born Untouchable, he was not supposed to have schooling, let alone learning. Even though the entire system was hostile to him, he was able to develop self-confidence because of the encouragement from some sympathetic professors and teachers like Prof. Muller and ultimately with the *munificence* of the ruler of Baroda Sayaji Rao Gaikwad, he was able to complete his BA examination creditably and gain admission to the prestigious Columbia University in the USA. Economics was his major area of study at Columbia. He obtained his MA degree in 1915 for the thesis 'Administration and Finances of the East India', which was an enlarged and detailed version of his earlier thesis 'National Dividend in India: A Historic and Analytical Study'. R.A. Seligman, the renowned Professor of Economics, was his supervisor. Later he went to the London School of Economics and Political Science for D.Sc. in Economics and worked under Prof. Edwin Canaan. He got his M.Sc. degree in 1921 for the thesis 'Provincial Decentralisation of Imperial Finances in British India', and D.Sc. for the thesis 'The Problem of the Rupee' in 1923.[3]

It is to be noted that Ambedkar was essentially an economist by academic training and a recognised researcher in problems pertaining to public finance and political economy. He studied thoroughly the economic problems facing British India and provided bold solutions to them which are relevant even today. It is also to be said to his credit that he build up an economic theory of his own on the organisation of society in independent India as a self-governing country. The establishment of free and egalitarian society was his goal. He endeavoured to build such a society as chairman of the Drafting Committee of the Constituent Assembly.

To achieve the goal, he propagated democracy, socialism, secularism and constitutionalism. He incorporated these ideas in memorandum he submitted to the Constituent Assembly even before he entered it. The memorandum, entitled 'States and Minorities: What are their Rights and How to Secure Them in the Constitution of Free India', was prepared by him in his capacity as the president of the All India Scheduled Castes Federation.[4] In this memorandum, he provides for remedies against invasion of fundamental rights of citizens, and guarantees freedom from economic exploitation and want and fear. He sought to achieve this through his theory of 'state socialism'. He pleaded for state ownership and management of all key industries and insurance. According to his theory of state socialism, agriculture was to be considered a key industry and it was to be organised on a collective basis. He wanted a collectivised system of agriculture and collective farming. He also works out the detailed implementation of the programme in Article II of Section II of the said memorandum. So, he developed in the course of his writings an economic theory which was wide-ranging, realistic and practical.

His Political and Social Philosophy

Political philosophy is the study of human ideals and thought which underlie political systems and institutions. It is a positive science besides being normative. Its main concern is nothing less than the 'moral phenomena of human behaviour in society'.[5] It gives to the political institutions such as state, government, etc. the human base and purpose of togetherness for social development. It also suggests the means to coordinate human ends of different social groups within the state. In fact, political philosophy tries to observe the actual in the light of the ideal, the momentary in the light of the eternal and the particular in the light of the universal. It is as part of this process that it becomes highly speculative.

But, Ambedkar's political philosophy was not at all speculative and idealistic. According to him, any philosophy, be it political, social or economic, has to be essentially related to actual human problems and issues. His political philosophy was an expression of vital human affairs as well as a sincere attempt to bridge the gulf between theory and practice. It was intended to be problem-oriented and conflict-resolving phenomenon. He naturally developed his own view of man and society as part of such a philosophy.

Man constitutes the focal point of his entire philosophy. Man is the chief object as well as subject of his study and investigation. He declared that every man should have an opportunity to live a dignified life. It was disgraceful for any man to live without self-respect which is so vital to an honourable life. Individual and individuality is the keynote of his philosophy. It is not enough for man to just manage to survive. Mere survival without culture is not enough. Ambedkar emphasises that 'what he (the man) must consider is the quality of his survival. If he does that, I am sure he will cease to take pride in the mere fact of his survival'.[6] He did not hold a static view of life. To him: '...a human being is always changing, always growing'.[7] He further says: 'Man is what his mind makes him'.[8] The mind should have opportunities to develop fully so that each develops his own individuality without any servility. He says: 'Lumping together of individuals into a few sharply marked-off classes is a superficial view of man not worthy of serious consideration. Consequently, the utilisation of the qualities of individuals is incompatible with their stratification of classes, since the qualities of individuals are so variable'.[9] Thus, he provides the required theoretical frame for his condemnation of the Hindu social order outright. He, naturally, does not accept Plato's concept of man and his classification of individuals under three categories of souls. He calls it demonstrably wrong. On the same premise he denounces and rejects the *chaturvarna* system of the Hindus by Manu as totally irrational, inhuman and unscientific.

Ambedkar's view of society is also different from that of others. To him it is not an organism. Society is essentially based on human attitudes. According to him: 'Men do not become a society by living in physical proximity any more than a man ceases to be a member of his society by living so many miles away from other men ... similarity in habits and customs, beliefs and thoughts, is not enough to constitute men into society. Things may be passed physically from one to another like bricks. In the same way, habits and customs, beliefs and thoughts of one group may be taken over by another group and there may thus appear a similarity between the two'.[10] He fully concurs with John Dewey, his professor a Columbia University, that 'society is the process of associating in such ways that experience, ideas, emotions, values are transmitted and made common'.[11] There has to be communication and 'social endosmis' if society is to be meaningful and egalitarian. The caste system of the Hindus 'prevents common activity and by preventing common activity it has prevented the Hindus from becoming a society with a unified life and a consciousness of its own being'.[12] It is on this premise and theoretical ground that he denounces caste system and gives a clarion call to the annihilation of caste. He condemns a society which makes a false basis of social organisation which leads to hypocrisy and wrong traditions. His ideal of a society is that it should be based on liberty, equality and fraternity. It should be open and mobile, open with opportunities for communicating and sharing common experiences. In other words, there must be social endosmosis.[13] So Ambedkar's political philosophy is based on the recognition that man and man alone constitutes the basis of all social relations. He fully agrees with Aristotle when he says: 'More than political or religious, man is a social animal. He may not have, need not have, religion; he may not have, need not have politics. He must have society; he cannot do without society'.[14] Thus Dr Ambedkar has attempted at an harmony between man and society as part of his social and political philosophy.

According to Ambedkar's political philosophy, even though society is basic, state is a necessary institution. So he does not hold an anarchic view, nor does he hold the absolutist view of state held by Hobbs, Hegel and others. He does not accept the view that state is an end in itself. To him, the state is a means to individual good. He advocated a stable state and the people should obey the laws made by the state from the well-being of the individual and the society. He said: 'Willingness to render obedience to the authority of the government is essential for the stability of government as the unity of political parties on the fundamentals of state. It is impossible for the same person to question the importance of obedience in the maintenance of the state. To believe in civil disobedience is to believe in anarchy'.[15]

Democracy is an important element of his political thought. He was an ardent believer in democracy. He held a comprehensive view of democracy. By philosophical persuasion, he was a liberal democrat. While pursuing the cause of justice for the Untouchables, he was in fact enunciating the democratic principle as the bed-rock of justice. According to him, democracy is 'a form and method of government whereby revolutionary changes in the economic and social life of the people are brought about without bloodshed'. Further, 'democracy is not merely a form of government. It is primarily a mode of associated living, of conjoint communicated experience. It is essentially an attitude of respect and reverence towards fellow-men'. He wrote that the society based on liberty, equality and fraternity should be the only alternative to a caste society. He was making purely a 'secular' approach to the problem of democracy and he believed in democracy that is complete and real. We see in him a burning desire to build democracy in the social, economic and political sphere in independent India. To him, the social and economic democracy are the tissue and fibre of a political democracy. He was painfully aware that this was not provided for in the Constitution of India. He did not make a secret of his anguish over this stark reality when he said it in the Constituent Assembly itself. He, in fact, was pleading for 'one man one value' instead 'one man one vote and one vote one value'. This was his philosophy all along. He pleaded for a share in the political power of the country so that they can influence decision-making in their favour. To him, political power is the key to all social progress. Such was the theoretical justification for his demand of separate electorate for the depressed classes. He was for socialism through democracy or democratic socialism which became so dear to Jawaharlal Nehru. Ambedkar wrote that the only way to have state socialism without dictatorship is '... to retain parliamentary democracy and to prescribe state socialism by the law of the Constitution so that it will be beyond the reach of parliamentary majority to suspend, amend or abrogate it. It is only by this that one can achieve the triple object, namely, to establish socialism, retain parliamentary democracy and avoid dictatorship'.[16]

Thus, in the views of Ambedkar we find the political and economic philosophy of John Locke, who stood for political and economic liberalism, is reflected. To sum up, we realise that the programmes and campaign of Ambedkar for the total emancipation and rehabilitation of all men in general and the depressed classes in particular were based on sound theoretical footing backed up by a philosophy of his own.[17]

Conclusion

Though Ambedkar was not a philosopher in the traditional sense, yet his concern for man all along led him into building up a body of philosophical thought that was not an idle, armchair, purposeless philosophy developed for its own sake without any concern for human beings. He realised fully well that no philosophy will be worth its name if it does not have its roots in humanism. Philosophy should serve human interests, and not the other-worldly or super-natural or super-human being. He accepts naturalism along with humanism. Naturalism denies the existence of anything beyond nature, behind nature of other than nature. There is nothing supernatural or other-worldly. Naturalism without humanism is meaningless. It is only a combination of the two that can bring about a better understanding and human welfare. His philosophy was guided by a kind of social dynamism. It was intended to provide solutions for the ills of mankind. It was this purposiveness that brought about a combination of thought and action and led him into practical politics. His politics was not for his personal gain, or politics of power to him. It was the politics of emancipation of the dumb, the downtrodden, millions of Indians. His ideas, ideals and philosophy revolved round the welfare of man through social and political action, respect for the dignity of man, respect for human rights, secularism, socialism, his belief in peace and non-violence, constitutional morality, social justice, etc. These are some of the most valuable and enduring elements of his social and political philosophy which guide us in building up a humane and progressive society. He was undoubtedly a great philosopher and theoretician of our times.

Notes

1. Jatava, D.R., *The Political Philosophy of Dr. Ambedkar*, Agra: Phoenix Publishing Agency, 1965, p. 2.
2. Rajasekharaiah, A.M., *Dr. B.R. Ambedkar: The Quest for Social Justice*, New Delhi: Uppal Publishing House, 1989, p. 15.

3. For his works on Economics, see *Dr. Babasaheb Ambedkar: Writings and Speeches*, Vol. II, Government of Maharashtra, Bombay, 1982.
4. For full text of the Memorandum States and Minorities see, *Dr. Babasaheb Ambedkar: Writings and Speeches*, Vol. I, Government of Maharashtra, Bombay, 1979.
5. Wayper, C.L., *Political Thought*, New Delhi: B.I. Publications, 1972, p. vii.
6. Ambedkar, B.R., *Annihilation of Caste*, Jalandhar: Bheem Patrika Publications, 1936, p. 55.
7. Ambedkar, B.R., *The Buddha and His Dhamma*, Bombay: Siddharth College Publication, 1957, p. 240.
8. Ibid., p. 359.
9. Ambedkar, B.R., *Annihilation of Caste*, op. cit., pp. 26–27.
10. Ibid.
11. Dewey, John, *Reconstruction in Philosophy*, Boston: Beacon Press, 1952, p. 161.
12. Ambedkar, B.R., *Annihilation of Caste*, op. cit., pp. 27–28.
13. Ibid., p. 38.
14. Ambedkar, B.R., *Pakistan or the Partition of India*, Bombay: Thacker & Co. Ltd., 1943, p. 119.
15. Ibid., p. 294.
16. Ambedkar, B.R., *States and Minorities*, Bombay: Thacker & Co. Ltd., 1947, p. 34.
17. For a complete discussion of the problem, see Rajasekharaiah, A.M. and Hemalata Jayaraj, 'Political Philosophy of Dr. B.R. Ambedkar', *The Indian Journal of Political Science*, Vol. LII, No. 2, April-June 1991. For a discussion on his Social Philosophy, see Rajasekharaiah, A.M., 'Social Philosophy of Dr. B.R. Ambedkar: The Quest for Social Justice', in *Dr. B.R. Ambedkar: The Man and His Message*, Commemorative Volume edited by Sudarshan Agarwal, published for Rajya Sabha Secretariat by Prentice Hall of India, New Delhi, 1991, pp. 139–148.

4

The Post-Ambedkar Indian Experience

K. Wilson

Much water has flown in the socio-political economic domain since the passing away of Ambedkar. There are things which went against the expectations of Ambedkar. Also there are several other developments—national and global—which Ambedkar did not anticipate. Times have changed. Perceptions too are either revised or modified. Hence, the imperative is to re-examine the issues that Ambedkar faced and see how Ambedkar would have reacted or responded to these issues particularly taking into consideration the nearly 50 years of post-Ambedkar Indian experience.

History reveals that no epoch-making person sought to bind future to the past. Every historic person looked far beyond his times and hinted at the burden that his followers should bear in tackling the issues at that particular period. So is the case with Ambedkar—the great Indian existentialist. In dealing with problems that he faced, Ambedkar neither looked to the hoary past nor threw the responsibility on someone else's shoulders; he responded to the situation in a way that, in his view, was correct for his response, reaction, and revolt. The enlightenment, the inspiration and the guidance given by Ambedkar to the posterity must inculcate in them enough courage to find new answers to new questions and new solutions to new problems. We, the present-day generation, will be bringing discredit to a great man like Ambedkar, if we shirk our responsibility and throw our burden back on Ambedkar, to tackle the post-Ambedkar Indian challenges. We can do so only at the risk of making Ambedkar a 'deus ex machine' who solves all problems of all times so that we may sit and enjoy the fruits of his labours. Such a stance amounts to abdicating our responsibility, acknowledging our incapacity, and celebrating our inactivity, passivity and therefore our right to exist as human beings. In order, therefore, to accomplish the task set before us, the present generation of Dalits must reflect and examine what could be the Ambedkarism in the post-Ambedkar Indian society. Ambedkar, who was not hesitant to go to any extent and do anything for the emancipation of Scheduled Castes would have, for a meaningful future of Scheduled Castes, radically revised his thinking on several key issues keeping in view the Indians of 1990s. In this context, it is proposed to discuss four important issues which Ambedkar wrestled with throughout his life. These are: (1) caste annihilation, (2) caste struggle, (3) religious conversion, and (4) political alternative.

1. Sharply reacting to the inhuman caste practices, Ambedkar affirmed that annihilation of caste is one way of achieving human emancipation for the Scheduled Castes. However, the post-Ambedkar Indian experience clearly indicates that annihilation of caste does not automatically guarantee the restoration of human standing for Scheduled Castes. For, the humanity of Scheduled Castes, or for that matter any caste, does not depend on either caste annihilation or caste affirmation.

Strictly speaking, 'caste' as such is not the problem of Scheduled Castes. They have never been allowed to be a part of the caste system. They are allotted a 5th class standing. There is no such thing as 'Harijan caste' or 'Dalit caste' or 'depressed caste'. All these terms indicate their cultural condition, such as poverty, alienation, dehumanisation, marginalisation, etc. Hence, the problem of Scheduled Castes is basically a human problem. Since there is no caste for Scheduled Castes, the questioning of denying caste to them does not arise. What is denied to them is something far more vital. And that is their very humanity. What is questioned is not the scheduledness of castes or scheduled casteness. It is the humanity of Scheduled Castes that is questioned.

In the context of India, the humanity of a person is celebrated through the assertion of caste. Here the term 'human' refers to a culture (view of life) which reflects one's inner confidence, or consciousness of unquestionable human standing, in terms of justice, dignity, equality, fraternity, liberty, etc. Even a poor illiterate, ignorant upper caste man feels assured of such a human standing. It is such self-understanding that emboldens a person to demonstrate the pride of his caste identity.

It is not, therefore, caste which confers or determines the humanity of a person. On the contrary, it is one's human standing that manifests itself in one's assertion of caste. Caste, therefore, functions as a mental frame through which one's humanity is either accepted or rejected. It is my assumption that if Ambedkar were to live today, he would have advocated not annihilation of castes but humanisation of castes. For, caste as such is a neutral phenomenon. We have to hasten the process of subjecting both the caste and the authority of Indian elitistic thought to humanistic critique. When castes are humanised, i.e. when all castes could celebrate their respective unique identity and humanity, real democratic foundations will be laid for genuine human transactions and relations. The human face of castes surfaces in their co-existence and functions as a sort of common wealth of castes where every caste functions on an equal footing. When human dimension dominates, castes may wither away.

2. The post-Ambedkar inter-caste and intra-caste dialectics and dialogues manifest that today caste relationships and affiliations function in different ways. Unlike in the days of Ambedkar, when even a peon could practise untouchability, today any Scheduled Caste high official is given all the honour and recognition as far as official status is concerned. However, in terms of personal relations, his humanity is questioned though not outwardly but inwardly. An upper caste person entertains in his consciousness, the idea, that a Scheduled Caste person in spite of his position and prosperity, is not equal to him. This amounts to questioning not his caste but his humanity. The Scheduled Castes, by virtue of their productive relations and friendships, get invited to social functions. But still, when the question of celebrating

social equality comes, the upper castes attribute to the Scheduled Castes the latter's human limitations. All this shows that the post-Ambedkar Scheduled Caste problem is not a caste problem, but a problem of human rights. Right to life, liberty, equality, property, etc. are some of the human rights. The Scheduled Castes must engage in organised struggles to achieve these rights. If Ambedkar were to live today, he would have unhesitatingly launched struggles for rights. The post-Ambedkar Dalit energy may have to be directed toward launching of human rights movements all over India.

3. Having determined not to die as a Hindu, Ambedkar opted to embrace Buddhism as a way of salvation for the Scheduled Castes. Several Dalits followed Ambedkar and embraced Buddhism. But the post-conversion experiences of Scheduled Castes to Buddhism shows that in spite of change of religion, caste system continues to follow them. This stigma is so unbearable, that Indian Scheduled Castes, in their search for human liberation, experimented with almost all the religions of India.

We have, in India, Christian Dalits, Muslim Dalits, Sikh Dalits, Hindu Dalits, Neo-Buddhist Dalits, etc. Did these conversions in any way help removing the stigma of caste? Certainly not. On the contrary, education and economic improvement greatly contributed to their self-confidence, freedom from dependency, and ultimately to the assertion of their humanity. Hence, my assumption that if Ambedkar were to be with us today, he would have, without any hesitation and reservation whatsoever, advocated secular and not religious path as the most and the best possible liberating answer to Dalits sections.

For, religious or metaphysical solutions may or may not meet the concrete human problems. Things such as 'protective discrimination' or 'separate electorate' may not find a place in any religion. They are evolved out of the existing concrete human conditions. In the ultimate analysis, it is the actual concrete human condition out of which emancipatory solutions must be developed, and not from any religious worldview.

4. In the thick and thin of political contours, Ambedkar took an independent stand. He was rightly critical of the traditional leftist, the rightist and the reformist positions vis-à-vis the Scheduled Castes. Both the Congress and the Communist parties

have equally come under fire with Ambedkar, of course, for different reasons. He founded the Scheduled Caste Federation and fought elections on that plank. Today, the times have changed. Apart from their ideological and theoretical differences, all national level political parties in this country, to a greater or lesser degree, are united at least on the single concrete issues, and that is caste. All these political parties theoretically condemn but in a very subtle way practice caste.

If, therefore, Ambedkar were to live today, he would have positively advocated some sort of political alliance with the 'leftist' parties in this country to dislodge the oppressive, and segregative, thought practices. By leftist parties, I do not mean Communist parties. We have for too long abdicated our freedom and indiscriminately used the western meanings of these terms. Time has now come for us to reinterpret the traditional cliché such as 'left', 'right', 'left to right', 'right to left', etc. These words have to be understood primarily from the background of Indian culture. From the standpoint of culture, only that thought or movement, which seeks to contest, protest, and revolt against the Vedic, elitistic, Brahmanical thought, that alone can be described as the true Indian leftist alternative. In this sense, even Communists may fail to qualify as leftists. It is in this sense, Dalit alliance with the leftists has to be understood.

Today, almost all national parties scrupulously follow this Vedic elitistic socio-economic political thought in deed, though in words all of them sound socialistic. The new phenomena which is very powerfully making its presence felt are the regional parties most of which are manifestations of protest against elitistic, Brahmanical thought. A critical study of Ambedkar's socio-political philosophy clearly indicates that he would have preferred for Dalits to align themselves particularly with such political alternatives to realise the task of establishing a humanised Indian society where equality, fraternity and liberty are celebrated by one and all not only in words but also in deeds. Let us critically and dispassionately examine this probable post-Ambedkar Indian experience and see to what extent it can contribute to the total human emancipation of all the weaker sections.

5

Ambedkar and Marxism

A Critical Examination of the Case for Synthesis

Sharad Patil

After the foundation of the Satyashodhak Communist Party in 1978, an intense and prolonged debate raged in Maharashtra on the issue whether Jotiba Phuley, B.R. Ambedkar's preceptor, and Ambedkar were just ideologues or philosophers. Sudhir Bedekar, owing allegiance to the CPI(M), took the former position and argued that Ambedkar's being a bourgeoisie ideology, it cannot be combined with Marx's probetarian philosophy. Communists, Marxist and socialist scholars were unanimous on this point. Philosophy being an extremely specialised subject, it is still the monopoly of the Brahmins. Hence, even the Dalits did not enter the fray to defend their master. I had to pick up the gauntlet and prove that Phuley and Ambedkar were philosophers.

Criterion of Philosopher

If philosophy is considered to be a worldview, then Buddha cannot be called a philosopher. For, he denied the primacy of either matter (*rupa*) or mind (*vijnana*) and prohibited his monks and nuns to discuss purely philosophical matters which he bade them, were not conducive to *nirvana*. Though Buddha's teaching of emancipation from sorrow (*dukkha*) was meant for individual salvation, by preaching, the five directives (*pancadhamma*) to the laity he called upon the slave owning householders to practically manumit their slaves. He and his monastic order led the social revolution that abolished the *varna*-based slave society which made way for the new and more productive *jati*-based feudal society. S.N. Dasgupta and Debi Prasad Chattopadhyaya say that Buddha's philosophy was revolutionary in the sense that it revolutionised the whole contemporary philosophical atmosphere which had reached a stalemate. But Ambedkar was the only person to declare in his *The Buddha and his Dhamma* that Buddha was the greatest social revolutionary of India. Hence, the traditional definition, either western or Indian, is not applicable to such philosophies. Only Antonio Gramsci's definition is applicable to them. He says in his *Prison Notebook*:

> ... it would not be exact to call by the name of 'philosophy' every tendency of thought, every general orientation etc., not even every 'conception of the world and of life'. The philosopher can be called a 'specialised worker' by comparison with the unskilled labourer, but this is not exact either, since in industry, in addition to the labourer and the specialised worker there also exists the engineer who not only knows it theoretically and historically. The professional or technical philosopher does not only 'think' with greater logical sigour, with greater coherence with more systematic sense than do other men, but he knows the entire history of thought. In other words, he is capable of accounting for the development of thought up to his own day and he is in a position where he can take up a problem from the point which it has reached after having undergone every previous attempt at a solution ... .

Ambedkar has aptly pointed out that the caste problem was taken up by high caste social reformers as one of reform of high caste Hindu family life and not for abolishing the caste system itself. That is why they did not go beyond the framework of Upanishadic or Christian monotheism and idealist philosophy. Phuley (died 1890) related social reform to caste abolition and national freedom to Sudras' (which included Untouchables and adivasis) emancipation. That is why he did not stop at adopting the theist mechanical materialism of the western bourgeois democratic revolutions but combined it with the non-Brahminical philosophies of India from *charvaka* materialism to Buddha's dependent origination. It should be noted that the term 'a Brahmana' (non-Brahminical) in Indian tradition means one opposed to the caste system and women's slavery to a lesser or greater extent. It, thus, can be seen that Phuley took the caste problem to a new philosophical stage. That is why Phuley was not just an ideologue but a philosopher. I call his philosophy non-Brahminical theistic materialism.

Before embracing neo-Buddhism in 1956, Ambedkar was an anti-caste social democrat. He opposed Indian communists only because they ignored the caste problem. He embraced Buddhist religion because he considered Buddha to be the greatest champion of equality. He equated Buddha's *dukkha* with economic (class exploitation) and social (caste) oppression and *dukkha-mukti* with emancipation from this exploitation and oppression. It should be noted that Buddha was not faced with the task of abolishing *jati* which was then a grouping and more productive social system, but he took every opportunity to oppose it. That is why, Ambedkar who was faced with the task of abolishing the moribund *jati* system, exposed Buddha's philosophy of dependent origination (*pratitya samutpada*). Dr Jatav, a Dalit scholar, calls Buddha's philosophy dialectical realism in his Hindi work on Indian philosophy. According to Buddha's dialectics (*a-nityatavada*), everything in the world comes into being and passes away, nothing is eternal (*nitya*). *Varna* and *jati* were not exception to this law. The Bhikkhu Maha-Katyayana tells the king of Mathura, who like other non-tribal kings of the times was considered a Sudra by the Brahmins, in the Madhuriya Sutta, that all four *varnas* are equal ('... *ime cattato varna sama sama honti* ...'). Buddha declares in the *Vasettha-Sutta* that *jatis* exist in the animal and plant world but not in human beings.

In his state socialism, Ambedkar called for nationalisation. It can be seen that Ambedkar took the problem of caste to a still more advanced philosophical stage. That is why Ambedkar was not just an ideologue but a philosopher. I call his philosophy socialistic dialectical realism.

Thus, both Phuleyism and Ambedkarism can meet Marxism on an equal philosophical ground.

Combination

Combination, electicism and synthesis differ from each other. Combination means mixing of two or more phenomena. Electicism means selective and subjective combination and synthesis means selective combination which results in the emergence of a qualitatively new phenomenon. Here, we will use the more simple and popular term 'combination'.

Can Ambedkarism and Marxism be combined? Marxists like Bedekar object to it by saying that Marxism, being a revolutionary philosophy of the proletariat, cannot be combined with a casteist bourgeois ideology.

It is well known that Marxism arose out of the combination of two philosophies—Hegel's dialectical (objective) idealism and Feurbach's mechanical materialism. Both were bourgeois democratic philosophies. How could a revolutionary proletarian philosophy arise from them? It is evident that Marxists visualise combination for Ambedkarism and Marxism, while they take for granted synthesis of Hegelism and Feurbachism.

Why is Marxism revolutionary? Because it wants to abolish classes. Ambedkar was also for abolishing classes, but he affirmed that classes cannot be abolished without prior abolition of castes, which indisputably proves that he was a revolutionary.

Communists argue by implication that Ambedkar preferred to become a leader of the Untouchables, i.e. he was a caste leader and not a class leader. Prof. Nalini Pandit, a Marxist, said in her review of Gail Omvedt's book on the non-Brahmin movement in Maharashtra in 1977 that only class struggles are progressive while caste and communal struggles are reactionary. She was but giving voice to a representative opinion of the Indian communists. Ambedkar led two famous anti-caste struggles in the 1920s and 1930s. The first was for drinking the water of the tank at Mahad in the Konkan and the second was the temple entry *satyagraha* at Nasik. In these, the Untouchables were raged against caste Hindus. Were these struggles reactionary? The organisational form of anti-caste struggles has undergone sea change during the post-Independence period. The struggle for changing the name of the Marathwada University to Dr Babasaheb Ambedkar Marathwada University was waged by a front of Dalit and non-Dalit organisations, i.e. its organisational form was of class, transcending caste. This is going to be the pattern of all future anti-caste struggles.

Communists regard the industrial working class of India the only proletariat in India and being a class, it is homogeneous. In his *Annihilation of Caste* (1936), Ambedkar challenged the homogeneity of the Indian proletariat, and pointing out that it was as much caste affected, he made his famous declaration that 'caste system is not merely division of labour. It is also a division of labourers'. In the conference of Dalit railway workers held at Manmand in 1937, he advised them to organise on caste line if their class union refuses to pay attention to their grievances arising out of caste discrimination. Since then he coined the term 'social proletariat'. Ambedkarism has now come to represent the social proletariat which is composed 'of the SC and ST workers'. Addressing a trade union conference of scientific workers in Calcutta on the eve of his death, B.T. Ranadive termed the SC and ST workers as 'the real proletariat' and warned the left trade union movement that it will be doomed if priority is not paid to solving the caste and community grievances of this section of the Indian proletariat.

Thus, Ambedkar was not a casteist leader but a revolutionary leader of the Indian social proletariat.

The existence of two proletariats is an established fact of Indian social reality and hence combination of these two proletariats and their philosophies is the most pressing need of the day.

Elements of Synthesis

Marxism

The first stage in synthesis of two or more philosophies is to set aside their outmoded elements and select the lasting ones.

The triad of Marxism consists of (1) dialectical and historical materialism, (2) scientific socialism, and (3) Marxist economics. In this triad Marxism stands head and shoulders above every other philosophy in the world.

Marxists world over consider last two of the triad to be capable of change and development, but the first to be inviolable. Nevertheless, Lenin seems to have thought otherwise. Debi Prasad

Chattopadhyaya in his *Lenin the Philosopher* quotes Lenin from his philosophical notebooks to say that a philosophical system will continue to grow out of each of the countless shades of reality.

Dialectics as living, many-sided knowledge with the number of sides eternally increasing, with an infinite number of shades of every approach and approximation to reality remaining the same (with a philosophical system growing into a whole out of each shade. p. 156).

The article containing this brilliant passage was published one year after the death of Lenin (1925). But, nevertheless, Marxist philosophy remained inviolable.

With the collapse of socialism in Eastern Europe and Soviet Union, the questions suppressed or ignored are roaring for answer.

The question as much applicable to the surviving socialist countries is: How could a classless society be built when class itself is still not adequately defined? Marx and Engels had left class undefined. Lenin defined it on the basis of ownership or non-ownership of the means of production. Speaking before the Third Congress of the Russian Young Communists League, he said: 'What is meant by classes in general? It is what permits one part of society to appropriate the labour of another. If one part of society appropriates all the land, we have the classes of landlords and peasants. If one part of society owns the plants and factories, shares and capital, while the other works for them, we have the classes of capitalists and proletarians' (Leontiev, *Political Economy*, 2002: pp. 14–15).

With the socialist revolution, private ownership in the means of production was abolished, and hence a classless society should have been established. But now it has been found that a class of party bureaucrats and technocrats controlled the means of production. A new dimension has been added to the definition of class which was visualised neither by Lenin who should have anticipated it after having written *Imperialism* nor by any of the ruling Communist parties.

But it should not be forgotten that Lenin's definition of class was historically correct. The first to define class was Plato (B.C. 428/427–347), who lived in the merchant democratic society of Greece which was based on the private ownership of the means of production. In his *Republic*, he said that in the process of socialism, growth of the division of labour leads to the division of classes (Jowet's trans., Vol. 1, 369 C–370 C). The classical economists confirmed the definition based on private property in the means of production.

The point now is that if the character of class can change from ownership also to control, class could have been preceded by institutions of exploitation and administration which controlled the means of production of their respective societies. This was not taken into account by Engels in his *The Origin of the Family, Private Property and the State* wherein he laid down that the slave society was preceded by the pre-class primitive communist society, without taking into consideration that this transition was mediated by the communal slave state called oligarchy, which survived in the form of the tribal slave state of Sparta. Hence, an unbridgeable gulf yawned between primitive communism and the slave society.

Confounded by this gulf, Dipankar Gupta surmised that the class methodology of Marxism is inapplicable to pre-class societies. The baby is, thus, being thrown away along with the bath water. Historical materialism is a methodology to study social evolution and not social evolution itself. Class methodology is the form of the present historical materialism and not its context. The content instructs us that in order to obtain real knowledge of a society, the study must start with its material base consisting of forces, means and relations of production and then proceed to the superstructure. Synthesising these two studies one arrives at the real knowledge of that society. This content helps us to study any society-pre-class *varna*, *jati*, race, etc. The class form of this methodology has become its fetter, restricting its scope and power of cognition. This contradiction between its form and context can be resolved by transforming its unilinear form into multilinear one.

M. Basavapunnaiah, a top CPI(M) ideologue, writing in the Marx centenary issue of *Social Scientist* (September 1983), criticised Mao for taking an anti-Marxist position in concluding that antagonistic and non-antagonistic contradictions do not exist in water-tight compartments but get transformed into each other, while according to Marx and Lenin, these contradictions existed in water-tight compartments and do not get transformed into each other. He stressed the point that class contradiction being the only antagonistic contradiction in society that can be resolved by revolutionary means, while all other contradictions, being non-antagonistic, can be solved by non-revolutionary means. By implication, it means that the caste-contradiction being non-antagonistic, it should be solved by non-revolutionary means. Marx, writing in *New York Tribune* on 8 August 1853, had declared that growth of modern industry in India would dissolve the hereditary divisions of labour, upon which rest the Indian caste. Indian communists transformed it into a dogma by formulating that caste will be abolished automatically in course of class struggle. Basavapunnaiah provided philosophical support to this outdated dogma. Outdated because S.G. Sardesai of the CPI had admitted in his booklet *Class Struggle and Caste Conflict in Rural Areas*, published in 1979 after the Marathwada anti-Dalit riots, that 50 years of communist movement has disproved this dogma and hence a minimum programme of caste abolition should be drawn up by the communist movement to implement which anti-caste struggle, in coordination with class struggles, should be waged. But like Ranadive's dying reprimand, Sardesai's call has gone unheeded. The left front has declared its intention to fight the new economic policy of the Rao Government tooth and nail, but has turned a blind eye to the proposed privatisation of public enterprises which will do away with present reservation to the SC and ST and future one to the OBC recommended by the Mandal Commission. It adamantly refuses to win over the 'real proletariat' and the OBC (peasantry in class terms) from the establishment.

Engels had declared at the end of his aforementioned book that democracy in future socialist society will be 'a revival, in a higher form, of the liberty, equality and fraternity of the ancient genes'. Maurice Bloch points out in his *Marxism and Anthropology* that no such primitive communist society ever existed. So the model for socialist democracy has proved to be totally a myth.

Only one democracy was in existence at the time of the first socialist revolution in the world, and it was bourgeois democracy. Lenin and Stalin had rejected it as bourgeois. Stalin was more outspoken in declaring in 1924 that 'the proletarian revolution had ... smashed bourgeois democracy' (*Problems of Leninism*, p. 14) Hence, what Stalin could offer to the Soviet people in the name of socialist democracy was proletarian dictatorship which inevitably turned into party dictatorship.

This tragic outcome was due to the non-dialectical and unhistorical conception of socialist democracy. Socialist democracy does not arise full grown as Draupadi arose out of the sacrificial fire. As it cannot be a 'resurrection' of the fictitious primitive communist democracy, it cannot also start from zero. It will have to make a synthesis of two historical democracies—tribal and bourgeois. Tribal democracy was either gynocratic or patriarchal. In tribal slave states, democracy was denied to the slaves. Even among the twice-born masters who enjoyed it, there was practically no scope for individual freedom. Rather the category of individual freedom was not born. Individual freedom is a produce of bourgeois democracy. The limitations of the bourgeois democracy have been discussed in detail world over; hence there is no need to go into it here. In passing it should be said that Ambedkar and Buddha will be of immense help in making this synthesis.

Ambedkarism

Phuley and Ambedkar had no systematised doctrines to offer like Marx's triad. Phuley had graphically depicted the social and economic woes of the Sudras (this term then covered the Untouchables and Adivasis or Ati-Sudras). Though he had not read Bachofer or Morgan or Engels, he drew his inspiration for a future society based upon total equality from the folktale of the Rakshasa Bali's kingdom. He was the first in modern India to characterise the struggle in India's history since the defeat of Bali at the hands of the Brahmin Vamana as the caste struggle between Brahmins and Sudras. He formulated his theory of the origin of the four *varnas* on the basis of this folk tradition and the western postulation according to which fair-skinned foreign invaders belonging to the upper three *varnas* (Brahmana, Kshatriya and Vaisya) enslaved the local dark-skinned people resulting in the formation of the fourth Sudra *varna*. He considered women to be superior to men and affirmed that women's emancipation is a pre-condition to men's emancipation.

Ambedkar developed Phuley's legacy, with the exception that he internalised the theory of the formation of the four *varnas*, in which he was influenced by the famous historian V.K. Rajwade. In his *Who were the Sudras*, he postulated that due to the refusal of the Brahmins to initiate a section of the Kshatriya *varna*, the uninitiated became Sudras and formed the fourth *varna*. Kosambi, who was one of four greatest Marxist historians, subscribed to the colour theory of *varna* by interpreting the word *varna* to mean colour though he left a pregnant suggestion to the effect that out of the seven primal sages (*saptarshi*), except Vishvamitra, all other sages belonged to pre-Aryan matrilineal stock (*The Culture and Civilisation of Ancient India in Historical Outline*, 1970, pp. 82–83). All scholars, Marxist or non-Marxist, subscribe to this colour theory, and are agreed that the *varna* system was of the standard four *varna* type. It has been proved in *Dasa-Sudra Slavery* that the original meaning of *varna* was moiety, meaning half of a tribe, and the *varna* system originated in a gynocratic tribe led by Nirrti in the early period of Indus civilisation. The *varna* system was never soley, of the standard four *vama* type. The gynocratic tribal state was of two *varnas* (Kshatra and Brahman), the non-Brahminical *rajaka* (monarchical) tribal slave States had three *varnas* (Kshatriya, Brahmin and Dasa) while the oligarchies (a *rajaka or sangha-gana*) again had two *varnas* (Kshatriya and Dasa).

Ambedkar defined caste as 'enclosed class' again under the influence of another Brahmin scholar, V.S. Ketkar. According to this theory, it seems that ancient India had a primary class system before it was transformed into a caste one. By caste here Ambedkar understood *jati*; for he considered *varna* society, which preceded the *jati* society more open and hence a class society. Except the gynocratic society consisting of two *varnas*, namely, Kshatra (women) and Brahman (men), all other *varna* societies mentioned above were tribal slave societies which were closed to their communal slaves called Dasa or Sudras. In the patriarchal four *varna rajakas* and oligarchies, women of even the twice born *varnas were* deprived of the right to initiation and hence reduced virtually to the status of Dasas or Sudras. Even among the twice-born *varnas* individuals from the Vaisya *varna* like the Suta Karna could not obtain Kshatriyahood though he was the bravest and one of the noblest of the age. Can then the *varna* society be called a class society?

Ambedkar could not completely shake off the influence of the Marxist class theory of caste, i.e. caste is a manifestation of class. All Marxist scholars, without exception, think that *varna* and *jati* are super-structural manifestations of class. Very few Marxist historians, e.g. Mohammad Habib, B.N.S. Yadav and Satish Chandra, treat caste as a separate category, and that is why their historical exposition is more fruitful. Nevertheless, no Marxist indologist as yet has posed the question: Was there class in pre-British Indian society?

Georgy Thomson points out in his monumental work *Studies in Ancient Greek Society* that there was no class in ancient Greek society up to the end of its oligarchic stage and class came into being when it passed from the oligarchic to the merchant democratic stage in which tribalism disintegrated to the extent of giving rise to private property, family and the state. As pointed out earlier, Vedic *varna* society was a tribal society and it started, disintegrating during the lifetime of Buddha. But Indian society did not pass from oligarchy to merchant democracy. It passed from oligarchic *varna* society to feudal *jati* society. Hence, private property and its resultant class could not arise in the feudal *jati* society. As far as linguistic evidence is concerned, the Vedic society did have the word *varga* which started being used to denote class in the last half of the 19th century. But Panini grammatical rules like *vargya-adayasca*' explain that *varga* meant moiety or half of any thing during the Vedic age.

Grammatical and Dharmasastra literature shows that during the pre-Turkish *jati* feudal period also, *varga* and its derivatives never meant class, but denoted institutions like *puga* and sreni and their members.

As far as the Indo-Turkish feudal *jati* period is concerned, the Arab, Turk, Afghan and Mughal rulers themselves hailed from their respective tribes and hence they could hardly be expected to break up the *jat*i society. On the contrary, they themselves were affected by the *jati* system. Even during this period, linguistic and historical literature furnishes us with no word for class.

The British capitalistic imperialism brought the institution of class for the first time in the history of India. But it did not destroy caste as understood by Marx. It's capitalistic imperialist interests needed caste for pumping out super profits and for keeping India divided. Gandhiji considered caste to be more 'useful' than class for national capitalistic interests. As shown by Jayant Lele in his *Elite Pluralism and Class Rule* (1982), the political representatives of Indian capitalist and landlord castes-classes and the elite of dominating peasant castes use caste now in a pluralist manner. That is why caste and class should be defined comparatively.

Jati	*Class*
(1) *Jati* is hereditary.	(1) Class is not hereditary.
(2) Profession is hereditary.	(2) Profession is not hereditary.
(3) Marriage outside one's *jati* class is prohibited.	(3) Marriage outside one's is not prohibited.
(4) Restriction on the food and drink of *jatis* other than one's own.	(4) No restriction on the food and drink of classes other than one's own.
(5) Separate and boycotted localities.	(5) No separate and boycotted localities.
(6) Council (panchayat) for internal administration of a *jati*.	(6) No council for internal administration of a class.

Common to both is the characteristic that both are instruments of exploitation and administration.

In spite of all modifications that have taken place during post-Independence capitalist development, *jati* as a system stays for reasons mentioned above.

Is caste material? Communists consider it to be superstructural, mental, and that is mainly why they deny the need to wage anti-caste struggles. Though Ambedkar did not clinch this issue, he conducted anti-caste struggles for caste abolition. The second characteristic in the table shows the inseparable connection of caste with the means of production. The Ati-Sudras, living outside Indian villages are the proletariat of the caste system. According to the Dharmasastra, they were *a-dhan* (propertyless). Manu lays down that the king should compel the Vaisya and Sudra producer to perform their hereditary professions; otherwise they would throw the whole society into confusion. The means of production were either owned or controlled by the two ruling feudal castes, namely, military and Brahmin. That is why caste was and is material.

The CPM(M) leaders like Godavari Parulekar still preach that by abolishing untouchability you abolish caste, while Ambedkar declared that untouchability is worse than slavery and that it being an inseparable part of the caste system, the former can be abolished only by abolishing the latter.

Strategies of Democratic Revolution

Though both Ambedkar and Marxists are agreed on the objective of accomplishing the democratic revolution, their strategies differ. Communists want abolition of landlordism (in whatever form it may be) and redistribution of the surplus land among the class of agricultural labourers and poor peasants (with priority to the SC and ST) in order to clear the way for industrial development. Contrary to this, Ambedkar did not want to stop at abolition of landlordism and redistribution of land. He demanded abolition of the caste system with it and nationalisation of land in order to guarantee abolition of the caste system. As an economist he was of the confirmed opinion that caste system is the greatest impediment to industrial development.

In the communist strategy, the worker-peasant alliance is headed by the working class and directed against the ruling alliance of capitalist and landlord classes. In Ambedkar's strategy, the alliance of Untouchable castes, *Adivasi* and criminal tribes and Sudra castes is headed by the Untouchable castes and directed against the three twice-born castes. Later on, he tuned from caste to caste-class strategy. For, he repeatedly declared that the main enemies of the Indian people are Brahminism (caste system) and capitalism (class system). Unfortunately, he did not live to elaborate it.

Enlightenment

Ambedkar had pointed out in 1936 itself that 'political revolutions have always been preceded by social and religious revolutions'. He clarified this statement by saying that 'the emancipation of the mind and the soul is a necessary preliminary for the political expansion of a people'. Emancipation of the mind is obtained by enlightenment. Marxists will, of course agree with Ambedkar on this point.

But after this agreement, disagreement starts. Should it be class enlightenment or caste one? If there was no class in pre-British Indian society, how can there be a class enlightenment regarding Indian society, history, literature, arts, philosophy, science and culture? It is due to their insistence on class enlightenment that Marxist scholars try to find class struggles in pre-British Indian society, history, literature, arts, philosophy science and culture, thereby failing to see the wealth of caste struggles, end up by imposing the identity of class struggle on some of the caste struggles themselves!

Though Ram Manohar Lohia was the only anti-caste leftist leader, the supreme heroes of India for him were Rama and Krishna and not Buddha. Communists in Maharashtra had no independent enlightened counterblast to Shiv Sena's stormy mass campaign against inclusion of the appendix 'Riddles of Rama and Krishna' in Ambedkar's Vol. 4, entitled *Riddles of Hinduism*. Two independent scholars, historian Dr T.D. Phadke and the Sanskritist Dr Rupa Kulkarni, put up a defence of Ambedkar's critique, but they did not differentiate themselves from the negative features of Ambedkar's non-Brahminical methodology. In criticising Rama and Krishna, non-Brahmanical methodology goes to the extreme of upholding Ravana and Kansa. This methodology is justified in espousing the cause of Sambuka and Ekalavya who were victims of the *varna* slave order, but it is unable to understand that this social order was more productive than the previous one and in this social context Brahminical heroes like Rama were revolutionary and that is why they became the idols of Indian people. Such a positive evaluation can be made only by Marxism. But due to its dogmatic adherence to class methodology, it tries to defeat BJP and RSS with their own weapons! When the BJP started its all India Ram-pierced *rathyatra* movement, Somnath Chatterjee, speaking in the Parliament, condemned the *rakshasas* and Ravanas, demons and evil incarnate, implying thereby that Rama was good incarnate. If a whole people can be condemned as demons and evil incarnate, why not condemn the Pakistani people similarly, equating them with their government? Not to be outdone in this eulogy of Rama, the CPI leader A.B. Bardhan, addressing a public meeting in Aurangabad during the election campaign that followed the *yatra*, compared Rama with V.P. Singh (who was on the dais) and Ravana with L.K. Advani. Thus, class enlightenment in India turns into Brahminical enlightenment.

Ambedkar's non-Brahminical enlightenment drove the OBCs into BJP's arms by its indiscriminate condemnation of Rama and Krishna while Marxist enlightenment drove them further into the Brahminical camp by unconditional eulogisation of Rama.

In Shivaji, we have a case in which both the camps tried with each other to appropriate him as their exclusive hero. The Brahminical camp glorified him as the nationalist champion of Hindu religion and its caste system. Phuley claimed him as a kind of the Sudra peasantry. Govind Pansare of the CPI tried again to hold him up as a leader of the peasantry. But the peasants live within the precincts of their villages, while the Untouchables and adivasis live outside them. If Shivaji did nothing whatsoever for these boycotted people, he cannot be considered to be anti-caste neither Phuley nor Ambedkar were able to prove him as anti-caste, while communists were not at all interested in showing him in that identity. In my recently published book *Who were the Real Enemies of Shivaji's Hindavi Svaraj, Muslims or Brahmins*, it has been proved that Shivaji, as a Sakta—a sect of the most anti-caste Tantrika religion—opposed the caste system and as a result of which he was poisoned by his Brahmin ministers with the help of his chief queen Soyarabai.

This proves that only synthesising the Ambedkarist and Marxist methodologies can an enlightenment be forged which will be capable of 'emancipating the minds' of the caste-ridden Indian people.

6

The Buddhist Ambedkar

B.V.S. Bhanusree

Born as an Untouchable, Ambedkar was not an exception to face and experience the same humiliation and tribulations, which every Untouchable had to face in those days. School, college, institution, or society wherever he entered, he was humiliated. He struggled continuously to face poverty and untouchability. In his own words: 'Owing to the poverty of my father I did not have the opportunity to enjoy any of these luxuries. Till late in life I suffered excessively and laboured very hard.'[1] He realised at his early stage itself that he was not alone in such a suffering world. He had seen people not having sufficient food to eat; women with no clothes to cover their bodies; no roof over their heads to give them shelter; no land to grow foodgrains. They were utterly downtrodden and poverty-stricken; they were oppressed and exploited; they had no dignity, and no value at all.

What was supposed to be the reason for only a particular section of people in a big society like India to suffer? Ambedkar struggled a lot to get the answer for it. He blamed Hinduism which, he thought, was the reason for this plight which was based on inequality and injustice. It divided men cruelly in the name of caste. In its fold some people became Untouchables and slaves. It never encouraged them to develop their minds and to advance in life. It suppressed the enthusiasm and inspiration of the students of the downtrodden class of people. He realised intensely that the Hindu religion did not appeal his conscience, and did not appeal to his self-respect. So, as long as the downtrodden remain in Hindu fold, they cannot lift their heads up and move fearlessly. To quote him: 'This religion and the social order had ruined us. But this is not going to stop here. This would ruin the Hindus themselves and ultimately India'.[2] So, he decided not to live any more in the Hindu fold. Though by chance he was born Hindu, he did not want, at least, to die a Hindu. Since then he went on constantly thinking and searching for the most appropriate form of religion that touches the heart of the grief stricken humanity.

Learning of his views, Sikhs, Muslims and Christians invited him to join their respective religions. They offered enormous funds and other amenities, not only for himself but for his followers as well. But, he flatly refused all these tempting offers.

In spite of all the atrocities that he had gone through, Ambedkar was not against religion. He considered it essential for the proper development of mankind. He did not agree with those who said that 'religion is a parasite' or 'is an opiate'. According to him, 'man cannot live by bread alone. He had mind which needs food for thought. Religion instils hope in man and drives him to activity'.[3]

What Sort of Religion does Mankind Need Today?

Keeping this problem in mind, Ambedkar carefully examined and analysed all the four major religions of the world, namely, Christianity, Islam, Hinduism and Buddhism. He found that Christ claimed that he was the son of God and those who wished to enter the kingdom of God would fail if they did not recognise him as the son of God. Mohammad went a step further. He claimed that he was the messenger of God and also, that one should accept that he was the last messenger. Both of them claimed that what they taught was the word of God and so infalliable and therefore beyond question. Krishna claimed that he himself was God and what he taught was original and final and the question of infalliability would not arise at all. But Buddha never made such claims. He asked his disciples not to follow him blindly, but accept him only after testing his words with reason.

Ambedkar felt that modern civilisation needed such a rational religion. He wished to have the religion in the sense of morality which remain the governing principle in every society. It must be scientific. As a social code of morality, it must recognise the fundamental tenets of liberty, equality and fraternity. The most important thing is that it has to enrich the lives of people mentally and materially and protect their dignity, value and self-respect. Ambedkar found that Buddhism was the only religion that satisfied all these tests.

Ambedkar also rejected the modern ideologies like Marxism and communism whose main principle is based on force. 'No doubt, the communists get quick results because when you adopt the means of annihilating men, they do not remain to oppose you'.[4] But, what the grief stricken men need is not such treatment. They need love, sympathy and persuasion. This, he found in Buddhism. Buddha wanted to conquer the opponent by inculcating love and not by exercising power. Ambedkar was deeply moved by Buddha's attitude towards humanity. To quote: 'Just as mother would protect her only child at the risk of her own life, even so, the Buddha cultivated a boundless love pervaded the whole world, above, below and across, without any obstruction, without any enmity'.[5] With this, the greatness of Buddha reached its heights in Ambedkar's view.

At the age of 16, Ambedkar was presented with a book, entitled *Buddha Charita* in Marathi, by his people, on the occasion of his success in matriculation. He was much fascinated by reading it. This was the first incident which associated him with Buddhism. Thereafter, he studied the vast literature of Buddhism and was inspired by its principles and ideals. Impressed by the speeches and discussions with the Italian Buddhist teacher, Ven Lokanatha, he moved much further towards Buddhism. He started associating himself with Buddhist monks and scholars, like Ven. L. Ariyawan sa, Ven. Jagdish Kashyap and Mahapandit Rahul Sankrityayan and so on. At last, on 14 October 1956, Dr Ambedkar converted himself from Hinduism to Buddhism along with millions of his followers in Nagpur.

Ambedkar's View of Buddhism

Ambedkar realised that Buddhism was the greatest of all the religions in the world, as it was not merely a religion but a great social doctrine. His research-oriented mind was fully convinced by the logical, empirical, humanistic and pragmatic teachings of Buddha. He observed that besides *ahimsa,* Buddha taught many other things, such as social freedom, intellectual freedom, economic freedom and political freedom. It would be difficult to find a religious teacher to compare with Buddha whose teaching embrace so many aspects of social life and whose doctrines are so modern and whose main concern was to give salvation to man in his life on earth and not to promise it to him in the heaven after he is dead.

Recognition of human suffering was the real basis of Buddhism. Ambedkar emotionally declares that 'never in the history of the world has any founder of a religion taught that the removal of this misery is the real purpose of it'.[6] This point touched his heart deep. He was much impressed by Buddha's interpretations of the traditional concepts. He observed that Buddha did not believe in soul. Indeed, in his opinion, the belief in the existence of soul is far more dangerous than belief in God. Regarding rebirth, Buddha seemed to believe in the regeneration of the matter and not in the rebirth of the soul. Buddha's view, so interpreted, felt Ambedkar, was in consonance with the science.

The law of *karma* in Buddhism is different from that of Hinduism. Buddha's doctrine of *ahimsa* does not say, 'kill not'. It says, 'love all'. He did not ban killing where there was a need to kill. He did not make *ahimsa* a matter of rule. He enunciated it as a matter of principle or way of life. Ambedkar tried to interpret Buddhism in modern terms and make it suitable for the present conditions. He compared the concept of *dukkha* with poverty, slavery, inequality, exploitation, depression and mental agony. Eradication of all forms of suffering and getting liberated is *nirvana*. He emphatically says that Buddhism is the most appropriate religion in which there is no place for the distinction of high or low, rich or poor, caste, colour, etc. It is the religion based on equality and universal brotherhood. Buddha never preached that there existed any superhuman person on earth. The aim of all human beings should be to attain *nirvana*, peace and prosperity for all. Nobody should rule over others simply because he took birth in a ruling family. One attains rank and respect by one's own actions not by birth. The doors of Buddhism are open for everyone. Just as all the rivers lost their identity when they entered into the sea, all the men lost their identities and become one when they join Buddhism.

Ambedkar says that the struggle of the downtrodden is not simply for economic progress, but for honour and self-respect. To say in his own words: 'For a man it is his birth right to lead an honourable life. To achieve this aim, we must do our utmost. We are prepared to make the greatest sacrifice for achieving this. We are struggling for human dignity. We want to make our life as full and whole-some as possible. We have started this movement to develop and educate our minds'.[7] One needs confidence, courage and will to rise. Ambedkar believed that Buddhism as a humanistic religion provides all these things.

The essence of Buddhism lies in working practically for one's freedom—economic, social and political. Buddha was the torch bearer of democracy and an ardent exponent of liberty, equality and fraternity. It is only in Buddhism he insisted, that a man can have freedom.

Another interesting observation made by Ambedkar in Buddhism was the equal treatment of women. According to him: 'It is true that Buddha did advise his disciples (*Bhikkus*) not to make it a habit to visit families of lay disciples for fear of human weakness yielding to frequent contact with women. But he did not forbid such visits nor did he express any disdain about women as such'.[8] He believed that Buddha did not regard women as inferior to men to treat them and regard them as mothers, sisters and daughters according to their ages. He knows that women were fully capable of realising his doctrine and discipline. That's why he maintained Bhikkuni Sangha along with Bhikku Sangha. The Bhikkuni Sangha has been opened for all classes of women—married, unmarried, widowed and even for prostitutes. All could acquire merit, freedom, dignity, and equality along with men.

The reason why Buddha had to maintain two separate *sanghas* was that he knew the sex instinct to be a great force in the lives of men and women. It is this instinct which drives a man into woman's bondage and a woman into man's bondage. This force, if given an opportunity to have its full force, the rule of celibacy could not last for a minute. To save the rule of celibacy he had to organise two separate Sanghas.

The Bhikkhus who were already instructed in his doctrine and trained in his discipline took the responsibility to instruct the Bhikkunis. By entrusting the work of training them, the relationship between them became one of teacher and pupil.

Though we find some passages that shows the negative attitude of Buddha towards womankind in Buddhist literature, Ambedkar firmly ruled them out as they are not the original words of Buddha. So many passages, according to him, are later interpolations. In the first place, the Pitakas were not reduced to writing till 400 years after the death of Buddha. And, as Rhys Davids says: 'All of them, narrators, teachers, editors were men whose choice of ideas of life differed from that of the rest of the world ... though this distorting medium he has to read, and asks himself which saying put into the mouth of a certain accredited 'teacher and way-shower' of truth are likely to have come from such a man as he is recorded to have been.'[9] Besides all these, Ambedkar was strongly convinced that being a rationalist, Buddha would not teach anything which is irrational, unempirical and unverifiable.

How to Practise Buddhism

In the preface of *Buddha Puja Paath*, Ambedkar wrote how to practise *dhamma*. He quoted from *Dhammapada*:

1. Not to do any evil to cultivate good to purify one's thoughts (183).
2. Arise! Be not negligent! Lead a righteous life. The righteous live happily in this world and the other (168).
3. He is not versed in the *dhamma* merely because he speaks much. He who hears little, but sees the truth mentally and observes it well indeed, he is called versed in the *dhamma* (259).

Ambedkar says that it is the duty of every Buddhist to visit Buddha Vihara on every Sunday and listen to the discourses. Unless this is done, the neo-Buddhists will not be able to understand Buddhism properly.[10] He also suggested his men not to encourage violence, work hard and educate themselves; face any problem with calm and in a peaceful way, without fear in mind. They must choose only Buddhism for their mental and physical upliftment and maintain dignity and value. In one of his speeches, he asked them to convert into Buddhism for, 'getting liberty, … . He expected that they should aim at building a society of humans, not of beasts. They should not do anything that brings bad name to the society'.[11]

Propagation of Buddhism

It is the duty of every Buddhist that he should not only liberate himself, but should try to elevate his country and the world in general. No religion can live without propaganda, in any form. One should work hard selflessly for this great task. Of course, propagation cannot be undertaken without men and money. It is the duty of not the individuals, but also of the nations. If the Buddhist countries do not develop the will to spread Buddhism, it will not be done. They must realise that the duty of a Buddhist is not merely to be a good Buddhist, but to spread Buddhism. They must have the belief that to spread Buddhism is to serve mankind.

Conclusion

I would like to conclude with the words of Ambedkar by way of summation. He said: 'India would rise once again to its glory only when people turn to Buddhism and practise the high ethical principles preached by Lord Buddha … .'[12] He further said, 'As long as man does not know how to behave with man and creates barriers between man and man, India can never attain the grandeur and glory of ancient days. To end all these ills, India must embrace Buddhism. Buddhism is the only religion based upon ethical principles that teaches how to work for the good and well-being of the common man'.[13]

Notes

1. Speech at the occasion of the Great Conversion Ceremony at Nagpur on 15 October 1956.
2. Ibid.
3. Quoted from Ahir, D.C. (Ed.), *Dr. Ambedkar on Buddhism*, Bombay: Siddharth Publications, 1973, p. 36.
4. Speech at the occasion of the Fourth Conference of the World Fellowship of Buddhists, held at Kathmandu, Nepal, on 20 November 1956.

5. Fausboll, V., *Sutta Nipata*, Oxford: Clarendon Press, 1881, pp. 148–149.
6. Ambedkar, B.R., *The Buddha and His Dhamma*, Bombay: Siddharth College Publication, 1957, p. 131.
7. Speech at the occasion of the Great Conversion Ceremony at Nagpur on 15 October 1956.
8. 'The Rise and Fall of the Hindu Women: Who was Responsible for It?', *Maha Bodhi*, Calcutta, 1950.
9. Davids, Mrs Rhys and F.L. Woodward, Preface to *The Book of Kindred Sayings*, Vol. II, Pali Text Society, London, 1989.
10. B.R. Ambedkar's written speech in Marathi at the conference held in Bombay on 30–31 May 1936. This speech was first published in the Maharashtra Government's special issue 'Laka Rajya' brought out on 16 April 1981. It had been translated into English by Vasant Moon and was first published in the 'Oppressed Indian', the organ of the BAMCEF. Also, published in the *Jantak Lehar*, Jalandhar (Punjab), Vol. 3, No. 4, April 1916.
11. *Baidha Dharma Hi Manav Dharma*, Speeches at Sarnath, Varanasi, from 24 to 27 November 1956, quoted from Ahir, D.C. (Ed.), *Dr. Ambedkar on Buddhism*, Bombay: Siddharth Publications, p. 57.
12. 'Buddha and the Future of His Religion', *Maha Bodhi*, Vol. 58, April-May 1950.
13. Speech in New Delhi on Buddha Jayanthi in 1950.

References

Ahir, D.C., *Dr. Ambedkar on Buddhism*, Bombay: Siddharth Publications, 1982.

Ambedkar, B.R., *The Buddha and His Dhamma*, Bombay: Siddharth College Publication, 1957.

Balley, L.R., *Ambedkarian Thoughts: Relevance of Ambedkar Mission*, Jalandhar: Buddhist Publishing House, 1946.

Davids, Mrs Rhys and F.L. Woodward, *The Book of the Kindred Sayings (Part-II: Sanyutta Nikaya)*, London: Pali Text Society, 1917.

Falboll, V., *A Collection of Discourses* (Suttanipate), Delhi: Motilal Banarsidass, 1968.

Kusuma, D.R., *Abhinava Buddha Ambedkar Suktulu* (Compiled-Telugu), Hyderabad: Ambedkar Memorial Society, 1970.

Ling, Trevor, *Buddhist Revival in India*, London: The Macmillan Press Ltd., 1980.

Max Muller, F., *A Collection of Verses* (Dhammapada), Delhi: Motilal Banarsidass, 1968.

Rhys Davids, T.W. and C.A.F. Rhys Davids, *Dialogues of the Buddha (Part-II: Digha Nikaya)*, London: Pali Text Society, 1921.

Setty, N.S., *A Brief Life Sketch of Dr. B.R. Ambedkar*, Hyderabad: Ambedkar Memorial Society, 1987.

Singh, Sanghasen (Ed.), *Ambedkar on Buddhist Conversion and its Impact*, Delhi: Eastern Book Linkers, 1990.

7

Buddhism, Secularism and Ambedkar

K.N. Kadam

We talk about secularism usually in a very loose manner, and we equate it in common parlance with *dharma nirapeksha vada* and *sarva dharma samabhava*, which to my mind, are not precisely the same as secularism. The ambiguity surrounding the concept of secularism is probably due to its being a relatively new concept in the realm of thought, so much is our thinking dominated by religion that it is difficult to think otherwise. In this paper, an attempt is made to understand the nature of secularism, and to explore the extent to which Buddhism is secular.

There are also doubts in the minds of some intellectuals whether Ambedkar may be considered to be a secular thinker especially on account of his spirited advocacy of Buddhism. An attempt is, therefore, made to adduce evidence of Ambedkar's secularism.

The relevance of this topic to our times cannot be underestimated. We are all apprehensive of the danger of fundamentalism in the world today: I mean the danger of Hindu fundamentalism, Islamic fundamentalism, Sikh fundamentalism, and so on. In fact, it was fundamentalism that drove Buddhism out of its homeland for quite a long time. It is, therefore, imperative that, if the human race, as a whole, is to live in peace, progress and prosperity, fundamentalism must be persuaded to see reason.

Historical Background

Confining ourselves to the story since the infiltration of the Aryan hordes through the mountain passes in the north-west into the sunny plains of India, around 1200 B.C., we see that religion and religious institutions have been dominating men's minds (Kadam, 1985).

The stranglehold of religion continues to this day, notwithstanding the protest of the Upanishadic philosophers against Vedicism and Brahmanism, and despite the protests of skeptics, materialists, hedonists and rationalists and secularists, from time to time. So long as Buddhism is not regarded as a religion, and wherever Buddhism is not viewed as a religion, Buddha will always be regarded as a secularist. It was his secularism that shook Vedicism to its foundations. And it was his object to reconstruct the world on the down to earth secular principles of justice, liberty, equality and fraternity—the very principles incorporated in the secular Constitution of independent India.

After the decline of Buddhism, India relapsed into Brahminism, casteism, ritualism, superstition and untouchability fortified and defended by the *Gita* and the *Manu Smriti*, thereby spreading darkness and ignorance and injustice into the world that had been enlightened by Buddha. Religious fundamentalism drove Buddhism out of India. This process started with the assassination of Brihadratha Maurya, in 185 B.C., and the enthronement of the Brahmin dynasty of Pushyamitra Sunga.

The way was now clear for fundamentalism and its Brahminical law-givers who gave us the world's most tyrannical laws loaded totally in favour of the Brahmin, and detrimental beyond comparison to the Sudra. A.R. Biswas (1990) observes in his essay on *Manu, Dr Ambedkar and the Supreme Court*: 'The Dharmasutras do not fail to remind us of the Brahmin's immunity. According to Gautama, this immunity is total. A Brahmin ought not to be beaten, not put in irons, nor condemned to a fine, nor banished, nor censured nor abandoned'.

From the point of view of legal history, it is important to note here that the Brahminical law since Vedic times was 'authoritarian', that is, based on the authority of the religious *Shastras*, or 'shabda pramanyas'. Subsequently, in the regions conquered by Muslim invaders, Muslim rulers administered the *Shariat* based on the *Koran* so far as Muslim were concerned. However, under Muslim rule, the *sultans* and emperors 'generally admitted that Hindus should remain subject to their (own) laws and customs in matters of private law, such as family law, inheritance, partition, adoption and the like. But the court of the *kadi* could only judge according to Islamic law' (Biswas, 1990). Biswas further observes that *kadi* (or *kazi*) was in practice 'assisted by a *pundit* in the case of Hindu law, and by a *mufti* in the case of Islamic law'. Furthermore, the Muslim authorities allowed local bodies a large measure of autonomy. Biswas says: '... village assemblies or caste tribunals, under the name of panchayats, became the ordinary courts for the Hindus, which gradually usurped the powers of the state courts and passed judgments for which there was no appeal'. This deference shown to the respective communities, to my mind, did not radically alter the nature of the law applied, nor did it make it secular.

With the advent of British rule in India, after the battle of Plassey, the old authoritarian system based on the words of the Shastras and Smritis underwent a radical change, substituting 'the role of law' or 'legality' in place of the old authoritarian system. As has been observed by Ambedkar in his *The Evolution of Provincial Finance in British India* (1925: 1–2):

> ... each Governor-in-Council was also empowered to make and issue such rules, ordinances and regulations for the good order and civil government of the territories he individually command, provided that they were just and reasonable and not repugnant to the laws of the British realm. To the codes promulgated by these authorities must be added the body of English statute law introduced in India so far as it was applicable by the character of George I, in 1776.

The process of secularisation gained momentum during the British period in India. As D.R. Jatava observes (1987: 159):

> The British rule brought with it a process of secularisation of Indian social life and culture, a tendency that gradually became stronger with the development of communications, growth of

> towns and cities, increased spatial mobility, and the spread of education.

He further says (1987: 160):

> The western Christian impact, therefore, enabled Indians to pay more attention in human life on earth and promote the general material attitude in social, political relationship. It made them conscious of their social and political ills and encouraged them to uproot these evils.

The British government in India, of course, had its own handicaps. Especially after the Mutiny of 1857, the British pledged not to interfere with the traditions of the people of India. The British parliament (perhaps due to its internal limitations) could not abolish the Hindu and Mohammedan laws, and introduce a common civil code of law for all. Even in independent India, Ambedkar resigned in utter disgust from his position as Law Minister, on 11 October 1951, when his Hindu Code Bill was opposed by the Indian Parliament (Kadam, 1998: 122).

What is Secularism?

In his *Sceptical Essays* (1934: 146–47), eminent philosopher Bertrand Russell says: 'I am myself a dissenter from all known religions, and I hope that every kind of religious belief will die out. I do not believe that, on the balance, religious belief has been a force for good'. It will be my endeavour, in the course of this essay, to maintain that religion and its extreme form of 'fundamentalism', both are social 'diseases' that must be cured for the sound health of the human body politic. It would, therefore, be necessary to understand these diseases before we analyse their remedy, namely, secularism.

What then is religion? The best analysis of religion, to my mind, is found in Ambedkar's *The Buddha and His Dhamma*. He says (1957: 315):

> The word 'religion' is an indefinite word with no fixed meaning … . This is because religion has passed through many stages. The concept at each stage is called religion, though the concept at each stage had a different meaning. In the evolutionary course of religion, it came to be identified with magic;

then with beliefs, rituals, ceremonies, prayers and sacrifices; belief in gods and God as the Creator; belief in the soul.

Ambedkar rejects this concept of religion, thereby rejects magic, and beliefs associated with religion. He rejects rituals, ceremonies, prayers, sacrifices, belief in gods and God, soul rebirth, etc. Religion, he believes, 'is personal and one must keep it to oneself. One must not let it play its part in public life' (1957: 316).

Let us read this with what Ambedkar had said earlier in his *Annihilation of Caste* (1979: 75): 'What is called religion by the Hindus is nothing but a multitude of commands and prohibitions. Religion in the sense of spiritual principles, truly universal, applicable to all times, is not to be found in them'.

To my mind, these words of Ambedkar clearly reject the concept of traditional religion, and pave the way for broader humanism and secularism.

Having briefly discussed the concept of religion, it would also be useful to understand the nature of the diametrically opposite concept of fundamentalism. The *Oxford Encyclopedia Dictionary* defines fundamentalism as 'strict maintenance of traditional, orthodox religious beliefs, such as inerrancy of scripture and literal acceptance of the creeds as fundamentals'. Thus, fundamentalism is 'anti-intellectual', revisionist, and revivalist, and would go even to the extent of preventing the teaching of the Darwinian theory of evolution.

What does the term 'secularism' mean? Brewer's *Dictionary of Phrases & Fables* says that secularism is 'the name given in 1846 by George Jacob Holyoake (1817–1906) to an ethical system founded on "natural morality" and opposed to the tenets of released religion and acclesiasticism'. I consider this definition important as it appears to be the earliest one. Secondly, let us take the *Oxford Encyclopedia Dictionary* which says: 'Secularism is concerned with the affairs of this world; not sacred, not monastic or ecclesiastical; temporal "profane" lay sceptical of religious truth or opposed to religious education'. Thirdly, *The New Webster's Dictionary of the English Language* defines secularism as the 'secular spirit or tendencies, especially, a system of beliefs which rejects all forms of religious faith, worship the view that public education and other matters be conducted without the introduction of a religious element'. Fourthly, the *Encyclopedia Britannica* distinguishes a 'secular society' from a 'sacred society'. 'In a secular society, there is willingness and ability amongst its members to respond to new cultural elements, whereas in a "sacred" society there is unwillingness or inability to change'. It says further: 'A secular society is accessible to contact with other value systems. Its value system is thereby impermeable. The movement towards secularism has been in progress during the entire course of modern history, and has often been anti-Christian and anti-religious'. Fifthly, *The Encyclopedia Americana* describes secularism as an ethical system founded on principles of natural morality and independent of revealed religion, or supernaturalism. Its first postulate is 'freedom of thought—the right of every man to think for himself … . Implied in this postulate as its necessary complement is the right to difference of opinion upon all subjects of thought …'. I may add, the right to difference of opinion comprehends the right to hereby. Sixthly, *The Encyclopedia of Religion and Ethics* says: 'It is impossible to ignore the fact that serious social wrongs produced the reaction of which secularism was one of the fruits'. It describes secularism as a movement intentionally ethical, negatively religious with political and philosophical antecedents. Seventhly, *The English and Marathi Dictionary*, edited by Molesworth and Candy, and published by the Deccan College, Poona, in 1847, defines the term 'secular' as relating to this present world, not spiritual. And lastly, *Angreji Kosh* defines the Hindi term the *dharam nirapekhsh* as 'secular'. If these terms are taken to mean 'aloof from religion', then secularism would mean 'keeping aloof from religious matters in public life'.

Our own improvised Marathi version of the term 'secularism' is worth noting. The nearest equivalent terms currently used are *sarva-dharma-samabhava* and *dharma-nirapekshate* (*Sarva-dharma-samabhava*, to my mind, is not secularism; it only means equal respect for all regions).

Having looked upon some of the various definitions of secularism, it would be useful to note some of its principal characteristics, which to my mind, are as follows:

1. Unlike religion which is concerned with God, souls and the other world, secularism is concerned with the affairs of this world.

2. Secularism is skeptical of religious profession of truth, and is opposed to religious education in schools.
3. Secularism accepts nothing as sacred, and nothing profane.
4. Secularism rejects religion and religious worship rites, rituals and ceremonies.
5. Secularism promotes freedom of thought and expression, and does not outlaw hearsay.
6. Secularism is accessible to contact with other societies.
7. Secularism is willingness and ability to respond to new cultural situations.
8. Secularism avoids stagnation of thought, and is open to change.
9. Secularism is an ethical system founded, not on divine commands and revealed religion, but on experience and reason, and is in consonance with science.
10. Secularism is opposed to monasticism.
11. Secularism is 'keeping aloof from religious matters and religious practice'.
12. Secularism must steer clear of fanaticism.

At this stage, it is perhaps necessary to distinguish between secularism as state policy, and secularism as an ethical principle permeating the social ethos of the community as a whole. As state policy, secularism is largely a negative concept of non-intervention in religious matters and the religious practices of a community; it is a policy of non-interference in the field of religious propagation of rival religious groups, subject, of course, to maintenance of law and order.

As has been observed by Sangharakshita (1983: 4), in the course of his talk on *Religion and Secularism* in the Vishwa Hindu Parishad, in February 1983: 'A secular state is one in which no religion in particular is favoured above the rest, i.e. favoured by the government. A secular state is one in which no particular religion is discriminated against, and in which each individual is free to follow the religion of his own choice. Moreover, in a secular state, everybody is free to propagate his own religion, subject to consideration of law and order and public decency, and provided in practising and propagating his own religion, he does not infringe the rights of other people'.

Secularism, as it is propagated and practised in India today, is generally speaking of the negative category. I propose to give here for the reader's consideration briefly my own understanding of the doctrine of secularism. Secularism, I believe, is a way of life that is directed away from other worldliness and religiosity, and away from transcendentalism and fundamentalism. Secularism essentially relates to this world of humanity. Secularism rejects meaningless rites, rituals and ceremonies. It rejects all dogmas. Secularism is rationalist and humanist in its outlook of life. It promotes freedom of thought and expression. Secularism transcends the man-made bounds of caste, creed, sex, race, colour, religion and even patriotism. It makes no distinction between the 'sacred' and the 'profane'. Secularism promotes openness of the mind, rendering it amenable to change. It is founded on principles of natural morality and justice. Secularism questions the need of the monastic life.

In brief, secularism is radical and revolutionary in its outlook and philosophy.

Buddhism and Secularism

In 1981, I wrote an essay on 'Buddhism as Rationalism and Humanism'. I am now tempted to add one more dimension to it, that of secularism, for, I believe, Buddhism is also secularism. But, as I look at it again, I think that such amendment would be redundant, because, on the positive side, secularism is nothing but rationalism and humanism. Though this be true, it is worth-while to take a quick look at it again and examine whether Buddhism fulfils the tests of secularism, as suggested by the various lexicographers and encyclopedists.

To take the first point, I maintain that Buddhism is secularism, because it is not founded on belief in gods, God, or soul; nor on belief in either heaven or hell. To my mind, there is no life after death. Or, if you wish to put it differently, even if the entire race of man is extinguished from the universe, there would be as much life on earth as there was, say about four millions years ago, i.e. before the human race began, its existence here (Tomkins, 1984: 50). Buddhism is concerned, out and out with our lives, with life in general, here on earth, and with how best to live our lives without reckoning with what will happen to us when we die. Buddhism is concerned with human morality. As Ambedkar (1957: 323) puts it: 'Morality is the essence of *dharma*. Without it, there is no *dhamma*'. Or again, as he says: '... in the religion of the Buddha, morality has been given the place of God'.

Secondly, there is nothing transcendental in Buddhism, for Buddhism is rationalism. Or, as Ambedkar (1957: 250) emphatically puts it: 'Buddhism is nothing if not rationalism'. The Kalama Sutta of Buddha himself, to my mind, is veritably the Magna Carta of free thought and rationalism (Kadam, 1981: 29), if one ponders over it dispassionately without being carried away by emotion.

Thirdly, I believe, there is nothing 'sacred' in the world, and nothing 'profane'. Only wrong thinking makes things appear so. 'To me all books are vulgar', says Ambedkar, in the sense that to him all books are on the same, common plane. The *Gita*, the *Bible* and the *Koran* are, to my mind, as important as Darwin's *Origin of Species*, H.G. Wells' *The Outline of History*, or Bertrand Russell's *History of Western Philosophy*. For, if one does not believe in the existence of God, all books and scriptures are by-products of the human brain.

Fourthly, I believe, Buddhism is the rejection of all rites and rituals and ceremonies. An example may be cited what the Buddha said to the Brahmin who had made a ritual of bathing in the river Bahuka for washing away his sins and producing religious merit. 'The Bahuka, the Adhika, the Gaya, the Sundarika, even the Sarayu or Prayaga, as also the Bahumati cannot purify the fool of his sin, bathe himself ever so often ... . Have the bath here, O Brahman ... Any water is Gaya to these' (Kadam, 1981: 38). Rites, rituals and ceremonies, I think, lead inevitably to priest craft and crafty priesthood. I am afraid that by bringing back ritualism in the practice of Buddhism, we are bringing back the priest by the back-door. The Buddha was against rites and rituals, because they were the home of superstition; and superstition was the enemy of 'Samma Ditti', the most important element in the *Ashtanga Marg* (Ambedkar, 1957: 54).

Fifthly, in his very first sermon to the *panchavaggiva bhikkhus*, Buddha exhorted them to abandon supernaturalism and superstition, and to seek right views. Thus, Buddha taught liberation of the mind from the authority of God and religion, and from the stranglehold of greedy priesthood, their sacred texts, and from the fear of Hall and the Lure of Heaven, and from the need to propitiate gods by rituals and wanton animal sacrifices.

Sixthly, one of the principal tenets of Buddhism is that everything is subject to change. Not stagnation and permanence, but change is the rule of existence. There can be no progress without change. In a changing world, man cannot hold on to anything obsolete, if one's outlook on the world and one's philosophy of life is to serve as an instrument for the good life. In the *Annihilation of Caste*, Ambedkar (1979: 79) quotes his teacher Professor John Dewey:

> Every society gets encumbered with what is trivial, with dead-wood from the past, and with what is positively perverse … . As a society becomes more enlightened, it realises what it is responsible not to conserve and transmit the whole of its existing achievements, but only such as make for a better future society.

And lastly, so far as monasticism is concerned, we are, perhaps trading on controversial ground. I believe, however, there is a need to reform and replace the old order of the Bhiku Sangh by a new organisation of secular social workers. I am inclined to believe that eventually all monasticism will die out.

We have seen that, by and large, Buddhism satisfies all the tests of secularism. Buddhism is a rationalist, humanist, and secularist way of life. To be a Buddhist and a secularist are not contradictory things. These are but two aspects of the same thing, if we regard the teachings of Buddha as rationalism and humanism, unless we turn the Buddhist way of life into a religion of ridiculous rites, rituals and ceremonies.

Ambedkar and Secularism

Let us now examine Ambedkar's image as a secular philosopher. To some it may appear incongruous to name him as a secular philosopher. How can the author of *The Buddha and His Dhamma*, and *Buddha and the Future of his Religion*, be called secular? How can the man who converted lakhs of his followers to Buddhism, on the grounds of the Deeksha Bhumi, at Nagpur, 1956, be called secular?

In his *Annihilation of Caste*, Ambedkar (1979: 76) says:

> While I condemn a religion of rules, I must not be understood to hold the opinion that there is no necessity for a religion. On the contrary, I agree with Durke when he says that true religion is the foundation of society, the basis on which all true civil governments rest, and (gives them) both their sanction.

It is clear that Ambedkar was in search of a 'Religion of Principles' as distinct from a 'Religion of Rules'. He makes his position clear when he says:

> Consequently, when I urge that these ancient rules of life be annulled, I am anxious that its place shall be taken by a religion of principles, which alone can lay claim to being a true religion.

While the Constitution was on the anvil in November 1948 and when a member of the Constituent Assembly suggested that the word 'secular' might be added in Article 11, Ambedkar opposed the amendment, and said that the Constitution should not 'tie down' the people to live in a particular type of society (Ahir, 1973: 66). Subsequently again, during the debate on the controversial Hindu Code Bill, in February 1951, referring to the question of state secularism, Ambedkar said that 'the idea of secular state in the Constitution did not mean that they could abolish religion'. It meant that 'government could not thrust any particular religion on the people' (Keer, 1981: 427). To my mind, these quotations go to demonstrate Ambedkar's genuine statesmanship.

Evidently, though the concept of the secular state was discussed in the Constituent Assembly, the founding fathers of the Constitution thought that, perhaps it was not wise to wrangle over the word 'secular', and decided to drop the matter here. The word 'secular' was subsequently inserted in the preamble to the Constitution in 1976.

Some critics may object to my description of Ambedkar as a secularist on the ground that he did not completely throw overboard the concept of religion. He was certainly not in favour of a 'religion of rules'. What he wanted was 'a religion of principles of universal application, to all races, to all countries, to all times' as 'the governing part' of one's life (Ambedkar, 1979: 75). Such, according to him, was the true religion. His quest for a philosophic, universal overview of principles governing human life was epitomised in his *magnum opus—The Buddha and his Dhamma* (1957). At this juncture, it is of interest to note what John Dewey, his eminent American teacher, had said in his *Ethics* (1991: 333):

> This brings us to the essential point in the consideration of the value of general principles. Rules are practical; they are habitual ways of doing things. But principles are intellectual; they are useful methods of judging things.

How far Ambedkar had travelled on the road of secularism is best seen in his article 'Buddha and the Future of His Religion' that he contributed to the *Maha Bodhi* (1950). This important essay reveals the frame of his mind while he was still engrossed in the writing of his *magnum opus*. In fact, to my mind, this article is a fitting prologue to *The Buddha and His Dhamma*. In the course of 'Buddha and the Future of His Religion', Ambedkar stressing the need of law and morality says:

> Religion must he in accord with science. Religion is bound to loss its respect and therefore become the subject of ridicule, and thereby not merely lose its force as a governing principle of life, but might in course of time disintegrate and lapse, if it is not in accord with sequence. In other words, religion, if it is not function, must be in accord with reason which is merely another name for science.

Ambedkar had full faith in the principle of secularism. In his *States and Minorities* which is virtually a forerunner to the Constitution of India subsequently drafted by him, Ambedkar says (1947: 12): 'The state shall not recognise any religion as the state religion'. When this principle was accepted in the Constituent Assembly, Jatava (1950: 192) says: 'He (Ambedkar) was very happy when the people of this great country declared India as a secular state'.

Is India a Secular State?

For a brief while, let us consider the nature of secularism as it obtains in India today. In effect, there are worthy intellectuals who find it difficult to accept the position that India is a secular state notwithstanding the nor, in this behalf, laid down in the preamble to the Constitution of India, as amended in 1976.

Justice R.A. Jahagirdar of the Bombay High Court, for instance, is not prepared to believe that the Indian Constitution is secular. 'The Indian Constitution', he says, 'is not a secular Constitution'; and 'the Republic of India is not secular Republic'. Clarifying his stand, he says ('Religion and Caste in Politics', *Faith*, 1982: 1):

> In my opinion that state is a secular state which is separated from religion by a firm and impregnable wall. That state is not secular state which merely tolerates all religions and encourages all religions equally. If one religion is allowed to play any part, large or small, in the affairs of a state, that state cannot be said to be a secular state. That is why, in America by a series of judgments of the Supreme Court, it has been held that there is a wall of separation between the Church and the State. As early as in 1892, Thomas Jefferson, the founding father of the American Constitution and later a president of the United States, had mentioned that the first amendment to the Constitution of the United States enjoining upon the establishment of religion or prohibiting the free exercise thereof necessarily meant the separation of the Church from the State. Indeed, he used the phrase: 'A wall of separation between the Church and the State was built up with the first amendment to the U.S. Constitution'.

Justice Jahagirdar, in the course of the same speech, says (1982: 3):

> A mere mention of the word 'secular' in the preamble does not convert the Constitution into a secular state just as a mere mention of the word 'paradise' in the preamble will not convert India into a paradise.

Finally, let us see what Ambedkar, the father of the Constitution of India, has to say on the subject. Writing in the *Maha Bodh* of Calcutta, in its issue of April-May 1950, he says:

> There cannot be a thesis more false than the thesis that all religions are true. However, this slogan gives the Hindus who have raised in the support of the followers of other religions. There are other Hindus who have come to realise that there is something wrong with their religion. The only thing is that they are not ready to denounce it openly. This attitude is

understandable. Religion is part of one's social inheritance. One's life and dignity and pride are bound up with it. It is not easy to abandon one's religion. Patriotism comes in: 'My country right or wrong'. So also: 'My religion right or wrong', instead of abandoning it, the Hindus are finding escape in other ways. Some are consoling themselves with the thought that all religions are wrong. So why bother about religion, at all?

There is, however, in the *Essentials of Dr Babasaheb Ambedkar*, a more specific meaning given by Ambedkar to the term 'secularism'. He says:

> A secular state does not mean that we shall not take into consideration the religious sentiments of the people. All that a secular state means is that this parliament shall not be competent to impose any particular religion upon the rest of the people. That is the only limitation that the Constitution recognises.

Conclusion

I hope, in the foregoing pages, I have made four points clear: (i) Ambedkar's rejection of the concept of religion, and all that goes by that name; (ii) Ambedkar's emphasis on the need of an adequate, overall moral philosophy to hold human society together; (iii) Ambedkar was not rigid and dogmatic, but a system that provides for change suited to the times; and (iv) Dr Ambedkar's ethical philosophy was based on rationalism and humanism, and was in consonance with science to make it universal and durable. In brief, it has been my endeavour to demonstrate that his system was neither fundamentalistic nor religious. It was tolerant of religion, but not religious. It was secular.

His life-long endeavour was to clean that stables of religion rendered unbearable to humanity. On the positive side, he gave India basic law of the land founded on sound jurisprudence and designed to promote justice, liberty, equality and fraternity. His jurisprudence was founded on rationalism, humanism, science and secularism, which he summed up in one word—*dhamma*. His jurisprudence and his *dhamma* constitute the two sides of the same gold coin. Underlying all Ambedkar's endeavour was his conviction.

References

Ahir, D.C., *Dr. Ambedkar and the Indian Constitution*, Lucknow: Buddha Vihara, 1973.

Ambedkar, B.R., *States and Minorities*, Bombay: Thacker & Co., 1947.

——, *The Buddha and His Dhamma*, Bombay: Siddharth College Publication, 1957.

——, 'The Buddha and the Future of His Religion', *Maha Bodhi*, Calcutta, 1950.

——, *The Evolution of Provincial Finance in British India*, London: P.S. King & Son, 1925. Also see, *Dr. Babasaheb Ambedkar's Writing and Speeches*, Vol. 6, Government of Maharashtra, Bombay, 1989.

Biswas, A.R., *Manu, Dr. Ambedkar and the Supreme Court* (unpublished), 1990.

Dewey, John, *Ethics* (in collaboration with John and J.H. Tufts), New York: G. Bell & Sons Ltd. and London: Henry Holt and Co., 1910.

Dr. Babasaheb Ambedkar's Officers Social Forum, *Essentials of Dr. Babasaheb Ambedkar*.

Jahagirdar, Justice R.A., 'Religion, Caste and Politics', *Faith*, 1982.

Jatava, D.R., *Evolution of Indian Social Thought*, Jaipur: Bohra Publications, 1987.

——, *The Political Philosophy of B.R. Ambedkar*, Agra: Phoenix Publishing Agency, 1965.

Kadam, K.N., *Buddhism as Rationalism and Humanism and Other Essays on Religion and Rationalism* (unpublished), 1981.

——, *Currents and Counter Currents in Ancient Indian History* (unpublished), 1985.

Keer, Dhananjay, *Dr. Ambedkar: Life and Mission*, Bombay: Popular Prakashan, 1981.

Moon, Vasant (Ed.), 'Annihilation of Caste', in *Dr. Babasaheb Ambedkar's Writings and Speeches*, Vol. I, Government of Maharashtra, Bombay, 1989.

Russell, Bertrand, *Sceptical Essays*, London: George Allen & Unwin Ltd., 1934.

Sangharakshita, *Religion and Secularism*, Pune: Dhammamegha Series, No. 11, 1983.

Tomkins, Stephen, *The Origins of Mankind*, Cambridge: Cambridge University Press, 1984.

8

Democratisation of Higher Education in India

Ambedkar's Vision

K.S. Chalam

I am grateful to Dr B.R. Ambedkar Open University, Hyderabad, for the opportunity given to me to present some of my views on the topic relating to Babasaheb Ambedkar's role in democratising higher education in India. I read in the newspapers, dated 4 April 2017 that the ranks for the universities in India were announced by the framework established by the MHRD. It is interesting to notice that universities that are in the news for a democratic upsurge like JNU, Jhadavpur University and others have obtained higher ranks while University of Hyderabad that had a good rank earlier has plummeted after the Rohith issue. It is now empirically established that education, much less university education, needs free flow of ideas and an atmosphere of freedom to express and experiment new ideas that would remain the sine-qua-none of higher education.

Education as a process of learning and disseminating of knowledge is alien to India as learning, from the very beginning,

---

Keynote address delivered at Dr B.R. Ambedkar Open University, Hyderabad, on 4 April 2017 on the occasion of 125th birth day celebrations of Dr Babasaheb Ambedkar.

was related to enlightenment and self-realisation of individual. A savant like Swamy Dayanand Saraswati whose clarion call 'Back to Vedas' is now found resonating had emphasised on the character formation as the chief function of education. He has also advocated for compulsory education of the masses and behooved the state ensuring it for every Indian including the Untouchables. His scheme of education was traditional but adopted by the British to a large extent, if we look at the curriculum of some of the courses taught in government colleges like Rajahmundry during nineteenth century. This is different from the western concept of education where it is defined as 'acquisition of the art of the utilisation of knowledge' (Whitehead). One of the most influential thinkers and a great educator who had a profound influence on Dr B.R. Ambedkar (as his student), John Dewey said that 'education is the process of re-construction or re-constitution of experience giving it more detailed value through the medium of increased social efficiency'. He further noted: 'What nutrition and reproduction are to physiological life, education is to social life'. As an author of *Democracy and Education*, he said that 'if education is equivalent to genuine living, then democracy is the moral foundation of education. The essence of education is the extension of shared areas of meaningful action and this is also the essence of democracy'. One would notice these ideas resonating in most of the writings of Ambedkar where he invariably quotes his teacher of Columbia University.

We are concerned here about higher education. It is just not an extension of school education, it has its own identity, content, process and objectives and functions. Though higher education in a country is related to the structure of educational system of the country, it need not necessarily follow it in view of the recent developments in educational technology particularly the market for higher education. Interestingly, a section of economists has made higher education a commodity rather a private good to be offered on sale in any part of the world at any time. Therefore discussing about democratisation of higher education in India, today is a very daunting task.

B.R. Ambedkar is one of our foremost statesmen and intellectuals of the last century who had experienced what freedom stands for in a western democracy, both in USA and England, wished that it should happen in India. Critiquing the undemocratic social institutions like caste, he brought out the democratic principles involved in Buddhist Sangha. He desired that democracy should prevail in all our relations; economic, social and political. We could notice in his speeches and writings that democracy should remain the bedrock of all educational endeavours as it remains the mother that provides the cultural background to sustain an equitable socio-economic order.

What do we mean by democratisation of education? Is it equality of opportunity to get a place in the system of education? Is it a system of providing additional inputs to those whose family background is different from others where traits of a particular group are taken as standards to get admission? Is it to normalise the inputs of education and the outcome? Is it J.P. Naik's Coefficient of Equality at different stages? Is it Jenck's measure of inequality in income related to education? Is it reduction in the intergenerational inequality in income? And so on. But in most of the studies of scholars, the enrollment of SCs or STs or OBCs in different educational institutions in relation to their respective populations is considered as a measure of equality or democratising education or the so-called JP Naik measure. Even the Indian judiciary, popular discourse of Dalit and Bahujan intellectuals look at these figures to interpret how they are discriminated. This measure, no doubt gives broad view of democratisation, but it doesn't take into account the disadvantages and the deficiencies suffered by the students of weaker sections for generations while getting admissions based on a particular score. It also doesn't carry the need for parity in the enrollment of students from different courses of study in higher education including the enrollment in private sector institutions. There are several other issues that need to be considered by scholars to find out solutions to the problem.

The demand for places in public educational institutions started with the social movement of Jothi Rao Phuley who submitted a memorandum to Hunter Commission along with the Muslims of Ganjam district of Madras presidency in 1882. In the princely states of Mysore, Kolhapur, Baroda and several other places, the local zamindars provided opportunities of admission for lower castes. In fact D.D. Gholap, C.K. Bole, Members of

Bombay Legislative Council, demanded free and compulsory education for Untouchables in 1921 before Babasaheb Ambedkar made a strong case for it in 1927–28. Ambedkar was not satisfied with free and compulsory primary education, he was interested in higher education. You will find that in his speeches, both in Legislative debates and in public platforms, he had made strong appeal both to the government and Dalits to get admissions into higher education and in science and technology courses. This has a cascading effect on the enrollments in higher education in different parts of the country. But, it is not uniform and varies from state to state.

Education as a Universal Right

The development of education in India as a universal right is considered to be of very recent origin. Though the British are given the credit of being the benefactors of universal education in India, the historical evidence does not support this claim. The argument between Mahatma Gandhi and Sir Hartog is a known controversy in educational history as Gandhiji could not substantiate his claim that there was universal education in India before the British came to this country. It is equally true that the British failed to provide educational opportunities to every citizen in this country. It was only after the Woods Dispatch of 1854 that the British Government took some interest in the educational development of the natives. As mentioned above, Jyoti Rao Phule who in his memorandum to Hunter Commission in 1882 accused the British for their penchant in providing educational opportunities only to the upper castes, while collecting huge revenue from the illiterate Sudras and Ati-Sudras. One can say that this is the beginning of a movement for mass education in the country. However, no systematic attempt was made by any known leader thereafter for the educational upliftment of everyone in the country. It is in this context, the role of B.R. Ambedkar as a pragmatist of universal compulsory education for all and higher education as compulsory qualification for Scheduled Castes to enter public service need to be noticed. Perhaps he is the only leader of the pre-Independence period who had a vision for a people's education movement in India.

While contextualising Ambedkar movement as a protest movement, M.S. Gore, Gail Omvedt and several social scientists placed Dr Ambedkar as a leader of the Untouchables. He was never projected by the mainstream scholarship as a positive contributor to the overall social and educational development of the country. He has been a victim of reductionism and in this context some of his followers are also responsible in joining the bandwagon of reductionism. Therefore, one of the important contributions of Ambedkar's to Indian society, the 'educational development', has remained obscured. It is brought out by scholars now that there were great leaders in South-India such as Ayothidas (1845–1914), Ayyankali (1863–1914) and others who had preceded Dr Ambedkar in their mission of amelioration of social and educational conditions of the Dalits. But, the contributions of these savants are limited to South while Ambedkar's contribution had an all India character due to several reasons. Therefore, it is necessary to evaluate the contribution of Ambedkar to the mass educational movement in India. It appears that there is no parallel to Ambedkar during the pre-Independence movement in matters of an intellectual input into the arguments that the country needed universalisation of education. In this context, Ambedkar seems to have been influenced by his teacher and philosopher, John Dewey of Columbia University. Very few Indians in the twentieth century had deliberately chosen to get educated in an open society like the USA. One among these was B.R. Ambedkar and the other prominent figure was Jayaprakash Narayan. Though both the leaders differ in their struggles and outlook, there was a common bondage that could put them together. It was their strong belief in democracy. United States of America at that time was trumpeted as the symbol of liberty and therefore, democracy. There was also a reason for this. One of the prominent advocates of democracy and a great pragmatist was teaching in Columbia University and spreading the message of democracy through his disciples. It was John Dewey, a great educationist and a democrat. This has perhaps, attracted the attention of Ambedkar and he chose to study in Columbia University. In fact, the formative years of Ambedkar were shaped by the academic atmosphere in Columbia and particularly the lectures of John Dewey.

Experts and scholars have written elaborately about the contributions of Ambedkar to Philosophy, Sociology, Religion among other fields. But there are very few attempts by scholars to project him as a great educationist. In fact, more than half of his life was spent in educational institutions. Even while he was in the thick of politics he took interest in the educational programmes of Dalits. Out of 65 years of his precious life, he spent around 50 years as student, scholar, teacher and promoter of education (till 1938). His last assignment was Principal, Government Law College, Bombay in 1938. Therefore, it is necessary to understand and analyse his contributions to the development of education in India in general and to the educational upliftment of weaker sections in particular. In the formulation of special provisions for Scheduled Castes and Other Backward Classes in the Constitution, Ambedkar seems to have consciously chosen the concept of 'educationally and socially backward classes'. He knew that those who were considered as backward or uncivilised at that time were the ones who were denied education. Therefore, Ambedkar had been assiduously fighting for the educational rights not only of Dalits, but for the illiterate and ignorant masses of the country.

It is essential that we should reconstruct here the educational philosophy of John Dewey. The influence of John Dewey on Dr Ambedkar is so profound that he himself has declared in June 1952, after he was conferred an honorary degree in Columbia University, that I owe my whole intellectual life to Prof. John Dewey. This intellectual allegiance of Dr Ambedkar to John Dewey can be seen in every aspect of his active public life including his social and educational movements. The essence of John Dewey's pragmatism or practical idealism is projection of the ideal of democracy. His concern is that democracy should permeate every aspect of people's lives, including the way people think and philosophise. As Gordon L. Ziniewicz observed that the term 'democracy', for John Dewey is not confined to actual or potential political regimes, but extends to every facet of human culture.

Democracy for John Dewey is a way of life, the method of thinking, a manner of approach, a habit of expecting the unexpected, an attitude of openness to novelties and variety of flexibility in actively attending to adjusting facts and conditions as they present themselves. The greatest influence of John Dewey on

Ambedkar can be seen in John Dewey's emphasis on the precept that 'the people and the relations have to be democratic before democratic institutions can have any meaning'.

Out of six important works of John Dewey, the book, *Democracy and Education: An Introduction to the Philosophy of Education*, published in 1916, had influenced the progressive world including Russia and China at that time. It is here that John Dewey says: 'democracy cannot go forward unless the intelligence of the mass of people is educated to understand the social realities of their own time'. The contributions of John Dewey including brief stints in China, Russia and as Signatory of Humanist Manifesto are very significant as he brought out the fact that education and society are not separate, each influencing the other. These ideals have swayed Ambedkar in taking up the agenda of development through democratic national building. Therefore, many of his programmes including education remained to be the foremost in his agenda for upliftment of depressed classes. Even from the beginning of his political career, he was interested in education. In the Bombay Presidency debates of 1927 and 1928, he has raised several issues relating to education which became important for policy formulations on education. In his memorandum to the Simon Commission on 'concerning the State of Education of the Depressed Classes in Bombay Presidency', submitted on behalf of the *Bahish Krita Hita Karini Sabha*, he gave numerical data to bring out the miserable condition of the Untouchables in the education sector. He had pointed out that enrollment of the Dalits constitute 0.87 per cent of the total primary education and 0.14 per cent in Secondary and zero in higher education. Therefore, he wanted protection for the Dalits through education guarantee by making the education for the depressed classes as the first charge on the State Revenue. He had also protested the practice of untouchability in municipal schools of Bombay where separate *lotas* were given to Dalit boys in his budge debates. This, he said, made them drop out from schools. This is a great economic wastage. He was the first economist who had realised the economic importance of education in India.

In his budget debates in Bombay Legislative Assembly in 1927, as an MLC, he remarked, 'I wish to remind him that the backward classes have come to realize that after all education is the greatest material benefit for which they can fight. We may forego material benefits, *we may forego material benefits of civilisation, but we cannot forego our right and opportunity to reap the benefit of the highest education to the fullest extent*'. That is the importance of this question from the point of view of the backward classes who have just realised that without education their existence is not safe. It is for this reason that the fight for increase of seats is being made.

It is necessary to bring here the total intellectual contributions of Ambedkar to the educational development of the mass of people. He is, perhaps, one of the first economists in the world who had realised the economic importance of education. In his debates in the Assembly and Parliament, one can find the tenor of his argument in favour of subsidies for education in general and for the weaker sections in particular. He was arguing in the Bombay Presidency Legislative debates in 1927 as follows, 'We should at least spend on education the same amount that we take from the people in the form of excise revenue. The amount of expenditure that we incur per individual in this Presidency on education is only 14 annas, but the amount of money that we recover in the form of excise revenue is Rs. 2-2-9 (Rs. 2.17). I think it is only fair that our educational expenditure should be so adjusted that we should spend on the education of the people as much as we take from them in the form of excise'. He has also calculated the fees income at different levels and argued that it financed 36 per cent of expenditure in collegiate education, 31 per cent high school and 26 per cent middle school education. Higher education should be made cheaper so that lower classes (not necessarily low castes) can enter in higher education and benefit from the opportunities it creates. He had lamented that educational institutes were running on commercial lines during the British Raj. His words are prophetic as today higher education has become a business that does not recognise 'merit', but only money power.

Views on University Education

Higher education is generally related to university education that provides undergraduate education in colleges affiliated to a university and UG and PG and research mostly on campus departments now. However, university system was just evolving in the first fifty years after 1857 as it was basically used as a body to conduct examinations and confer degrees and later on developed on the lines of London University. Ambedkar was the first Indian economist who had two PhDs in Economics from two premier universities of the World, Columbia and London School of Economics. Interestingly, he was offered a Lecturer post in Sydenham College while several others were directly offered Professorship in the university system after they returned with a foreign degree. If you read his debates on education in the Bombay Assembly, evidence submitted before University Reforms Commission, etc. you would notice that he carried the pain, but made constructive suggestions for the development of higher education.

Let us look at what Ambedkar noted in the Bombay Assembly in 1927. He said:

> Sir, the University is primarily a concern of the intelligentsia and of the educated classes, and that as the University is to function properly, it is necessary that it should be controlled by what are called the educated classes. I would accept that principle, if the educated classes who are going to control the University possessed what we called social virtues. If they, for instance, sympathized with the aspirations of the lower classes, if they recognised that the lower classes had rights, if they recognised that those rights must be respected, then probably we, coming from the backward communities, might well entrust our destinies to what are called the advance communities. But, Sir, for centuries we have had the bitterest experience of the rule of what are called the higher and the educated classes, Sir, I think it is hardly to the credit of the advanced classes that there should exist in this country a large part of the population which is known as the criminal tribes. It is certainly not to their credit that there should exist in this country a population which is regarded Untouchable. Surely, they could have raised the status of the depressed classes; they could have raised the status of the criminal classes. They could have brought their culture to us and made us equal to them, if they had only the desire to do so. But they have never done so in the past and do not mean to do anything in that direction in future. By their callous neglect of us and by their active hostility to our progress, they have convinced

us that they are really our enemies. There is no doubt that it is their desire to keep us where we are. I do not wish to refer to the debate that has gone on for the last few days. But there is not the slightest doubt about the fact that the opposition benches which looked upon Government as their enemy sided with it, now with the sole object of defeating us on this vital question. There is no other excuse for their conduct except that they wanted to defeat the claims of the backward communities for representation through nomination. It is for that reason that they have joined Government whom they opposed in season and out of season. Sir, can we have any trust in an intelligentsia so narrow, so illiberal in its views.

He continued by saying that:

I agree with the Inspectors of the Board of Education in England that the aim and functions of University Education should be to see that the teaching carried on there is suited to adults; that it is scientific, detached and impartial in character; that it aims not so much at filling the mind of the student with fact or theories as at calling forth his own individuality, and stimulating him to mental effort; that it accustoms him to the critical study of the leading authorities, with perhaps, occasional reference to first hand sources of information, and that it implants in his mind a standard of thoroughness, and gives him a sense of the difficulty as well as the value of reaching at truth. The student so trained should learn to distinguish between what may fairly be called matter of fact and what is certainly mere matter of opinion. He should be accustomed to distinguish issues, and to look at separate questions each on its own merits and without an eye to their bearing on some cherished theory. He should learn to state fairly, and even sympathetically, the position of those to whose practical conclusions he is most stoutly opposed. He should become able to examine a suggested idea, and see what comes of it, before accepting it or rejecting it. Without necessarily becoming an original student, he should gain an insight into the conditions under which original research is carried on.

In his deposition before the University Reforms Committee, Ambedkar said:

> If a University as a corporation of learning is to serve the community, then its constitution must provide (a) for a body which will keep it in touch with all varied requirements of the community; (b) for a body which will give the University a statesman-like guidance in the provision and also in accommodation of means to ends so as to bring about a working compromise between the possible misconceptions of the public and the possibly too narrow outlook of the scholar; and (c) for a body of scholars engaged in the work of teaching to give an authoritative direction to the academic business of the University. I want to impress upon the Committee that a University does not become a teaching University merely by engaging in the work of teaching through the agency of its own staff. That is not the criterion of a teaching University. A University may undertake teaching and yet may not be a teaching University. Whether or not a University is a teaching University depends upon whether or not the scholars engaged in the work of teaching have the authoritative direction of the academic business of the University in their hands. If it is in their hands then the University is a teaching University. If it is not in their hands then the University is not a teaching University. *A teaching University is a teachers' University*.

In making these comments upon the management of the educational affairs of the Presidency under the Reform in their bearing upon the depressed classes, the Bahishkrit Hitakarini Sabha is not oblivious to the special provisions made for the education of the depressed classes in the form of a few hostels and a few scholarships for higher education. But the Sabha begs to point out that it is useless to make provision for higher education of the depressed classes unless steps are taken to ensure the growth of primary education. Besides there is no guarantee that such concessions will continue. On the other hand, they depend a great deal upon the policy of the particular Minister in charge of Education and upon the voting strength of the depressed classes in the Legislative Council, both of which are uncertain factors and cannot be depended upon.

It is also necessary here to bring in the ideas of Dr Ambedkar about the university education in his written reply to the Bombay University Reforms Committee. Dr Ambedkar has expressed his opinions about the aim and functions of university education as follows:

1. That it is scientific, detached and impartial in character.
2. It aims not so much at filling the mind of the student with fact or theories as at calling forth his own individuality and stimulating him to mental effort.
3. It accustoms him to the critical study of the leading authorities, with perhaps occasional reference to first hand sources of information and that it implants in his mind a standard of thoroughness and gives him a sense of the difficulty as well as the value of reaching at truth.
4. The student so trained should learn to distinguish, between what may fairly be called matter of fact and what is certainly mere matter of opinion.
5. He should be accustomed to distinguish issues and to look at separate questions each on its own merits and without an eye to their bearing on some cherished theory.
6. He should learn to state fairly, and even sympathetically, the position of those to whose practical conclusions, he is most stoutly opposed.
7. He should be able to examine a suggested idea, and see what comes of it, before accepting it or rejecting it.
8. He should gain an insight into the conditions under which original research is carried on without unnecessarily becoming an original student.
9. He should be able to weigh evidence to follow and criticise argument and put his own value on authorities.

Democratic Functioning of Colleges

He has also expressed strong views about the relations between affiliated colleges and the university administration. He was of the view that government should have no control over the academic affairs of the university. He has put forward an innovative idea that the duration of study for post-graduate degree in social sciences should be four years. There are two stages of two years each. At the end of the first stage, the candidate should be entitled to the MA Degree, should specialise in one subject only which should be the subject of his major interest. The test should consist of a written examination accompanied by an essay of some 75 type written pages showing his familiarity with the art of using original source and commenting upon them. At the end of the second stage, the candidate should be entitled to the PhD Degree. There, the test would include an oral examination and a thesis of a respectful size fit for publication. He has always upheld the dignity of the teacher. In explaining the criterion of the teaching university, Ambedkar has proposed that both the teaching and academic business should be under the control of the teachers. He has argued for reservation of places in the universities senate and syndicate to represent the interest of the weaker sections. He wanted the use of vernacular as a medium of instruction at all stages of education. Some of his innovative ideas of pooling teaching resources at one place in urban areas appear to be more relevant today than ever before.

He was also emphatic in his arguments about the devolution of functions between college and university. He was not at all favourable for professorial positions in the university who did not bother to teach and benefit undergraduates. He gave written evidence before the University Reforms Committee wherein he had elaborately discussed the objects of higher education functions of various committees etc. which are still relevant. He has also argued in favour of more powers for the University Syndicate and also delineated the functions of senate, he considers it as a Legislative Council of the university and syndicate in debates in the Bombay Assembly. He was of the opinion that the object of post graduate education is to train the student 'to learn to distinguish what may fairly be called matter of fact and what is certainly mere matter of opinion'.

Ambedkar was found to be a thorough academic in his approach to problems with practical insights. He had a total understanding of education starting from primary to university level. He has expressed his scholarly vision on research. He spent most of his life for the development of education and even after retirement from active political life, he took interest in the development of educational institutions. He was the first among many Indians who had initiated a Peoples Education movement for the poor in India.

In his detailed note, Ambedkar mentioned that education under the British rule in the Bombay Presidency must have a beginning with the foundation of the Bombay Education Society. It was later named as Bombay Native Education Society and was headed by Mount Stuart Elphinstone but the progress achieved by this society was according to him minimal. He pointed out: 'what do these figures show? They show that although mass education was the policy of the Government, the mass were as outside the pale of education as they were before the years, 1854 and that the concept and aborigine classes of the Hindus still remained lowest in order of education'.

The lacunae in the British Policy of Education according to him were its partial attitude towards the elite. The Court of Director's mentioned that 'it is our anxious desire to afford to the higher classes of the Natives of India the means of instruction in European Sciences and of access to the literature of civilised Europe. The character which may be given to the classes possessed of leisure and natural influence ultimately determines that of the whole people.'

In this, he found that the education in the British, India was confined to few upper classes only. Ambedkar here provided the information and the arguments to show that the landlords, the higher employees and the Brahmins were the real upper classes who were benefitted by the British education. See Appendix Tables for data provided by him before 1930, reproduced. Therefore, he wanted that the educational subsidy given by the British should provide opportunities to every one of the depressed classes much less the Untouchables. He has provided sufficient data to prove what Mahatma Phuley had brought to the notice of the British in 1882. In fact, he had extended the argument of Mahatma Phuley as his spiritual heir, asking for the British support for universalising education. In his debates in the Bombay Presidency, he opposed the introduction of Compulsory Primary Education Act as the proposed Act shifted the responsibility of educating the people to the School Boards. He pointed out that the School Boards would again implement the mandate of the elite as the Boards are dominated by higher classes and with little funding. It is an irony that the country is still debating on the free and compulsory education to the mass of people even after 70 years of Independence. The Free and Compulsory Education Bill made as an Act and as a Right under Article 21A is not made fully operational. Had Ambedkar wisely included Article 45 in Directive Principles of State Policy, the Apex Court would not have directed the government to amend and incorporate Article 21A.

Ambedkar was a practical man as far as education is concerned. He registered the People's Education Society in 1945 in Bombay to start Siddhartha College. He sent an application to the government for an interest free loan of Rs 6 lakhs. While he was the Member of the Governor General Council, he made an appeal to people to contribute liberally for the establishment of the college. In his memorandum of association, he noted that the society is formed to establish a cosmopolitan college to provide education to Scheduled Castes, Buddhists and others and will be managed by Buddhists. J.H. Subbaiah of Secunderabad was also a member of the society. The foundation stone for Milind College was laid by President of India Dr Rajendra Prasad in 1950 in Aurangabad. The land for the college was donated by Nizam and it was affiliated to Osmania University. I had an opportunity to participate as Chief Guest of a National seminar at Milind College in 2004 where Dr Sahare and the principal have shown pictures of Babasaheb physically carrying construction material and was totally involved in building the institution.

Ambedkar was more interested in higher education and the above two examples are worth mentioning here. In his Manifesto of the Scheduled Caste Federation under Article 6 he mentioned that, 'the set of education which the SCF has in mind with regard to these classes is not primary education, not even secondary education. What is in mind is advanced education of such high order, both in this country and outside, which will enable these classes to fit themselves for taking hold of administration.' The SCF insisted on reservations in higher bureaucracy subject to minimum standards. Interestingly, in his memorandum to the government for loan to start Siddhartha College, he gave data relating to the enrollment of Dalits in higher education as very low and appealed to the government for assistance in view of Dalits being: 1. poor, 2. lack of accommodation for Dalit students, and 3. for diversity in education. He has noted that the institution would function effectively as it is headed by him and said, 'Having been a professor of Economics in the Sydenham College of Commerce, Bombay, Principal of the Government Law College, Bombay, a Member of the Senate and Syndicate of the Bombay University, I feel that I can get recognition for the proposed College more readily from the Bombay University than from a University outside that Province'.

He had a pragmatic approach as far as education was concerned. In his speech for Voice of America on 20 May 1956, he said, 'Can education destroy caste? The answer is "yes" as well as "no". If education is given as it is today, education can have no effect on caste. It will remain as it will be. The glaring example of it is the Brahmin caste. Cent per cent of it is educated, may be majority of it is highly educated. Yet not one Brahmin has shown himself to be against caste. In fact, an educated person belonging to the higher caste is more interested after his education to retain the caste system than when he was not educated. For education gives him an additional interest in the retention of the caste system namely by opening additional opportunity of getting bigger job .... But education may be solvent if it is applied to the lower strata of Indian society. It would raise their spirit of rebellion. In their present state of ignorance they are the supporters of the caste system. Once their eyes are opened they will be ready to fight the caste system.'

The data presented by Ambedkar from the reports of Hartog Committee and others clearly show that there were hardly a couple of graduates from Scheduled Castes in the presidencies in 1930, except in Bengal where there were 1670 graduates, Madras 47, Bombay 9 and in others nil. Now, SC enrollment constitutes around 10 per cent of the total enrollment of higher education, while the enrollment of the nation itself is below 20 per cent. We do not have data about other castes except the reserved groups and in public institutions. The emergence of private sector under the tacit support of all non-reserved castes helped the bourgeoning of Science, Technology and Management courses where the entry of the poor Dalits, Adivasis and backwards is formidable not only due to cost restrictions, but caste cleavages working against the reserved groups now.

The above analysis of Babasaheb Ambedkar and his understanding about education and its ameliorative character tells us about his vision for the future. It means that Babasaheb had visualised the present trend few decades before as noted in his Voice of America speech that unless higher education is democratised there is no future for the lower castes. It does not mean that by providing places in public institutions in proportion to the population of each caste, the inequalities and social discrimination would end. As we have witnessed during the last decade how Dalit and backward caste boys and girls committed suicides for not getting admissions into the system, but the system of higher education has become vicious for them to survive. Ambedkar himself has given the answer by saying that 'once their eyes are opened they will be ready to fight the caste system.' It is possible by popularising and educating the learned citizens, the 'others' about the long run benefits of higher education would be higher and perpetual if your own citizens are educated and admitted as part of a democratic society as the externalities would be fabulous human development, failing which it would lead to social disaster.

Appendix Table 1

Disparity in Education in 1923-24

Classes of Population in the Presidency	*Order in Respect of Population*	*Order in Respect of Education*			*Primary Edu. Students Per 1000 of the Pop. of the Class*	*Second Edu. Students per 1000 of the Pop. of the Class*	*College Edu. Students per 1000 of the Pop. of the Class*
		Primary	*Secondary*	*Collegiate*			
Advanced Hindus	4th	1st	1st	1st	119	3000	1000
Intermediate Hindus	1st	3rd	3rd	3rd	92	500	52
Backward Hindus	2nd	4th	4th	4th	38	140	14
Mohammedans	3rd	2nd	2nd	2nd	18	14	Nil (or nearly one)

Source: Dr Babasaheb Ambedkar Writings and Speeches.

Appendix Table 2

Educational Achievement During 1854–82

	Primary Education Total	*Secondary Education Total*	*Collegiate Education Total*
Christians	0.49	2.26	3.00
Brahmins	20.17	40.29	50.00
Other Hindus	64.69	34.84	22.30
Mohammedans	12.54	2.04	1.50
Parsis	1.12	19.66	21.50
Aboriginal and Hill Tribes	0.87	—	—
Low caste Hindus	0.87	—	—
Jews and others	0.12	0.86	0.40
Total	100.00	100.00	100.00

Source: Adopted from Dr Ambedkar as above.

Appendix Table 3

Higher Education in India by Social Category Access and Equity Program-Wise Enrollment 2004–05

Program	*Total*	*Per cent Girls*	*Per cent SC*	*Per cent ST*
PhD/DSc/DPhil	55,352	41.2	5.8	2.4
MA	469,291	46.6	16.2	4.9
MSc	198,719	45.7	10.4	2.8
MCom	122,257	34.0	9.2	3.0
Post-Graduate-sub total	790,267	44.4	13.6	4.1
BA/BA Hons	3,772,216	43.9	14.9	5.2
BSc/BSc (Hons)	1,490,785	38.9	11.3	3.3
BCom/BCom (Hons)	1,465,028	36.6	8.5	3.3
BE/BArch	696,609	23.7	8.5	3.1
Undergraduate—subtotal	7,424,638	39.6	12.3	4.3
Medicine, Dentistry, Nursing, Pharmacy, Ayurvedic, Unani and Homeopathy	256,748	34.7	11.5	3.7
BEd/BT	155,192	43.8	12.4	5.8
Others	3,095,099	37.9	6.0	2.1
Total enrolment	11,777,296	39.4	10.7	3.7
2015–16	–	–	18.5	13.3

9

Educational Philosophy of Ambedkar

K.P. Subba Rao

Ambedkar was one of the modem thinkers of India. He was more a social philosopher than an academician. Ambedkar strived for the upliftment of the Untouchables throughout his life. He was known to the world as a social thinker, jurist, economist, and a constitutionalist. His philosophy of education was seen through his practice in his lifetime. His educational ideas or thoughts are reactions to the social structure of the time he lived. Ambedkar was very keen to make the depressed classes avail the opportunities in public services. He could not devote sufficient time to give a form to his educational thought due to his relentless participation in the struggles of the oppressed classes. This paper attempts to give a shape to his educational philosophy.

Ambedkar's educational philosophy struck roots in the John Dewey's pragmatic theory of education. He was influenced by Dewey as the latter was the teacher of the former. According to Dewey, education, in its broad sense, is the means of social continuity of life. Ambedkar took these ideas of Dewey as the basis for his educational philosophy. He established 'depressed classes educational society' to organise the school education of his community with this philosophy. He wanted to see these depressed classes on par with other communities in the society. He could change his ideas of education in accordance with time. The educational philosophy of Ambedkar was a blend of pragmatism of Dewey and *dhamma* of Buddha. In 1956, on the eve of his conversion, he said untouchability cannot be removed by education alone. But he emphasised that Scheduled Caste students should have the technical education, not arts subjects as they do not serve the purpose of Scheduled Castes and even caste Hindus. In his view education, for that matter university education, without subjects like Science and Technology could not provide any job opportunities. It was in this background that Ambedkar formed ideas of education taking cognizance of Hindu stratification which gave the *varna* system. He said that Untouchables are neither Hindus nor Muslims. But they are really more backward than either of these communities. An amount proportional to their population should also be allotted to Scheduled Caste people for the education. 'With education, intelligence, knowledge and experience that I have, it is not difficult for me to oppose or fight against any evil,' he said. These ideas reveal his educational philosophy which give importance to knowledge and practice. He has opened educational institutions so that the Scheduled Caste people could join the public services so as to earn their livelihood. Dewey regarded education as a process of life; therefore, education itself is life. Ambedkar envisaged that education was an instrument for the change of the lives of Untouchables. He declared that the elevation of the depressed classes was recognised to be the cause of all the enlightened people in the country. He thought that education would enlighten his people and bridge the gap between rich and the poor to which the Untouchables belong.

Nature of Education

Human beings survive by maintaining their ideals and renewing them constantly. Education is the means by which this is done. Ambedkar believed in democratic socialism. He says: 'I think, my definition of democracy is a form and a method of government where by revolutionary changes in the economic and social life of the people are brought about without bloodshed'. He thought that the more the education in the society, the more social interaction among people. As our society is plagued with caste system, it is bound to breed inequalities. In order to remove these inequalities, education is to be geared to play a dominant role. Ambedkar was mainly concerned about the uplift and political struggle of the Untouchables. He believed that education was necessary to shake off their mental lethargy and satisfaction with their existing plight. He argued that education was effective as it could destroy the caste system. He opined that social legislation alone could not do much efforts, it must also be made to change the hearts of Untouchables themselves. He argued that Untouchables should be educated formally as well as informally to stop carrying dead animals, eating carrion and skinning carcasses and to begin observing cleanliness in their daily lives. He demanded facilities for improving the education among Untouchables. He has argued that a certain percentage of seats be reserved, and separate hostels should be started for the Scheduled Caste girls.

Aims of Education

Ambedkar upheld the democratic concept in education profounded by Dewey. Any education given by a group tends to socialise its members. The basis for the concept of education be upon society which really exists in order to have any assurance that our ideal is a practicable one. Ambedkar himself was an example of what education could do to the under-privileged section of the society. Education is not only a layer for their social mobility but also opens the doors for their modernisation. It also affects in reducing their dependence on the rural elite and offers them a chance for occupational change. It makes them aware of their humiliation and enslavement and has ultimately emerged as an instrument of liberation and empowerment. It was through education and exposure to outside influence that they could become aware of their exploitation. This was expected to reduce the inequality in the social and economic life of the nation.

Curriculum

Curriculum is a means to realise the educational aims. Ambedkar gave importance to science and technology courses. Earlier, he had established the 'Bharatiya Samaj Seva Sangh' whose motto was to read, read out and hear, understand, realise and give realisation.

Education was necessary to instil among the downtrodden a sense of self-respect and dignity and it could hasten the assimilation into mainstream of enlightenment of professional courses in Engineering, Medicine, Law, etc. He was a national man. He was of the view that the curriculum should go a long way in developing rationality among learners. The rationality tends to give them the capacity to distinguish truth from untruth.

Owing to the existing social system, the Scheduled Castes occupy economically a very low place in the Indian economy. The status and conditions of Scheduled Castes could be improved only through technical education which gives way to occupying executive posts.

Methodology

The process of teaching-learning occurs in human association. This human association is possible through formal education. Formal teaching and training facilitate transmission of all resources and achievement in a complex society. Formation of character by an intercourse with others becomes an increasingly important task with every development of special schemes. What maturity and reproduction are to physiological life, education is to social life. Taking cue from Plato's philosophical definition of slave, Ambedkar resounded that, call the slave as slave, he rebels.

Ambedkar has always reminded the depressed classes about what they were deprived of. Efficiency in production often demands division of labour. Hindu society was divided into innumerable castes and sub-castes. The democratic ideal of education, with which Ambedkar associated, was based upon the realisation of a different forum of society. Obviously, a society to which stratification into separate classes would be fatal, must see to it that intellectual opportunities are accessible to all on equal and easy terms. Therefore, there must be equal opportunities in education. Ambedkar affirmed Plato's view that the place of an individual in society should not be determined by birth or wealth or any conventional status but by his own nature as descended in the process or education.

Educational Management

Education is one of the basic needs along with food, clothing, shelter and medicine. Ambedkar was very particular in developing the primary education. He could see that free and compulsory primary education for the children up to the age of 14 years was included in the directive principles of state policy in the Indian Constitution. He argued that the children of the poor are admitted freely to government institutions. In the statement submitted to the Indian Statutory Commission in 1928, he said that unless compulsion in the matter of primary education is made obligatory and admission to primary school is strictly enforced, conditions essential for educational progress of the backward classes will not come into existence.

Conclusion

Pragmatism was the basis for Ambedkar's educational philosophy. In his view, education was a democratic process in which everyone gets their due share. He gave importance to character formation through education. Ambedkar has advocated that the education would be useful to the learner in particular and benefits the large society in general.

References

Ambedkar, B.R., *Conditions Prescribed for Successful Working of Democracy*, Speech delivered to the members of the Poona District Library on 22 September 1953, Lok Sangrah Press, 1952.

Dewey, John, *Democracy and Education: An Introduction to the Philosophy of Education*, New York: The Macmillan Company, 1954.

Dr. Babasaheb Ambedkar: Writings and Speeches, Vol. 2 and 10, Education Department, Government of Maharashtra, Bombay, 1982 and 1991.

10

Ambedkar's Life

A Search for Social Justice

P. George Victor

Ambedkar's life was a search for social justice. Like the Harijans (Dalits) of his times and their brethren in many parts of present-day India, Ambedkar had experienced the inhuman practice of caste system particularly untouchability, Today, Ambedkar's life, mission and eminence have become the source of inspiration to the downtrodden people in India.

Ambedkar's actual name was Bhima Rao. His surname was Sakpal, but he replaced it with Ambavadekar, which is derived from his ancestral village called Ambavedkar, near Mandangad in Ratnagir district of Maharashtra. The name 'Ambavadekar' was again changed by his teacher in the school register; thus comes to the word 'Ambedkar', a Sanskritised version imitating the Maharashtrian names like Bhandarkar, Veerasavarkar, Keluskar, etc. Owing to this, Gandhi thought for some time that Ambedkar was a Brahmin.

Ambedkar belonged to an Untouchable caste of Maharashtra called Mahars, which was a dominant caste among the Harijans in that region. He was born on 14 April 1891 at Mhow near Indore in Madhya Pradesh. His father was a headmaster in the Military School. Ambedkar inherited the military courage both from his maternal and also from his paternal source. Though influenced by the devotional path of Kabir, his parents were the followers of the rituals of Hinduism.

Ambedkar's high school and college studies were completed in Bombay. He studied in the Columbia University from 1913 to 1915 and got his MA and PhD degrees. In London, he stayed from 1920 to 1923 and got MSc and DSc degrees, and also did his law course there. He visited Germany to study at the Bonn University, but it could not materialise.

When Ambedkar was 17 years old, his marriage took place with Ramabai. They got four sons, and a daughter. Except the third son Yeswanta Rao, all others did not survive. Ramabai had to suffer ill health and financial troubles as Ambedkar was away from home either for his studies or to do social work. She died at the age of 35 in Bombay in 1935. After 13 years of life as widower, Ambedkar married Sharada Kabir, a Brahmin lady in 1948. He died on 6 December 1956.

Regarding his professional life, Ambedkar worked as Military Secretary to the Maharaja of Baroda, under an agreement with the Maharaja of Baroda who financed his education in USA. But Ambedkar discontinued the job due to the practice of untouchability and ill treatment by other employees in the office. Later with the recommendation of Lord Sydenham, he joined as Professor in Sydenham College, Bombay. For sometime, he worked as a part-time lecturer in an accounting institute. Basically, Ambedkar was academic by nature but social conditions made him to be a revolutionary for the liberation of his community.

Historical Background of Ambedkar Struggles

During his times, India had witnessed a movement against untouchability. The Depressed Classes Mission, which was started in 1906, held a meeting in Bombay in 1918 under the presidentship of the Maharaja of Baroda and passed the 'All India Anti-Untouchability Manifesto'. The Muslims' claim for separate electorates was admitted by Lord Minto in 1906. Shivaram Janaba Kamble, a depressed caste leader, started a Marathi monthly *Somavanishya Mitra* to educate the depressed classes by 1910. The Congress condemned the practice of untouchability in 1917. In South India, especially in the Madras Province, the non-Brahmins organised a self-respect movement during the

1920s to fight against the disabilities imposed upon them by the Brahmins. The Maharajas of Baroda, Kolhapur, Pithapuram, etc. had helped the Untouchables by providing them scholarships, free education with lodging and boarding facilities. The Montague Chelmsford Reforms of 1919 admitted the provision for nominating members from the depressed classes to the legislative councils. After the completion of his studies in USA, Ambedkar stayed one year in England and came back to India in 1917, and joined the service of the King of Baroda. By this time, many depressed classes associations were formed in India.

In the year 1917, Montague, the then Secretary of State for India, came to India to study different shades of political opinion. Three different depressed classes associations, which were formed at Madras by that time, met Montague and demanded the grant of separate electorates to the depressed classes on par with the Muslims. The heads of the Depressed Classes Mission also interviewed Montague.[1] At this time, Ambedkar was 21 years old and had not entered the public life.

Ambedkar entered the service of the depressed classes in the year 1920. He participated in two conferences in that year on the invitation of the Maharaja of Kolhapur with help of Raja Kolhapur. Ambedkar started a fortnightly *Mook Nayak* (leader of dumb) by the end of that year. The publication of this paper continued till 1933 with change in its title as *Bahishkrit Bharat* in 1927 and as *Equality* in 1932. In his crusade against caste oppression and discrimination, Ambedkar organised Hindu temple entry movements in the earlier phase of his life. From 1930 to 1936, he organised various movements to uphold the rights of the depressed classes on par with the other Hindus of India. He started an association called 'Bahishkrit Hatakarin Sabha' in the year 1924, and subsequently was nominated as a member to the Bombay Legislative Council in 1927 by the Governor of Bombay Province. He formed an independent Labour Party in 1936 and dissolved it after six years. In 1946, he established Peoples' Education Society to educate the depressed classes through establishing colleges. In the last days of his life, Ambedkar thought to establish a party called 'The Republican Party of India', for the depressed classes to contest the elections but he died without establishing the same.

A study of the biography of Ambedkar, with reference to social and political conditions in India and the related movements of the welfare of the Harijans, reveals that Ambedkar had not advocated any new principle that was not existing in his times for the upliftment of the Scheduled Castes. But he was the champion of them because he had made the depressed class movement more revolutionary and aggressive in nature. India witnessed the Untouchables walking in the streets demanding for their human rights. He says: 'Lost rights are never regained by begging and by appeals to the conscience of the usurpers but by relentless struggle. Goats are used for sacrificial offerings but not lions'.[2]

Ambedkar had worked out some programme of action to fight against untouchability and caste discrimination. In the earlier phase of his life, Ambedkar took interest to enter the Hindu temples at the Kurdwar in Bombay, Vithoba temple in Ratnagiri and Kalaram temple in Nasik. Though these attempts failed, they attracted public attention and arose an awakening in the minds of the depressed classes.

He made another attempt to take drinking water from tanks by the depressed classes. At first, Ambedkar and his followers did it at the Chowdar tank in Mahad town of Kolaba district in Maharashtra on 21 March 1927. But it was purified later by the upper castes. Therefore, Ambedkar gave a call to his people to assemble on 25 December 1927 to offer *satyagraha*. This time, due to the prohibitory orders of the District Magistrate, they failed to draw water from the tank. However, they made that day an historic one by not only condemning Hindu scriptures but also by burning a copy of the *Manusmriti* which prophesied the slavery of Sudras and women, and which also attributed a worst origin to the low castes. In his later phase of life, Ambedkar even went on saying that the Untouchables were not related to the Hindus and considered them as a separate stock. Ganni Raju, a writer on the life of Ambedkar, says that 'he advised his people to renounce Hinduism and embrace any other religion where there was equality between man and man with no stigma of untouchability'.[3]

Ambedkar questioned the relation of Hindus with Untouchables as the Hindus were practically alienating the later. He logically puts that: 'If you say your religion is our religion, then your rights and our rights must be equal. But, is this the case? If not, on what grounds do you say that we must remain in Hindu fold in spite of your kicks and rebuffs?'[4]

Later, Ambedkar has decided to renounce Hinduism and on 14 October 1956 at Nagpur, Ambedkar took Buddhism as his religion. About three lakh people joined Buddhism along with him on that occasion. He declared at that time: 'By discarding my ancient religion which stood for inequality and oppression today, I am reborn … . I am no longer a devotee of my Hindu God or Goddess'.[5]

Ambedkar has written and commented on all major socio-economic problems of India and his writings now run into around ten volumes.

Though some of his conclusions on the origin of Sudras and Untouchables were outdated in view of the latest discoveries, and his book on *Buddha and his Dhamma* was considered not true to the spirit of Buddhism and was denounced by some Buddhist societies and authors, but the literature produced by him is now educating the Harijans and motivating them to agitate and organise themselves. He passed on to the latter generations a profound record of his activities, experiences and feelings. The literature produced by Ambedkar, particularly his ideals and remarks made on the society, has contributed to awaken the Untouchables. His books, particularly his criticism on the evils of caste system and how it works in the society for oppression and exploitation by denying the basic value of life and human rights of the Untouchables or the classes, have made a tremendous impact on the development of Harijans. His analysis of caste system and Hindu religion and his explanation in hating them have inspired the Harijans, and will continue to do so in future.

He gave a voice to the sufferings Harijans and made them recorded, published and popularised. The age of Ambedkar in Indian history is an age of enlightenment for Harijans. Among other outstanding Harijan leaders who sacrificed their lives for their people, Ambedkar stands alone as a man of documentation. Every incident, speech, scheme, proposal and ideals connected with him were recorded and published, whereas the other Harijan leaders left no recorded evidence of their struggle and service. Thus, Ambedkar created a history and heritage of the Harijans of India.

Ambedkar picked up every thought that helped the Harijans or the depressed classes and took every action to promote their status. On behalf of the depressed classes of India, he attended the two round-table conferences in 1930 and 1931. In 1937, Ambedkar was selected to the Bombay Legislative Assembly and worked for the welfare of the labourers. Subsequently, in 1942, he was nominated as a member of the Viceroy's Executive Council and given the portfolio of labour. In this period, he asserted for the establishment of Minimum Wages Act, etc. and maintenance of proper industrial labour relations. During the Second World War, Ambedkar supported the British, while the Congress has denied such support. Ambedkar has said that fascism was more dangerous than the British and therefore he supported them and toured all over India and addressed many meetings during this period.

His Last Days

With the help of Jogendranath Mandal of Bengal, the Law Minister in Interim Government, Ambedkar was elected to the Constituent Assembly by the support of the opposition members in Bengal Legislature. He argued before the Constituent Assembly in 1945 that 'the Scheduled Castes were a separate and a distinct element in the national life of India and that they had no connection with the caste Hindus'.[6] In view of the partition of Bengal, Ambedkar lost his place in the Constituent Assembly, according to the Indian Independence Act, 1947. The Maharashtrians have a special affection for Ambedkar and therefore the Bombay Legislative Congress Party placed him in a vacancy. Subsequently, in the first cabinet of free India, two opposition leaders were given the portfolios in the cabinet of Nehru, and Ambedkar was one of them. He was made as the Minister of Law. As Law Minister, he was elected as the chairman of the Constitution Draft Committee. Again, as the member of the Advisory Committee on Minorities, he argued for separate electorates to the Harijans but he could not succeed. Therefore, he criticised the Constituent Assembly as the 'assembly consisted of a majority of the waste Hindus'.[7] In 1948, Ambedkar introduced the

Draft Constitution in the Constituent Assembly, and after one year of debate and modifications, the Constituent Assembly adopted it in 1949, and it actually came into force on 26 January 1950. Later, Ambedkar prepared the Hindu Code Bill. As there was much controversy over it, it received little support from the members including Nehru. Ambedkar resigned as the minister. Later, Ambedkar participated in the 1952 general elections. Though he and his party were defeated in the elections for Lok Sabha, the Bombay State Congress Party elected him in the same year to the Rajya Sabha and he continued in the office till his death. Ambedkar has criticised Nehru's policies on military budget, foreign policy, Harijan welfare, etc.

In the last days of his life, Ambedkar lost his eye-sight, probably due to the result of his relentless work of drafting and editing of the Constitution of India and Hindu Code Bill. He was the first Untouchable in Indian history, who revolted against Hinduism and its tradition. He was the first man to herald the oppressive nature of caste system and how it works against the natural rights of man: equality, liberty and fraternity. Again he was the first man to write and record the status and history of Harijans and voice their grievances which no European writer and researcher could do it. Ambedkar was the first Indian who argued and supported the religious conversions.[8] Lastly, he was the first man who asserted that Harijans were a separate stock of people among the Indians. This is what Ambedkar has contributed actually for Harijans. Ambedkar was primarily a theoretician, political thinker and revolutionary for the emancipation of Harijans and for the enrichment of Indian society. He built up revolutionary struggles for the emancipation of Harijans which the other Indian leaders and the Congress have not done. Therefore, they were forced to yield to his proposals or accept the present-day benefits which the Harijans are enjoying today.

Notes

1. Raju, G. Ganni, *The Life of Dr. B.R. Ambedkar*, Babasaheb Dr. Ambedkar Memorial Society, Hyderabad, 1979, p. 24.
2. Ibid., p. 47.

3. Ibid., p. 51.
4. Keer, Dhananjay, *Dr. Ambedkar: Life and Mission*, Bombay: Popular Prakashan, 1981, p. 92.
5. Thangaraj, P., *Selected Thoughts of Dr. Ambedkar*, Madras: Puratchikanal Publications, 1977, p. 61.
6. Ganni Raju, op. cit., p. 222.
7. Ibid., p. 179.
8. Ibid., p. 184.

11

The Socio-Political Philosophy of Ambedkar

T. Krishna Kanth

The aim of this paper is to analyse the institution of caste and its hold on the Indian society even in a democratic set-up. The solutions offered by Ambedkar on the caste system will be re-casted to focus in a different perspective so as to find mechanisms to eradicate the untouchability in India.

Ambedkar was born in a Scheduled Caste family in Maharashtra. Throughout his childhood he was subjected to inhuman treatment based on untouchability which has been an inherent feature of Indian society. Ambedkar after experiencing the ill-treatment at the school and in the society, had determined to fight against the social evil imposed on Scheduled Castes and other lower castes. He also realised that the root cause of untouchability is in the institution of caste order and its practice. Throughout his life he had championed the cause of Untouchables and other lower castes. He put up a valiant struggle all his life to help his neglected brethren to lead a better life in dignity and with self respect.

Ambedkar analysed the problem of caste and its fall out in every sphere of activity. He had aimed to achieve democracy and in turn has tried to democratise the Indian society. Education, he felt, could bring awareness among the downtrodden and enlightenment in the society. A great man must be motivated by the dynamics of a social purpose and must act as the scourge and scavenger of society.[1]

Genesis of Caste System

Dr Ambedkar systematically analysed the institution of caste. The caste system is a pivotal institution in Hindu society. It shapes and directs the relationships of its members in a number of ways. Caste has been considered both as a unit and as a system of social stratification. As a system of social stratification, it places its units, sub-units and all its members in an order of high and low ranks. These ranks are ascribed by birth in particular caste.

According to Hindu tradition, the caste system owes its origin to the four *varna*, which are respectively derived from the Brahmin who sprang from the mouth of the deity, the Kshatriya who was created from his arms, the Vaishya who was formed from his thighs, and the Sudra who was born from his feet.[2]

The caste system, thus, has general characteristics of social stratification—exclusiveness, inclusiveness, and hierarchical relations are endogamy, commensality, ritual status, hereditary specialisation, cultural differences, domination and power.[3]

Ambedkar after having understood the social malady came out with different solutions to eradicate the social evil and to pave the way for a more democratic society.[4]

Caste consciousness is essentially a result of the sentiments of belonging to a particular caste group. By virtue of hereditary caste membership, people share common socio-religious norms and values in regard etc. occupation, commensality, and marital relations etc.[5] Some European scholars have tried to equate caste with class. Though both operate in similar manner but they differ in many ways. They might share the consciousness of being one and belong to one but caste as a group achieved crudity by getting a religious sanction to practice it as separate entities while class has mobility and circulation. Anybody by virtue of his hard work and wealth can change his status, but it is not the case with caste.[6]

Caste Malady and Its Evil Effects

Ambedkar imbibed the ideas of western education and political philosophy, understood perfectly the great ideas of liberty, equality and fraternity. He cautioned his followers to achieve political education among the depressed classes and organised them to fight against the socio, economic and political inequality. So much has been written and talked about the institution of caste and its evil effects on Indian civilisation. In fact, it is Arnold Toynbee, who in his monumental work on history, made a wonderful observation that slavery, the pernicious institution, which had contributed largely to the decline and fall of the Hellenic society and in the Indian case, caste is always on the verge of being a social enormity, but when it is keyed up by receiving a religious interpretation and a religious sanction, its enormity is bound to grow to monstrous proportions. Toynbee emphasises that the institution of caste played with the Indian civilisation and seen its decline and fall.[7]

What really shook Toynbee is notwithstanding the pernicious role played by caste in Indian society, there has never been any effective move to abolish or even to mitigate untouchability on the part of the Brahmins, the hierarchical caste became the master of the ceremonies of the whole system.[8] In the similar vein, a noted thinker and novelist, V.S. Naipaul, made a striking observation: 'To the ancient Aryans the Untouchables were walking carrion ... rural untouchability as serfdom maintained by terror and sometimes by deliberate starvation ... . In the country itself, the practice of slavery had attained such a sophistication that the victims themselves were made to feel a moral 'obligation to remain in slavery'.[9]

In fact, Kosambi observes that in ancient Indian society it was the ideology which was largely a substitute to physical violence with the result that violence in society remained invisible and survived for thousands of years. In the West, slavery has vanished with a strong and determined effort by dominant group, whereas in Indiagi case dominant group colludes to perpetuate the caste system.[10]

Indian Civilisation Questioned

Naipaul questioned the Indian civilisation on the practice of untouchability and enslavement of a quarter of the population. Hinduism has not been good enough for the millions. It has exposed us to a thousand years of defeat and stagnation. It has given men no idea of a contact with other men, no idea of state. Hinduism, by sanctifying the caste made the society fragmented and vulnerable. Its philosophy of withdrawal has diminished men intellectually and did not equip them to respond to challenge, stifled growth, that again and again in India history has repeated itself: vulnerability, defeat, withdrawal.[11]

In India, interesting thing is that every politician and political party involves in rhetoric of eradication of untouchability and improving their lot to sway the masses. But in practice they encourage the caste equations to gain political mileage. Ever since India became independent, there has never been an attempt to implement the rights guaranteed to Untouchables in the Constitution. No serious attempt is being made by any upper caste intellectual or political leaders of different faiths to mobilise a public opinion and organise large scale movement to inculcate new cultural and ethical values by incorporating the downtrodden masses on the similar lines of America's civil rights movement.[12]

In fact, the shocking thing is that most of the intellectuals (and political conspirators) tried to find solution to Indian problems by excluding the Scheduled Castes. The seats of higher learning have been denied to the Untouchables and to lower castes. Education as a path seeker of knowledge and truth monopolised by the upper castes. As far as Marxists are concerned, they too have failed to take cognizance of the problem. Instead of addressing the problem of untouchability they escape in the camouflage of political revolution. Ambedkar has foreseen these developments in India and has written therefore on revolution and counter-revolution and indicated the prerequisites of Communism.

It is very important to find a solution to the problem of untouchability and their plight in the Indian society. Certain groups did make some progress. India has emerged into a modern world with the similar problems faced by the West, important being the fight for self-determination and other secessionist movements. Given the nature of divergent cultures, religions, and castes, the malady of modern age is found to be terrorism.[13] It is going to stay and consolidate its position and spread its tentacles in India, unless the elite classes realise the urgent need to compromise, accommodate and reform the society. While addressing these secessionist movements in India they should also address the problems of Scheduled Castes. Otherwise in the fast changing world, people would ascertain their rights by resorting to terrorist and militant activity, which may play havoc with the fabric of Indian society and its economic development.[14]

Remedial Measures to Regenerate the Society

There are certain mechanisms which were applied in America to eradicate social discrimination. If the same are applied to Indian situation under the spirit of Ambedkar one may get the model as follows: (a) offering punishment by denying highest offices, once the person has been identified practicing untouchability or denying opportunity or ill-treating a schedule caste person, (b) take open stand on caste inequalities (c) there is need to organise a civil rights movement by bringing people from all walks of life to rebuild new values and norms for a social awakening, (d) compulsory implementation of reservations, (e) a holistic approach should be made in uplifting the downtrodden, i.e. helping the downtrodden should be considered as helping India to achieve all-round progress of her people, (f) destructing the Indian society and culture by nullifying the caste system.

Conclusion

The upper strata of society should make a genuine effort to bring socio-economic and political changes in the society. If they fail to do it, the lower castes will have an option of changing their religion by joining Islam.[15] By doing so they can claim equal respect, status and dignity in the Indian society.

It is interesting to note that the great persons and their ideas can not sustain or continue to sway the minds of people. In any society, dominant group plays a vital role and their patronisation or adherence is very crucial for survival of particular ideology. The dominant group in India has failed to come to terms with

Ambedkar's philosophy as far as his ideas on reforming the social structure is concerned. The author, therefore, strongly feels that the dominant group should play the role of harbinger of emancipation, equality and builder of new India.

Notes

1. See for a detailed analysis of Dr. Ambedkar's contribution, Keer, Dhananjay, *Dr. Ambedkar: Life and Mission*, Bombay: Popular Prakashan, 1981.
2. Hutton, J.H., *Caste in India: Its Nature, Function and Origins*, New Delhi: Oxford University Press, 1981, p. 148.
3. Ibid.
4. Ambedkar, B.R., *Annihilation of Caste*, Jalandhar: Bheem Patrika Publications, 1971.
5. Ginsberg, Morris, 'Social Class', in *Encyclopedia of the Social Sciences*, Vol. III-IV, New York: The Macmillan Co., 1959.
6. Bose, N.K., 'Class and Caste', in *Culture and Society in India*, New York: Asia Publishing House, 1967.
7. Toynbee, Arnold L., *A Study of History*, Oxford University Press, Oxford, 1978, p. 276.
8. Ibid., p. 302.
9. Naipaul, V.S., *India: A Wounded Civilization*, London: Andre Deutsch, 1977, p. 43.
10. See Kosambi, D.D., *An Introduction to the Study of Indian History*, Bombay: Popular Prakashan, 1976, p. 5.
11. Naipaul, op. cit.
12. Myrdal, Gunnar, *An American Dilemma: The Negro Problem and American Democracy*, New York: Carnegie Corporation, 1944.
13. See Clutterbuck, Richard, *Guerrillas and Terrorists*, London: Faber and Faber, 1967.
14. Hanton, Rosalind, *Caste, Conflict and Ideology*, Hyderabad: Orient Longman Ltd., 1985.
15. In earlier times, the lower castes to escape from the oppression and inhuman treatment 'from the Hindu rituals and upper castes have embraced Christianity, Sikhism, Buddhism and Islam. It is only Islam that threatened Hinduism and Indian civilization'. See Toynbee, op. cit., p. 302.

12

Ambedkar as a Theoretician and Policy-Maker

G. Saibaba

Bharat Ratna Ambedkar was a distinguished economist, an eminent educationist, a great social reformer, a unique politician, a revolutionary, a radical philosopher, and an ardent advocate of social democracy and welfare state. He ranks on par with Mahatma Gandhi, Nehru and Loknayak Jay Prakash Narayan in public recognition in modern India. Indeed, he is more popular today than ever before as his intellectual ideas are ebbing with public policy formulation and social action as the emancipation of the downtrodden sections of the Indian society is taking shape from the riddles of poverty, social backwardness and centuries old inertia. The recently concluded birth centenary celebrations of Dr Ambedkar are a fitting tribute to the unique role of his intellectual vision inscribed in the Constitution of India for achieving social development to secure social justice to the depressed classes. Ambedkar's life-long crusade was for the liberation of the depressed classes which has no parallel anywhere in the world.

Ambedkar as a Theoretician

It is surprising to note that in recent years several social scientists attempted to examine Ambedkar's ideas in the classical paradigms of economic development.[1] Some others try to analyse the relevance of Ambedkar through Marxian framework. A selected few advocated the need for a methodology to read, analyse and understand Ambedkar.[2] Anyone who attempted to analyse Ambedkar without a proper methodology will be a venture without drawing meaningful conclusions. To avoid such dangers, there is a need for a methodological approach to understand Ambedkar.

Ambedkar's economic ideas are mostly developed in an analytical frame with deep roots in an inter-disciplinary approach broadly covering social, cultural, political and legal dimensions of economics. Thus, he emerged as a competent researcher and theoretician in economics since 1923.[3] Since then he shifted his focus from economics to studies in social, legal and political problems. Indeed, Ambedkar may be regarded as one of the early Indian economists who introduced the ideas of institutional economics to the Indian economic studies (perhaps R.K. Mukherjee may be the first).

Ambedkar's training at Columbia University (U.S.A.) has provided him an opportunity to acquaint himself with the institutional economics and has given the basis for his institutional approach for Indian economic issues. There are several instances of the real bearing of the intellectual traditions developed by the institutional trio, namely, Veblen, Commons and Mitchell. It is interesting to observe that he acquired all the theoretical ideas of this institutional trio. He has demonstrated tremendous analytical powers to explain simple economic issues with a unique inter-disciplinary framework which is very much popular with present-day theoreticians. Perhaps, Ambedkar may be regarded as one of the early Indian economists who introduced an inter-disciplinary methodology to the Indian economic studies.[4] It is of great interest to note that Ambedkar has specialised in the legal basis of the Indian economic studies with an inter-disciplinary approach which is now developed in recent years by the noble laureate Prof. Ronal Harry Coase, a product of London School of Economics.

Like Coase, Ambedkar has challenged the way economists formulated several issues in Indian economic studies. His theoretical frame has strong roots in social, cultural, political and historical approach. Interestingly, Ambedkar has demonstrated an unusual capacity and great skill in building up several powerful theoretical arguments on various issues. In his development paradigm, one can identify socio-cultural factors based on legal foundations with constitutional safeguards and political content in Buddhism. All his economic ideas, it appears, were developed only to subserve his main analysis and ideas on several issues. Against this background, the general recognition of Ambedkar as a theoretician is valuable.

Ambedkar's paradigm of poverty and development of Dalit is a conscious effort which challenges the recent approaches to poverty eradication programmes. In fact, it questioned the foundations of the concept of poverty developed by Dandekar and Rath and even World Bank. His legacy to Dalits is primarily the constitutional safeguards for Scheduled Castes as a means for liberating and enabling their deliverance from deprivation and social stigma.

His deep theoretical insights into India's economic problems are to be found in his doctoral dissertations, pamphlets and articles. There are several insights into India's economic problems in numerous memoranda and statements submitted by Ambedkar to government at different times. In spite of such varied and adequate contributions in economics as in law and social activities, there is general negligence of Ambedkar's theoretical contributions in economics. The surprising fact is that there appears to be a total blackout of his contributions in economics until 1991.[5] Thus, there is a great need to rectify this lapse and greater efforts need to be made to make people aware of his economic thought, particularly his insights into India's economic problems. In this context, it is highly interesting to note the arguments of Prof Adiseshaiah who advocated to develop a relevant economic theory for India. He has given several examples how we are missing relevance of economic laws in various analytical tools and several used to understand Indian economic situation. He made two observations on present-day economics: one on the pedagogy of economics in India and the other on economic policy for the country.[6] Against this background, Ambedkar's theoretical approach need to be examined because he has developed some original ideas.

Ambedkar's Thought on Indian Monetary System

His major contribution in the area of monetary economics is his DSc dissertation on 'The Problem of Rupee'. Subsequently, he made a statement and gave evidence in 1924–25 before the Royal Commission on Indian Currency and Finance whose findings gave way to the establishment of Reserve Bank of India. Ambedkar has given an excellent exposition. Ambedkar as an original thinker and analyst dwells into the hitherto unemployed areas of Indian currency spanning for nearly 10 decades from 1800 to 1893. His analysis of the Indian money market came true. The dream of Ambedkar that 'conversion of good commercial paper in to currency best suited to the needs of seasonal demands' came true in the form of introduction of various new instruments like 182 days treasury bills, inter-bank participation certificates, certificate of deposit and commercial deposits.[7]

Public Finance

His contribution to the field of public finance is of great significance. His dissertation on 'The Evolution of Provincial Finance in British India' (1921) and another publication on 'The Problem of the Rupee' (1923) are the two notable books on economics. In these two books, Ambedkar exposed the designs and objectives of British imperial system and also brought clearly the way the vested interests at home collude with the European imperialists. He has further exposed the manner in which the British manipulated the exchange relationship between the rupee and pound in such a manner that they could maximise their profits. He clearly explained how this settlement of exchange rates adversely affected the lives of the Indian masses.

Agricultural Economics and Rural Development

His contribution to agricultural economics can be seen in his publication 'Small Holdings in India' and his book *States and Minorities*.[8] Ambedkar's ideas on agricultural development was based on industrial development. Institutional reforms which include land reforms and state socialism are also pursued by Ambedkar. His ideas on land reforms are mostly the by-products of his famous paper. As an economist, he predicted and projected the input and output relations that may emerge as a consequence of land reforms. The ills of the Indian agriculture do not relate primarily in the matter of enlarging holdings but failure to increasing capital and capital goods. This implies a production function for agricultural sector. This idea makes it clear that Ambedkar was keen in treating agriculture as an industry. Thus, he had argued that to step up agricultural output, land reforms should come in a manner that they resulted in creation of economic holding. He clearly examined the merits and demerits of the concept of economic holding and pointed out: 'The remedy for the ills of agriculture in India does not lie primarily in the matter of enlarging holdings but in the matter of increasing capital goods'.[9] His ideas on land reforms were highly practical and original. Ambedkar presented data to show the economic effects of idle labour. Thus, he advocated to shift this idle labour to non-agricultural activities, where it is productively used. This means industrialisation of India is the soundest remedy for the agricultural problems of India. In his book *States and Minorities*, he advocated for a plan of economic life of the people on the lines which would lead to the highest point of productivity without closing any avenue to the private enterprises. As an institutional economist, he advocated for several institutional reforms such as nationalisation of insurance and transport sector along with land. All these ideas gave an impression that Ambedkar was able to visualise as a true economist. He was able to grasp the nature of production function of agriculture, political changes of land reforms and the backward and forward linkages of industrialisation. Thus, he emerges as an institutionalist who was concerned with persistence of archaic rural institutions.

Ambedkar as a Policy-Maker

Ambedkar's prime concern was the uplift of the depressed castes population. He anticipated the imperative of human development/social development long ago. The current emphasis on human resource development in India which endorses public policy for social development is in reality anticipated by Ambedkar.[10] Proper appreciation of the role of Ambedkar's social policy in public policy warrants the consideration of the dynamics of public policy. A historical review of public policy reveals that intellectual tides have played a vital role in shopping and changing public policy. Ambedkar's legacy for the Dalits is mainly in the form of constitutional safeguards, planning for the life of the people (i.e. state socialism) and educational planning and development.

It was found that Ambedkar has developed his ideas on education mainly in his writings and speeches in the form of (a) memorandum to the Simon Commission, and (b) written statements before the University Reform Committee and speeches in the Bombay Legislative Assembly on grants for education. He clearly stated his ideas on the economic value of education in India for all sections of the population. Ambedkar has covered a wide area of educational planning and development issues which broadly includes (a) cost and benefits of education, (b) finances of education, and (c) management and administration of education. Perhaps, as an economist, Ambedkar is the first to calculate the costs and the benefits of education in India. He has calculated the sources of finance for education at different levels. It is interesting to note that he had argued that Mohammedans are given due share in the education sector by treating them as a minority and similar benefits should also be extended to the depressed classes. He supported all his arguments with necessary data. In fact, the influence of Mahatma Jyothi Rao Phuley and John Dewey, his teacher at Columbia University, on Ambedkar is very well known. His written arguments before the University Reforms Committee in 1925 provide a major source of information on his ideas on administration of higher education. Ambedkar advocated for the teaching of undergraduates by university professors from the beginning of their university career to secure best men for research and best work out of them. Thus, Ambedkar proposed inter-collegiate teaching. These ideas have great relevance in the context of recent emphasis on orientation and refresher courses for college and university teachers. In fact, the pragmatic approach of Ambedkar based on strong statistical data on education and his analytical arguments before various educational bodies and his own experience as a teacher of economics greatly contributed to the planning and the development of educational policy in India.

Thus, Ambedkar has emerged as an eminent policy-maker of modern India. Some of his ideas are gaining relevance in recent years on several policy measures, such as the founder of human development theory and architect of social democracy.

Notes

1. Saibaba, G., *Ambedkar Ideas on Poverty and Development of Dalits: A Study of Emerging Perspectives*, UGC Seminar Volume, S.K. University, Anantapur, January 1992, pp. 87–89.
2. Several social scientists specialised in Marxian lore adopted this approach. Notable among them are Prof. Hari Gopal, D.N. Reddy and Seshaiah. For details, see papers of these scholars in recent seminar volumes on Ambedkar, S.K. University, Anantapur and Open University, Hyderabad.
3. Saibaba, G., *Ambedkar Ideas on Agricultural Development*, Seminar Paper, A.P. Open University, Hyderabad, July 1992.
4. Ibid.
5. Naidu, K.M., *Highlights of Economic Thoughts of Babasaheb Ambedkar*, UGC Seminar Volumes, S.K. University, Anantapur, 1992, pp. 103–11.
6. Adiseshaiah, Malcolm S., 'The Relevance of Economics', *The Indian Journal of Labour Economics*, Vol. XVI, No. 4, January 1974, p. 356. In this, he advocated the need for the Indian approach and, if possible, Indian theories.
7. For an excellent account on the relevance of Ambedkar ideas on monetary economics, see Chauhan and Elumalai's.
8. Ambedkar, B.R., 'Small Holdings in India and their Remedies', *Journal of Indian Economic Society*, 1918 and *States and Minorities*, Bombay: Thacker & Co., 1947.
9. *The Writings and Speeches of Dr. Babasaheb Ambedkar*, Vol. I, Education Department, Government of Maharashtra, Bombay, 1979, p. 478.
10. Chalam, K.S., 'B.R. Ambedkar on Economics of Education and Educational Development', paper presented in the UGC seminar on B.R. Ambedkar's Economics Philosophy held at Hyderabad, 17–19 July, 1992.

Part II

Socio-Economic Ideas of Ambedkar and their Relevance

13

Development Philosophy of Dr B.R. Ambedkar

K.S. Chalam

Babasaheb Dr B.R. Ambedkar was one of the greatest thinkers of modern India who blended the western thought with Buddhist ideals. It is very difficult to come to any conclusion about his contributions merely on the basis of his biography written by some individuals or merely going through his debates in the Parliament and in Bombay Legislative Assembly. In fact, the profusion in his thinking and the philosophical thrust given to his political strategies had reached its zenith by the time he completed his *Buddha and his Dhamma*. Therefore, one should relate his insightful thoughts with his analytical approaches to understand India and see how he provided solutions to the existing evils in the country. At the same time one can see the continuity in his thinking from that of his *Annihilation of Caste* through his economic writings and *Buddha and His Dhamma*. In part IV of the book *Enlightenment and the Vision of the New Way*, Dr Ambedkar has clearly understood the Gautama's dilemma. He said that when he sat in meditation for getting new light, he was in the grip of Sankhya philosophy. As we all know that Sankhya is one of the enlightened schools of Indian thought that has influenced *Bhagavad Gita*. But, the problem with the Sankhya according to Ambedkar was that Gautama was riddled with how to do away with suffering. Sankhya has limited tools to deal with this problem. In fact, Sankhya was one of the greatest schools of thought in ancient period and even preceded the western thought as far as the proof of truth was concerned.

But it was least concerned about social issues. Therefore, Ambedkar has come to the conclusion that Buddha had finally developed his own teachings without much reliance on Sankhya. Thus, Buddha became an independent philosopher and teacher. He has explained that there were four important distinguishing features in the teachings of Buddha. They are; (1) Mind precedes things, mind is leader of all its faculties etc. (2) Mind is the fount of all the good and evils, (3) Avoidance of sinful acts, and (4) Real religion lies not in the books of religion, but in the observation of the tenets of the religion. He went on explaining the greatness of Buddha and said that Buddha's doctrine of anicca, (*transitoriness*) is confirmed as modern science is echoing the Buddhist doctrines of transitoriness (*anicca*) and of agelessness (*anatta*). Ambedkar seemed to be emotional at the end of the book and says that 'who would not say let such a one be our Master?' The essence of Babasaheb's work was that knowledge was essential to salvation and ignorance was one of the two main causes of failures to attain it (craving or attachment being the others). Modern scholars might evaluate Ambedkar as an idealist in interpreting the importance given by him to mind over matter. But, definitely he cannot be compared with that of Sankaracharya as Ambedkar himself has critiqued him in his writings. He may be considered to some extent as an epistemological idealist in interpreting Buddha. But Babasaheb had a profound understanding about the materialist conditions of the people in general and Dalits in particular. Therefore, he had given a practical guide to achieve equality in an egalitarian society.

There is some kind of a passion for Buddhism among some sections of Dalits and to that extent are idealising and some times vulgarising Babasaheb's personality also. One must understand here that why Babasaheb wanted Buddhism to be a tool for the emancipation of Dalits. He was not interested to give the Dalits salvation as there were several religions under which Dalits were already thrown without emancipation. I consider that the Hindu philosophy including Sankhya and *Karma* yoga of Gita were supporting the social exclusion (castes) as a metaphysical elucidation of *karma*, transmigration of souls, sin, etc. It was never challenged. Perhaps, it was the greatness of Babasaheb in discovering in that the core of Hinduism that supported the existence of castes and divisions among humans was contested and defected by Buddhism. The Buddhist approach to philosophy was largely borrowed from the native Ajvikas; Buddha had propounded the theory of *paticca samuppada*, dependent origination. This theory speaks about *anitya* and the process of continuous change and elucidated nothing like ego, personality, soul, etc., remains. Therefore, no transmigration takes place. Then where is the need for *varna* based on past *karma*. In other words, in one go the whole edifice of caste, based on past *karma* and transmigration of souls was destroyed by Buddha. This was a great revolution in the ancient period to denounce the existence of caste. It is still valid and is not available in other religions including the Mediterranean Islam and Christianity. I have been searching for the reasons why Babasaheb embraced Buddhism. I found the above philosophical underpinnings as possible explanation for this. It is already known that Buddhism demolishes the metaphysical Hinduism that supports caste. And, at the same time, it provides sufficient grounds for emancipation of the Dalits in the modern society. But it should be creatively used and not limited to the worship of the idol alone that makes Buddha as an Avatar.

I feel that philosophical indulgence is always necessary to sustain a programme. Unfortunately, some of the activists in the movement do not understand or are sometimes led away by competing religious discourses to come to a different conclusion. I am of the opinion that among different communities in the country, it is only the so-called Scheduled Castes, or Dalits who are in great confusion or divided on the basis of religion, sub-caste region, language and other considerations. This has been the curse of the community. But, we have today the writings of Babasaheb and they are to be interpreted to the changing times of the country and the world. The kind of changes and developments in India and in the world today are never seen before in history. The speed and the methods with which these are implemented need to be understood by the scholars and activists to make Babasaheb relevant to the times.

II

It is in the above philosophical context that I have tried to bring out the following programmes of Babasaheb which I consider are important. Dr Ambedkar has written books and made presentations in the Legislative Assembly, Bombay Constituent Assembly and formulated policies as Labour Member, in Governor General's Council that gave him an opportunity to project a vision about the future of Dalits. However, it is very difficult to find a specific theory of Dalit development exclusively written by him at one place. Except, in his detailed memorandum on the safeguards for the Scheduled Castes for being submitted to the Constituent Assembly on behalf of the SC Federation in March 1947, nowhere Dr Ambedkar has formulated detailed programme for Dalit development. It is also true that scholars and activists have focused more on the social and political contributions of Dr Ambedkar than his economic and educational ideas. In fact, Babasaheb Dr Ambedkar had two PhD's in Economics from two premier universities of the world in the early part of the 20th century. He was aware of the fact that economic development is essential for the survival of the Dalits. But, his existential condition and the social circumstances that prevailed during the British India forced him to concentrate more on the problems of social exclusion, untouchability and made him to fight for human dignity for Dalits. It does not mean that he has not written anything about the economic upliftment of the Dalits in India. There are occasions in which Dr Ambedkar has clearly formulated a vision for the upliftment of the Dalits in India. Some of the ideas are scattered in different parts of his writings. Therefore, it is the responsibility of the scholars to bring all of them together to bring out a vision of the great son of India for the upliftment of the Dalits in particular and the poor in general. I have gathered the following sources from which I have put together a comprehensive vision of Dr Ambedkar about the Dalit development:

Philosophical background is based on his books, *Buddha and Dhamma*, *Annihilation of Caste* and *Buddha or Karl Marx*.

1. States and minorities.
2. Small holdings in India and their remedies.

3. Economic writings and his speeches delivered in the Bombay Legislative Assembly and in the Parliament.

The Philosophy of Development

The theories of development and growth have appeared only during the de-colonisation period particularly with reference to less developed countries. Development during the colonial rule was understood as emancipation from want and destitution. Dalits were considered during the 18th and 19th centuries as destitute and depressed classes. Therefore, if there is any single theory propounded by Dr Ambedkar about the economic emancipation of the Dalits in India, it is about his ideas relating to State socialism. It has a philosophical and theoretical understanding of the fact that development according to him is possible for the Dalits only through parliamentary democracy. In his paper on Buddha or Karl Marx he has clearly mentioned that the route cause of *dukkha* in the Buddhist tradition is poverty.[1] One can remove *dukkha* only through abolition of poverty with the State's ownership of agriculture, industry and insurance. But, this is to be achieved not through violence but through a peaceful means of democratic socialism in India. He has evaluated the means through which socialism can be achieved as per Marxist and Buddhist principles. On an evaluation, he has found that it is through non-violence and by following *panchashila* and the eight-fold path of Buddhism, it is possible to achieve equality and socialism for the Indians in general and Dalits in particular. It is said that 'philosophical achievement of Dr Ambedkar consists in working of a conception of individual without being an individualist of modern western brand conception of individual, which is not conflict with *Nairatmya Vada*. Dr Ambedkar has interpreted Buddhism as a vibrant world view and way of life to a whole people who were systematically denied any opportunity for engaging in philosophy and religion. He made the traditional religion morally reprehensible in a society which has expected to emulate secularist values'.[2] In other words, he has used Buddhist principles to blend with Marxist principles of annihilation of classes so that the Dalits will remain peaceful in a new society. I think, this has remained as the backbone of his vision of Dalits development.

Democracy as the Backbone of Development

Scholars like Amratya Sen are now elaborating on the need for a democratic polity to sustain development. In fact, Dr Ambedkar was one of the earliest to formulate a thesis that development can sustain only in a democratic set-up. He has elaborated on this point that political democracy rests on four principles:

1. That the individual is an end himself.
2. The individual has certain inalienable rights which must be guaranteed to him by the Constitution.
3. That the individual shall not be required to relinquish any of his constitutional rights as a condition precedent to the receipt of a privilege.
4. That the State shall not delegate powers to private persons to govern others.

In the above, Dr Ambedkar has observed that the rights of individuals are not negotiable, much the same for the Dalits. He knew that in a country like India where groups of individuals are placed in hierarchical order and are traditionally treated as unequal, it is essential that the primacy of the value that, 'all are born equal' is to be restored. It is difficult to envision development for all in India without first reinstating this universal value. That is the reason why Dr Ambedkar was insisting on the State socialism which is to be adopted for the Dalits and others in an equal footing. This is to be achieved through provisions in the Constitution and not through Legislative process.[3] That is the reason why he wanted to become a Minister for Planning so that he could implement this development programme. But Nehru did not give him this opportunity and he made him the Chairman of Drafting Committee to produce the Constitution. Dr Ambedkar played his historical role very well in this job by incorporating directive principles of State Policy where socialism and secularism were enshrined.

Economic Development for Dalits

Dr Ambedkar has worked for PhDs on Provincial Finances in British India, the problem of the rupee and written treatises like small holdings in India and their remedies, wherein we can find an economist par excellence. But the subjects that he dealt with in his PhD dissertations are not directly related to Dalits development. Therefore, no one has seriously examined the contents of those writings except the one on his contributions to Irrigation Policy and Planning by S.K. Thorat and P. Abraham. But one can find out from his book on 'the evaluation of Provincial Finances in British India', wherein he maintained that there is no relation between the revenue and expenditure due to bad fiscal policy of the British.[4] Dr Ambedkar has vehemently criticised the British India Government like that of Dadabhai Naoroji who proved that the draining of the Indian economy had taken place through excessive taxation. He has provided the data to show that the ratio of total land revenue to total revenue during the period 1772 to 1855 has remained at 54 per cent, while the customs income has remained around 6 per cent. Dr Ambedkar has commented that justice in taxation was conspicuous by its absence. He has observed that it was a cruel satire that the many, European Civil Servants who fattened themselves on pay and pickings were supremely exempted from any contribution towards maintenance of the Govt.'[5] He has also indicated in his dissertations that the most oppressive tax at that time was salt tax which remained at 11 to 14 per cent of the revenue during the same period. He has explained how the income was not spent on the development of the people. He found that around 60 per cent of the income was spent on military during the period 1809 to 1850. This, according to Dr Ambedkar was an imperial system which has drained the Indian-economy. Therefore, he wanted that India should have a federal structure, where the taxes should be based on rational principles. If one is inclined to formulate a theory of development as developed by Dr Ambedkar in his writings, this can be considered as the background on which one can develop his other writings such as making the agriculture sector as productive. In fact, the article published in the journal of the Indian Economic Society in 1918 preceded the theories of Arthur Lewis, the noble laureate in Economics.[6]

However, Dr Ambedkar was not really interested in the agricultural economy as indicated by him in the same article which is ends with the quotation from Sir Arthur Cotton, 'there is danger of too much agricultural in India'.[7] It is now clear that Dr Ambedkar was one of the greatest economists of the early part of the twentieth century who has analysed the ills of the Indian economy and suggested the measures to overcome the problems of underdevelopment in an agrarian economy where the Dalits did also suffer from low agricultural productivity along with others. The remedy seems to be indirectly hinted by Dr Ambedkar by saying that Dalits should be provided with opportunities in Public Sector and in Services.

Protection Against Economic Exploitation

The profound wisdom of Dr Ambedkar relating to economic upliftment of the Dalits could be seen in his memorandum on States and Minorities. In Article II, Section 2 on remedies against invasion of fundamental rights, Dr Ambedkar has provided provisions of protection against economic exploitation. It means that Dr Ambedkar wanted State socialism by means of constitutional remedy against economic exploitation for Dalits. The following text from his memorandum on States and Minorities clearly indicates what he wanted to provide for the economic development of Dalits. I am reproducing below the original text for the purpose of clarity of thought of Dr Ambedkar.[8]

1. That industries which are key industries or which may be declared to be key industries shall be owned and run by the State;
2. That industries which are not key industries but which are basic industries shall be owned by the State and shall be run by the State or by Corporations established by the State;
3. That Insurance shall be a monopoly of the State and that the State shall compel every adult citizen to take out a life insurance policy commensurate with his wages as may be prescribed by the Legislature;
4. That agriculture shall be State Industry;
5. That State shall acquire the subsisting rights in such industries, insurance and agricultural land held by private individuals, whether as owners, tenants or mortgagees and pay them compensation in the form of debenture equal to the value of his or her right in the land. Provided that in reckoning the value of land, plant or security no account shall be taken of any rise therein due to emergency, or any potential or unearned value or any value for compulsory acquisition;

6. The State shall determine how and when the debenture holder shall be entitled to claim cash payment;
7. The debenture shall be transferable and inheritable property but neither the debenture holder nor the transferee from the original holder nor his heir shall be entitled to claim the return of the land or interest in any industrial concern acquired by the State or be entitled to deal with it in any way;
8. The debenture-holder shall be entitled to interest on his debenture at such rate as may be defined by law, to be paid by the State in cash or in kind as the State may deem fit;
9. Agricultural industry shall be organised on the following basis:
   (i) The State shall divide the land acquired into farms of standard size and let out the farms for cultivation to residents of the village as tenants (made up of group of families) to cultivate on the following conditions:
      (a) The farm shall be cultivated as a collective farm;
      (b) The farms shall be cultivated in accordance with rules and directions issued by Government;
      (c) The tenants shall share among themselves in the manner prescribed the produce of the farm left after the payment of charges properly leviable on the farm;

   (ii) The land shall be let out to villagers without distinction of caste or creed and in such manner that there will be no landlord, no tenant and no landless labourer;

   (iii) It shall be the obligation of the State to finance the cultivation of the collective farms by the supply of water, draft animals, implements, manure, seeds, etc.

   (iv) The State shall be entitled to—
      (a) to levy the following charges on the produce of the farm: (i) a portion for land revenue; (ii) a portion to pay the debenture-holders; and (iii) a portion to pay for the use of capital goods supplied; and
      (b) to prescribe penalties against tenants who break the conditions of tenancy or willfully neglect to make the best use of the means of cultivation offered by the State or otherwise act prejudicially to the scheme of collective farming;

10. The scheme shall be brought into operation as early as possible but in no case shall the period extend beyond the 10th year for the date of the Constitution coming into operation.

The main purpose behind the clause (protection against economic exploitation) is to put an obligation on the State to plan the economic life of the people on lines which would lead to the highest point of productivity without closing every avenue to private enterprise, and also provide for the equitable distribution of wealth. The plan set out in the clause proposes State ownership in agriculture with a collectivised method of cultivation and a modified form of State socialism in the field of industry. It places squarely on the shoulders of the State the obligation to supply capital necessary for agriculture as well as for industry. Without the supply of capital by the State neither land nor industry can be made to yield better results. It also proposes to nationalise insurance with a double objective. Nationalised insurance gives the individual greater security that a private insurance firm does inasmuch as it pledges the resources of the State as a security for the ultimate payment of his insurance money market at a high rate of interest. State socialism is essential for the rapid industrialisation of India. Private enterprise cannot do it and if it did it would produce those inequalities of wealth which private capitalism has produced in Europe and which should be a warning to Indians. Consolidation of Holdings and Tenancy legislation are worse than useless. They cannot bring about prosperity in agriculture. Neither Consolidation nor Tenancy legislation can be of any help to the 60 millions of Untouchables who are just landless labourers. Neither Consolidation nor Tenancy legislation can solve their problem. Only collective farms on the lines set out in the proposal can help them. There is no expropriation of the interests concerned. Consequently there ought to be no objection to the proposal on that account.

The plan has two special features. One is that it proposes State socialism in important fields of economic life. The second special feature of the plan is that it does not leave the establishment of State socialism to the will of the Legislature. It establishes State socialism by the Law of the Constitution and thus makes it unalterable by any act of the Legislature and the Executive.

Students of Constitutional Law will at once raise a protest, said Ambedkar. They are sure to ask: Does not the proposal go beyond the scope of the usual type of Fundamental Rights? My answer is that it does not. If it appears to go beyond it is only because the conception of Fundamental Rights on which such criticism is based is a narrow conception. One may go further and say that even from the narrow conception of the scope of the Constitutional Law as comprising no more than Fundamental Rights, the proposal can find ample justification. For what is the purpose of prescribing by law the shape and form of the economic structure of society? The purpose is to protect the liberty of the individual from invasion by other individuals which is the object of enacting Fundamental Rights. The connection between individual liberty and the shape and form of the economic structure of society may not be apparent to everyone. None the less the connection between the two is real.

The Future of Dalits

Dr Ambedkar never wanted that the Dalits should remain in the scattered settlements of the villages. He was against the proposal to make the village as a unit of governance while Gandhiji romanticised the village. In his Constituent Assembly debate, Dr Ambedkar gave a strong reply to his critics who were very critical about him in not making the village as a unit of governance in the Constitution. In his reply Dr Ambedkar said that 'what is a village but a sink of localism, a den of ignorance and narrow mindedness'. What a profound vision that Dr Ambedkar had about the position of Dalits in India which is not different today from what he has described about the village about 60 years ago. Though Dr Ambedkar wanted the expansion of the Public Sector and creation of opportunities for Dalits in the services, it is lamented that the opportunities for the Dalits after 1991 Economic Policy have dwindled. I have the details in my forthcoming book *Economic Reform and Social Exclusion*. It is sad that most of our activists have neglected this part and are concentrating more on social issues. But economic issues as explained by Dr Ambedkar have social implications as were. This needs to be elaborated in the given conditions of liberalisation.

It is instructive to look at the proposal of industrialisation which Dr Ambedkar has mentioned in his States and Minorities here. It is good to find that the language and tenor of his argument on industrial policy for development was reflected in the Congress Government policy of 1948. The Industrial Policy Resolution of 1948 is almost the same as that of Dr Ambedkar's proposal in his memorandum. It is this policy that had made the country strong economy and the rate of growth of the economy during the operation of the policy before 1980 was around 5 per cent. The Dalits were anticipating a lot of opportunities in the Public Sector consisting of agriculture and manufacturing sectors. After the introduction of the Industrial Policy in 1948, the Congress Government eulogised it as sine-quo-non of socialism in their resolution at Avadi Congress in 1956. This was a policy to translate some of the provisions in the directive principles of State policy which Dr Ambedkar so laboriously developed and incorporated in the Constitution. It was also found that both Nehru and Ambedkar were influenced by the policies of the labour party in Great Britain in the 1940s. In fact Dr Ambedkar was the first to start an independent labour party in India, may be on the lines of British labour party. This is all shattered now. There is no leader like Dr Ambedkar now to argue and negotiate for the upliftment of Dalits in the twenty-first century. However, there is hope that the small section of the Dalits who are transforming themselves as organic intellectuals can draw abundantly from the writings of Babasaheb to fight for a casteless and egalitarian society in future.

Notes

1. Vasant Moon, *Dr. Babasaheb Ambedkar: Writings and Speeches*, Vol. 3, Government of Maharashtra, Bombay, 1987.
2. S.G. Kulkarni, 'Philosophy of Ambedkar: Some Observations', in K.S. Chalam (Ed.), *Relevance of Ambedkarism in India*, Jaipur: Rawat Publications, 1993.
3. Vasant Moon, op. cit., Chapter on States and Minorities.
4. Vasant Moon, op. cit., Vol. 6.
5. Ibid.

6. Vasant Moon, op. cit., Vol. I.
7. Vasant Moon, op. cit., Chapter on States and Minorities, last sentence.
8. Ibid.

References

Ambedkar, B.R., *Buddha and His Dhamma*, Bombay: Siddharth College Publication, 1957.

Arthur, Lewis, 'Economic Development with Unlimited Supplies of Labour', *Manchester School*, Vol. 22, 1954.

Chalam, K.S., *Economic Reforms and Missing Safety Nets*, Mumbai: Vikas Adhyan Kendra, 1999.

——, *Modernization and Dalit Education: Ambedkar's Vision*, Jaipur: Rawat Publications, 2008.

——, *Relevance of Ambedkarism in India*, Jaipur: Rawat Publications, 1993.

——, *Social Economy of Development in India*, New Delhi: Sage Publications, 2017.

Christophe, Jaffrelot, *Dr. Ambedkar and Untouchability*, New Delhi: Permanent Black, 2005.

Gore, M.S., *The Social Context of an Ideology*, New Delhi: Sage, 1993.

Thorat, S.K., *Ambedkar's Role in Economic Planning and Water Policy*, New Delhi: Shipra Publications, 1998.

Zelliot, E., *Dr. Ambedkar and the Mahar Movement*, University of Pennsylvania, 1969 (PhD dissertation).

——, *From Untouchable to Dalit: Essays on Ambedkar Movement*, New Delhi: Manohar, 1992.

14

Socio-Economic Ideas of Ambedkar and their Relevance

S.K. Sarkar

The mission of Ambedkar was to arouse the passion for right relations. Ambedkar studied deeply the social history of India and analysed the origin of social evils. His whole life was shaped and influenced by his bitter experiences. He inquired into the origin, growth, and development of caste and untouchability in India. These Untouchable Hindus were denied the use of public wells, and were condemned to drink any filthy water they could find. Their children were not admitted to schools attended by the caste Hindu children. Though they worshipped the gods of Hindus, observed the same festivals, the Hindu temples were closed to them.

Ambedkar studied the ancient social and religious literature including the Hindu scriptures like the *Vedas*, the *Upanishads*, the *Gita*, the *Mahabharat* and the *Ramayana*. But he was disgusted with social evils like caste and untouchability in society, which led him to withdraw himself from Hinduism. He thought in terms of introducing a radical change in Hindu society. In a changing society, there must be a constant re-adjustment of old values and the Hindus must realise that. He contended that if India were to advance, the Hindu social system must be overhauled.

He argued that the Untouchables were a separate element in the national life of India. The move for separate electorate and separate settlement was fully opposed by Gandhi and his comrades. During this time, Ambedkar became an ardent student of Buddhist literature. He found that the Buddha was really a man, who showed much sympathy for the common people and had a synthetic outlook on life. By 1951, Ambedkar developed in his mind a strong feeling that social emancipation and political aspiration must be subordinated to religious reform. So, he entirely turned to the religious awakening of his people. He found refuge in Buddha's *dhamma*. Ambedkar said: 'By discarding my ancient religion which stood for inequality and oppression, today I am reborn. I have no faith in the philosophy of incarnation, and it is wrong and mischievous to say that Buddha was an incarnation of Vishnu. I am no more a devotee of any Hindu God or goddess. I will not perform *shradha*. I will strictly follow the eight-fold path of Buddha. Buddhism is a true religion and I will lead a life guided by the three principles of knowledge, right path and compassion.'[1] The realisation of good life, combined with knowledge and guided by the spirit of love and equality, was the fundamental aim behind his religious conversion.

There is no doubt that religious conversion requires a man to sacrifice all that is traditionally attached to him. Religious conversion cannot be possible unless there is a strong mind and clear thinking in the person who wants it. Ambedkar's religious conversion was not a revenge. It was not even against the tradition of this country. He said: 'Buddhism is a part and parcel of Bharatiya culture. I have taken care that my conversion will not harm the condition of the culture and history of this land'.[2] In May 1956, he said: 'I prefer Buddhism, because it gives three principles in combination which no other religion does. Buddhism teaches *prajna, karuna and samata*. This is what man wants for a good and happy life'.[3]

Ambedkar gave a theory of the origin of the Sudras. According to his view, the Sudras were not of the Aryan communities of the solar race and ranked as the Kshatriya *varna* in the

Indo-Aryan society. There was a time when the Aryan society recognised only three *varnas*, namely, the Brahmins, the Kshatriyas and the Vaishyas. The Sudras were not a separate *varna*, but a part of Kshatriya *varna*. There was a continuous feud between the Sudra kings and the Brahmins, in which the Brahmins were subjected to many tyrannies and indignities. As a result of the hatred towards the Sudras generated by their tyrannies and oppressions, the Brahmins refused to perform the *upanayana* of the Sudras. Owing to the denial of *upanayana*, the Sudras became socially degraded, fell below the rank of the Vaishyas and thus, came to form to fourth *varna*.

Ambedkar thinks that had there not been Buddhism, and had the 'broken men' been stopped from beef-eating and induced to worship the cow, there would have been no 'broken men' in the form of Untouchables. There was, as he says, not only a struggle between the settled tribesmen and the 'broken men', but the Buddhists. The 'broken men', instead of being assimilated in the proper village community, became Untouchables for two reasons: (1) that they embraced Buddhism, and (2) that they retained the habit of beef-eating. According to his view, there is no racial difference between the Hindus and the Untouchables. The distinction between the Hindus and Untouchables, in its original form before the advent of untouchability, was the distinction between tribesmen and 'broken men' from alien tribes. It is the 'broken men' who subsequently came to be treated as the Untouchables. Just as untouchability has no racial basis, so also it has no occupational basis. The two roots from which untouchability has sprung are: (a) contempt and hatred of the 'broken men' as Buddhists by the Brahmins, and (b) continuation of beef-eating by the 'broken men' after it had been given up by others.

According to Ambedkar, endogamy is the essence of the caste system. The rule of endogamy is largely responsible for the caste mechanism. It is since Manu that the marriage rules became more rigorous. Manu codified these rules, and he gave them a religious sanction. The penalties were prescribed for those who broke the rules of the code. It is very difficult to check the exogenous tendencies of the people. Ambedkar says: 'Caste is an artificial chopping off of the population into fixed and definite units, each one prevented from fusing into another group through the custom of endogamy'. He regards endogamy to be a characteristic feature to caste as also a key to the understanding of its genesis and mechanism.

Ambedkar states that castes have no mercy for a sinner who has the courage to violate the code. As a result of the penalty of ex-communication, a new caste is formed. According to him, *chaturvarna* degenerated into the caste system. He strongly denounces this system. According to Ambedkar, caste has killed public spirit, destroyed the sense of public charity, and made public opinion impossible. Virtue has become caste-ridden and morality has become caste-bound. There is no sympathy for the deserving. There is appreciation of virtue but only when the man is a fellow caste-man.

Ambedkar was a total social revolutionary. He denounced the traditional values and placed before the society new values. He exhorted his followers to abolish slavery themselves and not to depend upon God for some superman for its abolition. Ambedkar pointed out that the roots of untouchability are in the caste system. Hence, for the eradication of untouchability, annihilation of caste was absolutely essential. In his presidential address to a conference at Lahore in 1936 (which was not delivered because the reception committee could not agree with all the revolutionary views expressed in it), Ambedkar pleaded for the annihilation of castes and reform in Hindu religion. He pointed out that the caste has completely disorganised and demoralised the Hindus. He observed: 'Hindu society being a collection of castes and even caste being a close corporation there is no place for a convert. Thus, it is caste that prevented the Hindus from expanding and from absorbing other religious communities. So long as castes remain, Hindu religion cannot be made a missionary religion'.[4] In the same speech, Ambedkar pointed out that his ideal society will be based on the principles of liberty, equality and fraternity. Caste will cease to be an operative force only when inter-dining and inter-marriages become matters of common course. But as the roots of caste system are in the Hindu religion, Ambedkar denounced the Hindu religion. At a conference held at Yeola in October 1935, he exhorted his followers to severe their connections with Hinduism and seek solace and self-respect in another religion. Ambedkar was not against religion as such. He agreed with Burke who said that true religion is the foundation of society. At the same conference, he declared that he would not die as a Hindu. Indeed, he did not die a Hindu, but a follower of Buddha.

In his Lahore speech, Ambedkar pointed out how Hindu religion can be reformed. His suggestion in this regard were:

1. There should be one and only one standard book of Hindu religion acceptable to all Hindus and recognised by all Hindus.
2. Hereditary priesthood among the Hindus should be abolished. Every person who professes to be a Hindu must be eligible for being a priest.
3. A priest should be a servant of the State and should be subject to the disciplinary action by the State.
4. No ceremony performed by a priest who does not hold a *sanad* should be deemed to be valid.
5. The number of priests should be limited by law.

Man and Woman on Equal Footing

Ambedkar was the staunch supporter and prime mover of Hindu Code Bill. The Hindu Code Bill places women at par with men in the matter of property, adoption and marriage. It contained: (1) She can now choose her spouse from any caste—high or low—a privilege enjoyed by men only. (2) She has been given absolute right on her property. (3) She can inherit as mother, sister or daughter in the property of deceased equally with sons. (4) The adopted son cannot deprive her of her share in her husband's property. (5) A girl can also be adopted. (6) For adoption wife's consent is necessary. (7) A destitute man can claim maintenance from his more fortune wife.

The Bill was introduced in Central Assembly in 1947 and passed through various stages by August 1948. But due to division in the Congress party on the Bill, nothing could be done during 1949 and 1950.

Sharp criticism of the Bill, inside and outside the Parliament, led many to believe that it might inflict heavy damages on the Hindu society. Even the then President of India, Dr Rajendra Prasad, issued a threat that he would withhold his assent even if it had been passed by the Parliament. Prime Minister Nehru then had to clarify to him that there was very little revolution in the Bill. 'Indeed it was very largely a codification of the existing laws'.[5] He further added that 'in his codification even custom has often been accepted as a guiding factor'.[6] Ambedkar said that the Bill aimed at removing the legal obstacles in the social advancement of women. He even went to the extent of throwing challenge to show him which of these sections in the Bill are not based on distastes of the Smritis.

Because of the division in the Congress party and also due to the forthcoming general elections of 1952, Nehru was not in favour of bringing the entire Bill before the House. The law members, therefore, as desired, split up the Bill into three parts and the one relating to marriage and divorce was introduced in the House in February 1951. But when the truncated Bill came up for consideration on 17 September 1951, the MPs with a view to taking out the Bill, indulged in long speeches. When Ambedkar found the Prime Minister keeping mum he became desperate and resigned as Member of Law on 27 September 1951.

People's Education Society

Ambedkar set up hostels for Untouchable students at different places like Panvel, Pune, Nasik, Sholapur, Thane and Dharwar with public donations and grants from district and local authorities. Having facility of free boarding to the hostel inmates, these were of considerable help in spreading education among Untouchables. Though colleges were open to Untouchable students, apart from financial constraints social and cultural stigma also affected full development of their personality in the Hindu dominated colleges. Therefore, Ambedkar wanted to set up separate institutions for the Untouchables. He established the People's Educational Society in July 1945. The main objectives were to (1) search after the truth; and (2) start, establish and conduct educational institutions or give aid to such institutions. In 1946, he started the Sidharth College of Arts and Science in Bombay. He gave a cosmopolitan character to the institution which was open to all, irrespective of caste or creed. In 1946, out of a total of 1,363 students on its rolls, only 60 belonged to the Scheduled Castes.

In 1950, Ambedkar established a full-fledged college at Aurangabad with a loan of Rs 10 lakhs from the Scheduled Castes Trust Fund of Hyderabad. This college was named as *Milind Mahavidyalaya* after the Greek King, Millinda, who carved out a kingdom in India in second century B.C. and later embraced Buddhism. In 1953, Sidharath College of Commerce and Economics was established. Later, in 1956, the Sidharath College of Law was also set up in Bombay. Ambedkar was fond of learning as well as teaching. Whenever he visited colleges, he preferred to stay in the hostels and mingle with the students. He repeatedly emphasised the need to explode the myth created by the Hindu orthodoxy that the Untouchables were incapable of learning.

Ambedkar strives for an ideal society which is based on liberty, equality and fraternity. He says: 'Positively, my social philosophy may be said to be enshrined in three words—liberty, equality and fraternity. Let no one, however, say that I have borrowed my philosophy from the French Revolution. I have not. My philosophy has roots in religion and not in political science. I have derived them from the teachings of my master, the Buddha'.[7]

He gives an important place to religious freedom. He stands for individual's religious freedom for intellectual and spiritual enlightenment. Every individual should be free to choose his own religion. He wants that the state should guarantee to all its citizens the liberty of conscience and free exercise of their religion including the right to profess, to preach and to covert within limits compatible with public order and morality. His ideal society emphatically provides choice.

Ambedkar supported the socialistic society. He pleads for a socialism with moral foundations. He does not want to confine socialism only to the sphere of economic reform. He says: 'If liberty is the ideal, if liberty means the destruction of the dominion, which one man holds over another, then obviously, it cannot be insisted upon that economic reform only. If the source of power and dominion is, at any given time or in any given society, social and religious, then social reform and religious reform must be accepted as the necessary sort of reform.'

He attempts to build a rational view of life with full utilisation of machinery and modern civilisation. He declares that the slogan of a democratic society must be machinery and more machinery, civilisation and more civilisation in order to provide every person some leisure for leading a life of culture.

Ambedkar stands for the emancipation of the poorer sections of Indian society. He suggested State socialism. He said: 'the main purpose behind state socialism is to put an obligation on the state to plan the economic life of the people on lines which would lead to the highest point of productivity without closing every avenue to private enterprise, and also provide for the equitable distribution of wealth'. His advocacy of State socialism amounts to an advocacy of the mixed economy. He does not want annihilation of any class, but the actual reformation of class structure so that the economic benefit may reach the doors of all persons. Ambedkar was against complete nationalisation of economy and state monopoly. He favours state ownership in the fields of insurance, industry and agricultural land only. He does not want the suppression of private property. He believes that India should industrialise otherwise it would perish.

In India, where a large section of people are landless, the changes in agriculture planning cannot bring material prosperity to all in rural areas. Only collective forms, Ambedkar insists, can help them, provided that agriculture becomes a state industry. He undoubtedly wants to bring about economic stability through the law of the Constitution. He sought to establish a balance between state control and private enterprises through his rational approach of state socialism. He does not indulge in any extreme type of individualism or of socialism. His formulation of state socialism does not suppress individual liberty and also retains the system of private enterprise, while giving the greatest benefit to the poorer sections of society. His concept of State socialism stresses the three economic processes of human society: (1) adaptation of the key industries and agricultural land to meet the demands of the poorer sections of society; (2) maintenance of the productive resources by the state; and (3) a just distribution of the common produce among the different people without any distinction of caste or creed.

He wants to establish State socialism without abrogating parliamentary democracy. He pleads that those who want the economic structure of society to be modelled on State socialism, must realise that they cannot leave the fulfilment of so fundamental a purpose to the exigencies of ordinary law, which simple majorities have a right to make and unmake. ln his view, the only alternative to parliamentary democracy seems to be dictatorship. He hopes that those who believe in individual freedom must strongly object to dictatorship and he insists upon parliamentary democracy as proper form of government for a free society. The problem is to have State socialism without dictatorship, to have State socialism with parliamentary democracy. He said: 'The way out seems to be retain parliamentary democracy and to prescribe state socialism by the law of the Constitution, so that it will be beyond the reach of a parliamentary majority to suspend, amend or abrogate it. It is only by this that one can achieve the triple object, namely, to establish socialism, retain parliamentary democracy and avoid dictatorship'.[8] He observes that the political structure of society is largely governed or dominated by the forces, which emerge from the economic structure.

The ideal of economic realism, that Ambedkar proposes, stresses on the following points: (1) Nationalisation of industries is necessary, if the interests of the public at large are to be safeguarded adequately. This is the only way by which economic order can be profitable to all men and women. (2) The object of nationalisation is to better the lot of the workers. Wages should be sufficient to live happily and which may also allow the development of mind, body and character. The number of the working hours should be reduced and workers be given equal pay for equal work. It is the responsibility of the State to prevent unemployment and exploitation. (3) Economic realism stands for the best utilisation of natural resources. These natural resources should be concerned for the present and future happiness of all men and should not be destroyed by the individuals whose only concern is their own private good. A socialist State should be guided purely by considerations of service motives. (4) The idea of economic realism wishes a complete transformation of society under the new set-up. (5) Ambedkar's economic thought does not want that all factors of production should be nationalised. Some of them should be put under democratic control, i.e. in the hand of private organisations. It is the will of the people, which is also to determine whether a particular thing has to be realised through democratic control or through state control.

Ambedkar's approach to humanism is ethical, social and secular. To him, the moral order in the universe is not maintained by God. lt is maintained by man. Man occupies the highest place. There is nothing absolute. Everything is related to man and society. Ambedkar holds that religion, based on the concept of the soul, is based on speculation. He says that the thing that exists is not the soul but the mind and mind is quite different from the soul. Believe in a soul only ends in creating superstition and priesthood, rather is unprofitable. For not only does it create a priesthood, not only is it the origin of all superstition, but it gives the priesthood complete control over man from birth to death.

Ambedkar's concept of ideal society is most suited to the needs of modern Indian society. To him, society is an integrated whole, and each individual is related to another with social ties. His views of society fully endures that an individual is mainly responsible for his own welfare, and at the same time, he shares the collective responsibility for the good of society. His cherished goal of an ideal society is to guarantee to all its members justice—political, social and economic, and according to him the attainment of this human ideal should be by democratic process. His advocacy of non-violence along with a democratic way of life is highly commendable in the existing conditions in India. Non-violence is the main feature of his philosophy of social humanism which is utmost necessary in India today for its national unity and integrity.

Notes

1. Vasant Moon, *Dr. Babasaheb Ambedkar's Writings and Speeches*, Vol. 1, 5 and 7, Government of Maharashtra, Bombay, 1979, 1989 and 1990.

2. B.R. Ambedkar, *The Buddha and His Dhamma*, Bombay: Siddharth College Publication, 1981.
3. Dhananjay Keer, *Dr. Ambedkar: Life and Mission*, Bombay: Popular Prakashan, 1981.
4. B.K. Ahluwalia and Shashi Ahluwalia, *B.R. Ambedkar and Human Rights*, Delhi: Manas Publications, 1990.
5. D.K. Baisantry, *Ambedkar: The Total Revolutionary*, New Delhi: Segment Book Distributors, 1991.
6. K.S. Bharathi, *Foundations of Ambedkar Thought*, Nagpur: Dattsons Publications, 1990.
7. W.N. Kuber, *B.R. Ambedkar*, Publications Division, Government of India, Delhi, 1987.
8. Thomas Mathew, *Reform or Revolution*, New Delhi: Segment Books, 1991.

15

Ambedkar on Economic Development and Social Justice

G. Nancharaiah

This paper is attempted with two-fold objectives of (1) analysing the important views of Ambedkar on social order, based on caste and its implications for economic development in India; and (2) presenting the salient features of his development strategy.

Ambedkar was one of the very few Indians who struggled to restructure the Indian society on the most egalitarian and humanitarian principles.[1] He believed that the state has to play crucial role in restructuring the society under democratic polity and the foundation of democracy would be feeble and shaky if there was no social and economic democracy consistent with political democracy.[2] He proposed a strategy of development based on growth with justice. Various scholarly works of Ambedkar indicate his contribution to economic thought and explain his deep insights into the socio-economic problems of Indian society and his perspective of development.

Ambedkar opined that the existing social and economic institutions, particularly caste and land tenure system, were not conducive for accelerating economic development with social justice and there was a need for reforming them. He believed that the desired social and economic change could be brought about under democratic polity through constitutional measures.[3] For him, democracy means not only political democracy but also social and economic democracy and emphasised the need for removing these inequalities as per condition for stable democracy[4] and rapid economic development with justice. He strongly believed that the social order based on caste system was mainly responsible for the existing social and economic inequalities and economic backwardness and hence the need for annihilating caste system.

Caste and Its Economic Implications

Ambedkar argued that caste system as a social institution did not promote the unity and integrity of nation and as economic organisation did not result in efficiency.[5] But even today, the defenders of the caste system argue that it is another name for division of labour and if division of labour is necessary feature of every civilised society then there is nothing wrong in caste system.[6] Ambedkar dismissed this kind of arguments and emphatically argued that caste system does not represent division of labour on the following grounds.

Caste is not nearly division of labour. It is also a division of labourers. It is hierarchical. The division of labourers are graded one above the other. Civilised society undoubtedly needs division of labour. But, in no civilised society division of labour is accompanied by this unnatural division of labourers into water-tight compartments. In no other country the division of labour is accompanied by the gradation of labourers.

The division of labour represented by caste system is not spontaneous. It is not based on natural aptitudes. Social and individual efficiency requires the development of the capacity of an individual to the point of competency to choose and make his own career. This is violated in the caste system to the extent it involves an attempt to assign tasks to individuals in advance not on the basis of trained original capacities, but on the basis of social status of the parents. This is positively pernicious from the point of view of economic development which is a dynamic phenomenon. Industry is never static and undergoes rapid changes. Individual must be free to chose his occupation compatible with such change. Otherwise it becomes very difficult for him to gain his livelihood. If a Hindu is seen to be starving rather than taking to new occupation not as-signed to his caste, the reason is to be found in the caste. Thus, by not permitting readjustment of occupations, caste becomes a direct cause of much of the unemployment existing in the country.

Caste system as a form of division of labour suffers from another serious defect as it is based on the dogma of predestination. Individual preference has no place in it, and certain occupations assigned by caste system are degraded and the people engaged in such occupations were treated as defiling group and were put to social stigma untouchability. As a result, people engaged in such occupations were provoked to aversion and there was constant desire to avoid and escape from such occupations. In a system under which neither men's hearts nor minds are at their work there can not be any efficiency. As an economic organisation caste is therefore a harmful institution in as much as, it involves the subordination of man's natural powers and inclinations to the exigencies of social rules.[7]

Untouchability and Economic Exploitation

Untouchability, which was the by-product of caste system, was not only a form of social discrimination but also a source of economic exploitation. Untouchables for centuries were not allowed to enter the villages during day time and to use the public utilities such as roads, wells, tanks, etc. They were made to live on the outskirts of the village and physically segregated from the mainstream of life.[8] They were assigned those occupations which were unclean and filthy and they were forced to remain in the same occupations. They were discriminated in the product market and in the factor market on the ground of untouchability.[9] Under such circumstances, there was no possibility of vertical mobility and there was underutilisation of labour. Economy ought to suffer on this account.[10] The Untouchables were denied right to education. They were denied the right of owning land and wearing jewellery.[11] They were also denied the right of bargaining for wages and they should accept whatever was paid to them. They had to perform a number of duties in villages without any remuneration.[12] Ambedkar observed that untouchability was more than a religious system. It was also an economic system worse than slavery. In slavery, the master at any rate of slave would decline. But under untouchability, the maintenance of the Untouchable was the responsibility of nobody. Untouchability as an economic system permits exploitation without obligation. 'Untouchability is not only a system of unmitigated economic exploitation but also a system of uncontrolled economic exploitation'.[13]

In view of the above reason, Ambedkar felt that there was an immediate need of annihilating caste[14] so that there was no contradiction between socio-economic conditions, existing in the Indian society, and political democracy. It was the precondition for accelerating economic development through democratic methods. Ambedkar, in his speech delivered to the Constituent Assembly on 25 November 1949, referred to contradiction, that is, equality in politics and inequality in social and economic life, the country was going to enter upon after the inauguration of the new Constitution on 26 January 1950. Ambedkar said: 'How long should we continue to live this life of contradiction? How long shall we continue to deny equality in our social and economic life? If we continue to deny it for long, we will do so only by putting our political democracy imperil. We must remove this contradiction at the earliest possible movement or else those who suffer from inequality will blow up the structure of political democracy which this assembly has so laboriously built up'.[15]

Ambedkar's Strategy of Development

'States and Minorities', a memorandum which Ambedkar prepared and submitted to the Constituent Assembly on behalf of the All India Scheduled Caste Federation, depicts the blueprint of Ambedkar's model of economic development. His model of economic development further represents a modified form of State socialism which has two special features: (1) it proposes State socialism in important fields of economic life, and (2) it does not leave the establishment of State socialism to the will of legislature.

Salient Features of State Soclallsm[16]

The salient features of State socialism proposed by Ambedkar are as under:

1. Industries which are key industries or which may be declared to be key industries shall be owned and run by the State.
2. The industries which are not key industries but which are basic industries shall be owned by the State and shall be run by the State or by corporation established by the State.
3. The insurance shall be the monopoly of the State and that the State shall compel every adult citizen to take out a life insurance policy commensurate with his wages as may be prescribed by the legislature.
4. The agricultural industry shall be State industry.
5. The State shall acquire the subsisting rights in such industries, insurance and agricultural land held by private individuals, whether as owners, tenants or mortgages and pay them compensation in the form of debenture equal to the value of his or her right in the land.
6. The State shall also determine how and when the debenture holder shall be entitled to claim cash payment.
7. The debenture shall be transferable and inheritable property but neither the debenture holder nor the transferee from the original holder nor his heir shall be entitled to claim the return of the land or enter in any industrial concern acquired by the State or be entitled to deal with it in any way.
8. The debenture holder shall be entitled to interest on his debenture at such rate as may be defined by law, to be paid by the state in cash or in kind as the state may deem it fit.
9. Agricultural industry shall be organised on the following basis:
   (i) The State shall divide the land acquired into farms of standard size and let out the farm for cultivation to residents of the village as tenants (made up of group of families) to cultivate on the following conditions.
      (a) The farm shall be cultivated as a collective form.
      (b) The farm shall be cultivated in accordance with rules and directions issued by government.
      (c) The tenants shall share among themselves, in the manner prescribed, the produce of the farm left

after, the payment of charges properly leviable on the farm.

(ii) The land shall be let out to villagers without distinction of caste or creed and in such manner that there will be no landlord, no tenant and no landless labour.

(iii) It shall be the obligation of the State to finance the cultivation of the collective farms by the supply of water, drought animals, implements, manure, seeds, etc.

(iv) The State shall be entitled to:

(a) Levy the following charges on the produce of the farm:

- portion for land revenue,
- portion to pay debenture holders, and
- portion to pay for the use of capital goods supplied, and

(b) to prescribe penalties against the tenants who break the conditions of tenancy or willfully neglect to make the best use of the means of cultivation offered by the State or otherwise act prejudicially to the scheme of collective farming.

10. The scheme shall be brought into operation as early as possible but in no case shall the period extend beyond the tenth year from the date of the Constitution coming into operation.

Thus, he proposed state ownership of agriculture with a collectivised method of cultivation and a modified form of state socialism in the field of industry. He explains the merits of this scheme on the following grounds.[17] It should be the obligation of state to supply capital, necessary for agriculture as well as for industry. The insurance was also proposed to be nationalised with a double objective. Nationalised insurance firm does in as much as it pledges the resources of the state as a security for the ultimate payment of his insurance money. It also gives the state the resources necessary for financing its economic planning, in the absence of which, it would have to resort to borrowing from the money market at higher rate of interest. State socialism is essential for rapid industrialisation. Private enterprise cannot do it and if it did, it would produce those inequalities of wealth which private capitalism has produced in Europe and which should be a warning to Indians. He also opined that consolidation of holdings and tenancy legislation are worse than useless. They cannot bring about prosperity in agriculture. Neither consolidation nor tenancy legislation can be of any help to the 60 millions of Untouchables who are just landless labourers. Only collective farms can help them.

Ambedkar also proposed that the above scheme of State socialism should not be left to the will of the legislature and it should be established by the law of Constitution so that it will be beyond the reach of a parliamentary majority to suspend, amend or abrogate it. This guarantees State socialism while retaining parliamentary democracy. 'It is only by this that one can achieve the triple object of namely to establish socialism, retain parliamentary democracy and avoid dictatorship'.[18] Ambedkar also believed that his plan of State socialism was essential for increasing productivity without closing every avenue to private sector and also distributing wealth equitably. 'The main purpose behind this clause is to put an obligation on the State to plan the economic life of people on lines which would lead to highest point of productivity without closing every avenue to the private enterprise and also private for the equitable distribution of wealth'.[19]

Further, Ambedkar also argued that if democracy was to live up to its principle of one man one value, it was essential to define both the economic structure as well as the political structure of society by the law of Constitution.[20] But due to strong opposition in the Constituent Assembly, Ambedkar could not incorporate his scheme of State socialism under fundamental rights as a part of the Constitution.[21]

Conclusion

It follows from the above analysis of Ambedkar's strategy of development that the State has to play very active and crucial role in accelerating the growth with justice through democratic methods. The foundation of democracy would be feeble and shaky if the contradictions between political democracy, enshrined in the Constitution and social and economic inequalities which are existing in our society are not resolved. The shape and form of the economic structure should be defined and prescribed by the law of the Constitution without leaving it to the will of the legislature along with that of the structure of the political democracy so that social and economic democracy consistent with political democracy is established.

Notes

1. Nanchariah, G., 'Dr. Ambedkar's Political and Economic Thought', *Journal of Social Development and Justice*, Vol. 1, March 1991, p. 64.
2. Government of Maharashtra, *Dr. Babasaheb Ambedkar's Writings and Speeches*, Vol. 1, 1979, pp. 408–412.
3. Ibid., p. 412.
4. Narayan, K.R., 'The Rebel', in B.L. Ahluwalia (Ed.), *Human Rights*, Delhi: Vivek Publishing Company, 1981, p. 7.
5. Government of Maharashtra, *Dr. Ambedkar's Writings and Speeches*, op. cit., pp. 50–58.
6. Ibid., p. 47.
7. Ambedkar, B.R., *Annihilation of Caste*, Jalandhar: Bheem Patrika Publications, 1936, pp. 75–77.
8. Government of Maharashtra, *Dr. Babasaheb Ambedkar's Writings and Speeches*, Vol. 5, 1989, p. 21.
9. Nanchariah, G., *Land and Caste*, Bombay: Himalaya Publishing, 1988, pp. 93–94.
10. Mishra, Vikas, *Hinduism and Economic Growth*, Oxford: Oxford University Press, 1962, p. 19.
11. Government of Maharashtra, *Dr. Babasaheb Ambedkar's Writings and Speeches*, Vol. 9, 1990, p. 194.
12. Government of Maharashtra, *Dr. Ambedkar's Writings and Speeches*, Vol. 5, 1989, p. 94.
13. Government of Maharashtra, *Dr. Ambedkar's Writings and Speeches*, Vol. 9, 1990, pp. 1961–87.
14. See Ambedkar, B.R., *Annihilation of Caste*, Bheem Patrika Publications, Jalandhar, 1936, which is also reproduced in Government of Maharashtra, *Dr. Babasaheb Ambedkar's Writings and Speeches*, Vol. I, 1979, pp. 67–80. For the detailed method of annihilating caste, I did not discuss these details as they fell beyond the limited scope of my paper.
15. Baisantry, D.K., 'Economic and Political Thought of Dr. Ambedkar', *Journal of Social Development and Justice*, Vol. 1, March 1991, p. 77.

16. Government of Maharashtra, *Dr. Babasaheb Ambedkar's Writings and Speeches*, Vol. 1, 1979, pp. 396–397.
17. Ibid., p. 408.
18. Ibid., pp. 411–412.
19. Ibid., p. 408.
20. Ibid., p. 412.
21. Baisantry, D.K., op. cit., p. 77.

16

Ambedkar's Views on Small Holdings in India

C. Sivarama Krishna Rao

Among his multi-faceted writings on Indian economy, Ambedkar had written on 'small holdings' in India and their remedies in the year 1918.[1] Ambedkar's perceptions on this agrarian question has many insights that have relevance even today. Though I know that the ideas of a great thinker need more elaboration, I would like to highlight some of his views that are of great importance to our present-day debates.

Ambedkar's views on importance of agriculture clearly bring out the problems of agricultural economy dealing directly with agricultural production, the size of holdings, the tenures of land, etc. In his discussion on size of holdings, Ambedkar had presented data on small holdings from various parts of the country. The first table that highlights the average area of holdings in acres shows that of the four regions, only central provinces show evidence of an increasing trend in the size of landholding unlike other provinces.[2] Ambedkar also utilises Mann's data to show how in a village, a majority have small holdings. Hence, he comes to the conclusion that the diminutive size of holdings is said to be greatly harmful to Indian agriculture. One observation made by

Ambedkar shows his perception of the problem which I would quote: 'The evils of small holdings, no doubt, are many. But it would have been no slight mitigation of them if the small holdings were compact holdings. Unfortunately, they are not. A holding of a farmer though compact for purposes of revenue is composed of various small strips of land scattered all over the village and interspersed by those belonging to others. The number of separate plots in each holding will show how greatly fragmented it is.'[3] The situation in the country today is no better than what he had observed in the early 20th century. He further presented data and had drawn two inferences that India is largely an agricultural economy and its agricultural productivity is the lowest.[4] These inferences may require some modifications in view of the reduced contribution of agricultural sector to national income, but its validity has to be viewed from the point of view of the dependence of population on agriculture, which remains high even today and Ambedkar also views this problem from that angle.

Ambedkar's later discussion on the problems of consolidation and enlargement of holdings gives an impression, rather a dialectical one, that he is arguing the case for large holdings. He makes a thorough discussion of Baroda Committee report, the views of H.S. Jevons and G.F. Keatings.[5] One observation that supports the above views is the critical comment he makes on their methodology, wherein he cautions that it must be borne in mind that consolidation may obviate the evils of small holdings unless the consolidated holding is an economic, that is, an enlarged holding.

His discussion on enlargement of holdings further gives an impression that the large holdings are more viable than small holdings. He cites the law of primogeniture for the inheritance of land as in the case of England.[6] But a careful perusal shows that he is more interested in trying to seek methods by which productivity on a small holding can also be improved. Hence, he observes that Prof. Jevons' view of an economic holding from the standpoint of consumption rather than production leads to an error, for according to Ambedkar, consumption is not the correct standard to judge the economic character of holding. Further, he observes: 'If the relation between out-turn and investments is a true economic relation, we can only speak of a farm as economic, i.e. paying in the sense of production and not in the sense of consumption. Any definition, therefore, that leaves on consumption, mistakes the nature of an economic holding which is essentially an enterprise in production.'[7] Here he brings in the law of proportion and draws an inference that mere size of land is empty of all economic connotation. He goes on to make an important observation that it cannot be possible for the language of economic science to say that a large holding is economic, while a small holding is uneconomic. It is the right or the wrong proportion of other factors of production to a unit of land that renders the latter economic or uneconomic. Thus, a small farm may be as economic as a large farm, for economic or uneconomic does not depend upon the size of land but upon the due proportion among all the factors including land.[8] These observations are much in consonance with the inferences drawn by many authors later in the size-productivity debate, highlighting the fact that Ambedkar is a forerunner in this debate.[9]

Ambedkar, in his critique of the remedies makes certain interesting observations. One observation is that existing holdings are uneconomic, not however in the sense that they are too small but that they are too large.[10] Consequently, the remedy for the ills of agriculture in India does not lie primarily in the matter of enlarging holdings but in the matter of increasing capital and capital goods. Adjunct to this, the evil of small holdings in India is not fundamental but is derived from the parent evil of the maladjustment in her social economy. Added to this, notwithstanding the vastness of land under village, so little land is cultivated in proportion to her population. Herein he brings the concept of idle labour when he observes that a large agricultural population with the lowest proportion of land in actual means that a large part of agricultural population is superfluous and idle. The economic effects of the idle labour have been traced as first, it adds to the tremendous amount of pressure that agricultural population exerts on land; and secondly, this enormous pressure is the chief cause of the sub-division of land. In this regard Ambedkar observes: 'To say that the law of inheritance causes sub-division of land is to give a false view by investing the real situation. The mere existence of the law cannot be complained of as a grievance. The grievance consists in the fact that it is invoked ... when fanning is the only occupation, to get a small piece of land is better than to have none.'[11] Hence, Ambedkar surmises that a population that has little else to prefer to agriculture will try to invoke every possible cause to get a piece of land however small. It is not, therefore, according to him, the law of inheritance that is the evil, lent it is high pressure on land which brings it into operation. He further observes: 'People cultivate the small piece not because their standard of living is low as Prof. Jevons seems to think, but because it is the only profitable thing for them to do at the present.'[12] His views clearly provide a clue to why landless yearn for a piece of land and also why small holding persist despite their less profitability. His arguments also lend support to the redistribution of surplus lands after the implementation of law on ceilings on land holdings.

As Ambedkar had been aware of the Hindu social order,[13] he could pinpoint that it is our bad social economy that is responsible for the ills of our agriculture. But one should not miss his insistence on the role of capital. He observes that our economic organisation is conspicuous by want of capital.[14] His observations about idle labour in rural areas, again a forerunner to Nurkse, and providing jobs to them in industries and lack of capital in agriculture confirm our view that he had been pleading for small-scale capitalist agriculture. This may not be in consonance with his later ideas about the abolition of private property, a common trait he finds in both Buddha's and Karl Marx's writings which also perhaps may be a viable solution as other ideas like cooperative farming or nationalisation of land did not catch up the imagination of our farming community, is capitalistic agriculture as he stresses once again that this type of agriculture will not need as many hands as are not required by our present-day methods of cultivation.[15]

A perceptive observation of Ambedkar that had been the hallmark of our development strategy is: 'If small and scattered holdings are the ills from which our agriculture is suffering then to cure it of them is undeniably to industrialise.'[16] Hence, Ambedkar's views on small holdings are based on pragmatism and his understanding of the agrarian question and the remedies that he offered are highly relevant to the present-day agriculture.

Notes

1. Government of Maharashtra, *Dr. Babasaheb Ambedkar's Writings and Speeches*, Vol. I, Education Department, Bombay, 1979, pp. 455–479.
2. Ibid., p. 456.
3. Ibid., p. 457.
4. Ibid., p. 458.
5. Ibid., pp. 460–464.
6. Ibid., p. 462.
7. Ibid., p. 466.
8. Ibid., p. 468.
9. For instance, Ashok Rudra and Prannoy Roy highlight this view, though the discussion had been essentially carried out that large sized holdings have essentially an inverse relationship with productivity per acre.
10. Ibid., p. 472.
11. Ibid., p. 471.
12. Ibid.
13. Government of Maharashtra, *Dr. Babasaheb Ambedkar's Writings and Speeches*, Vol. III, Education Department, Bombay, 1987, pp. 95–129.
14. Government of Maharashtra, *Dr. Babasaheb Ambedkar's Writings and Speeches*, Vol. I, Education Department, Bombay, 1979, p. 475.
15. Ibid., p. 475.
16. Ibid., p. 479.

17

Ambedkar and Democratic Socialism in India

K.S. Chalam

Ambedkar's writings and views can be divided into two distinct categories. One, the views of Ambedkar as an academician; and two, his views and opinions as a leader of the masses. Ambedkar's serious writings, including his PhD dissertations, could not attract the attention of common man as they were mainly related to economics, currency and finance. Ambedkar had started reflecting on the social economy of the Indian society only after he entered the political life. Therefore, his views on socialism and his mature opinion on the economic problems of the country can be found in his speeches in the Bombay Legislature, Constituent Assembly and references to economic issues in his writings on social and philosophical problems.

An attempt is now being made by communal forces to Hinduise Ambedkar and also project him as a crusader against communism so that he can ultimately be alienated from the toiling masses of this country. This is a conspiracy hatched against the leader of the masses so as to use him against the battle which he started to fight inequality in the Hindu society. Ambedkar himself has exposed such conspiracies in the Indian history in his writings on 'Revolution and Counter-Revolution'. But, the same conspiracy is now being used by the communal forces against him. Unfortunately, some of the gullible followers of Ambedkar who did not get the essence of Ambedkarism are becoming a prey in this conspiracy and are now religiously quoting some of his earlier and more often friendly criticisms of socialism to show that he is an opponent of socialism. Therefore, there is a need to project the real Ambedkar who is a socialist and who in his writings portrayed socialism as an ultimate reality.

Ambedkar made a distinction between socialism and communism and has even commented on the scientific socialism as propounded by Karl Marx. Though the discussions on Marx and Buddha are brief, he has raised some fundamental questions relating to socialism. He has compared the basic tenets of Buddhism with Marxism and concluded that both fought against the evil of private property. He has interpreted the Buddhist *dukkha* as the existence of poverty and opined that the removal of poverty is possible through State ownership in agriculture as enunciated by Buddhist principles. As a labour leader and member of the independent labour party, he has opposed the Workers Civil Liberties Suspension Act. As the chairman of the drafting committee of the Indian Constitution, he has included the directive principles of State policy which speak about socialism and equality.

Friends quite often quote the title of his writings on 'Marx or Buddha' as an indicator to show that he wanted Buddha in place of Marx. But, his last speech at Kathmandu, Nepal, on 20 November 1956 clearly shows that he wanted to reconcile Marx and Buddha in his analysis of society that he was contemplating to achieve. This does not mean that Ambedkar was merely interested in the two personalities. What he was interested in them is their deep concern for the suffering masses. Therefore, Ambedkar interpreted writings of both Buddha and Marx and pointed out that there are three common principles. These are: poverty, exploitation and private property. According to Ambedkar, 'the language of Buddha and Marx is different but meaning is the same'.[1] Ambedkar wished that the means to achieve the abolition of *dukkha*, i.e. poverty is made through non-violent path of following the 'Panchasila' as preached by Buddha. I do not know how many Buddhists of Ambedkar movement are really following the Panchasila, which includes: (1) abstaining from destruction of living things, (2) abstaining from stealing property of others, (3) abstaining from telling untruth, (4) abstaining from lust, and (5) abstaining from intoxicating drinks. Along with Panchasila, the Buddhists are expected to follow the eight–fold path as preached by Buddha. Ambedkar has interpreted Buddha in such a way that he wanted to show him as an ancient democrat and socialist. If Ambedkar is really interested in Buddhism, he would have interpreted him as a religious leader. There is no need for him to bring in Marx and to compare the basic tenets of Marxism with Buddhism. He was interested to reinterpret Buddha so as to be acceptable to a communist also. He appealed to the communist countries to adopt the principles of Buddhism and avoid violence in the process of achieving communism. In this context it is pertinent to quote Ambedkar: 'The Russians do not seem to be paying any attention to Buddhism as an ultimate aid to sustain communism when force is withdrawn'.[2]

It has been claimed that the communist dictatorship in Russia has wonderful achievements to its credit. There can be no denial of it. That is why, I say that a Russian dictatorship would be good for all backward countries (emphasis added). We welcome the Russian Revolution because it aims to produce equality. But, it cannot be too much emphasised that in producing equality, society cannot afford to sacrifice fraternity or liberty. Equality will be of no value without fraternity or liberty. Can any of our liberty publicist dare to say this today and still remain as socialists? But, the basic problem that a serious academic finds in these writings of Ambedkar is to relate the process of social development with the materialistic basis of the society. It is further not clear from his available writings whether the principles of Classical Buddhism including the concept of *dukkha* and the ownership of personal belongings of 'parivrajakas' are applicable to the Buddhist *sanghas* or to the entire community. There are no historical evidences or studies to show that during the Buddhist period, people did not possess private property. It is now left to the researchers and the Ambedkarists to work on such themes to prove these interpretations of Ambedkar rather than vaguely and superstitiously interpreting him. The most fundamental problem which Ambedkar had encountered in his analysis of socialism is a reconciliation of religion with equality. He was of the opinion that religion will sustain if force is withdrawn and it is essential for the survival of a society. It is to be seen whether religion in the modern sense of the organised religion would really benefit the common man and whether the structure would help eliminate inequalities particularly the hierarchically laid inequalities in the Hindu society, is a question to be answered by all of us who are interested in Ambedkar and to make him up-to-date to be able to be acceptable to the next century.

Most of the writings of Ambedkar on equality and occasionally on socialism are serious philosophical discourses and therefore need to be interpreted to understand their practical application. Philosophical discourses like precepts quite often avoid practical problems. However, in order to understand Ambedkar as a socialist, particularly as a democratic socialist, his philosophical writings are sufficient to prove that he is a democratic socialist but not an anti-socialist as some groups are trying to interpret him with an ulterior motive. In this sense, even the Indian communists and socialists have failed to understand Ambedkar as to why he was interested to interpret Marx along with Buddha in the Indian context. It is now necessary for those who are interested to go to the majority of the exploited masses to study, understand and interpret Ambedkar in the changed context and situation in India.

Ambedkar has clearly laid down his ideas relating to State socialism. He has explained what he meant as 'modified form of State socialism in the field of industry' in his draft Constitution of India prepared on behalf of the All India Scheduled Caste Federation in 1947 which is popularly known as *States and Minorities*. One must remember here that he has given this explanation in the appendix on explanatory notes to Clause 4 of Article II which is incorporated in the draft under protection against economic exploitation. After explaining the plan of how State socialism can be achieved to protect the people from economic exploitation, Ambedkar mentioned that liberally from the control of the State is another name of the dictatorship of the private employer. He further added that this liberty is the liberty to the landlords to increase rents, and for capitalists to increase hours of work and reduce rate of wages. These sentences contain grains of scientific socialism which Ambedkar would have elaborated had he lived longer.

The core of the economic and political arguments of Ambedkar in relation to socialism centre round abolition of exploitation through non-violence. He has argued that the consolidation of holdings does not improve the economic efficiency of land unless supported by capital investment made on the cultivable land. Industrialisation, according to Ambedkar, facilitates consolidation in agriculture and slowly brings in full employment by making use of the surplus labour. Therefore, he did not agree with Gandhi's views on machinery and said that instead of criticising the evils of machinery, we need to reformulate our social system to overcome the evils of machinery and involve more people in the process of industrialisation. In this respect, the views of Ambedkar resemble with that of Arthur Lewis, the Black American Nobel laureate who wrote on economic development with unlimited supplies of labour. Ambedkar has advocated collectivisation of agriculture and the Buddhist principle of ownership of land by the state. In a country like India, nationalisation of land and social control of industry, insurance, etc. lead to the total control of the economy by the State. The State, according to Ambedkar, has the obligation to plan economic life of the people and bring equalisation of wealth. He was also critical of the village community as a polity and wanted that individual be made as the unit of the Constitution that he was making, instead of the village. In support of his argument, quoting Metcalfe, he had said in the Constituent Assembly of India: 'Dynasty after dynasty tumbles down. Revolution succeeds to revolution. Hindu, Pathan, Mughal, Marhatta, Sikh, English are all masters in turn, but the village communities remain the same. In times of trouble, they arm and fortify themselves. A hostile army passes through the country. The village communities collect their little cattle within their walls, and let the enemy pass unprovoked'.[3]

Such is the part of the village communities have played in the history of their country. Knowing this, what pride can one feel in them? That they have survived through all vicissitudes may be a fact. But mere survival has no value. The question is on what plane they have survived. Surely, on a low, selfish level. I hold that these village republics have been the ruination of India. I am, therefore, surprised that those who condemn provincialism and communalism should come forward as champions of the village. What is the village but a sink of localism, a den of ignorance, narrow-mindedness and communalism? I am glad that the draft Constitution has discarded the village and adopted the individual as its unit. We can find a similar paragraph in Marx's *Capital* while analysing division of labour and manufacture in the Indian context.

The Marxian theory of State according to Ambedkar is weak and therefore the dictatorship of the proletariat in the context of Marxian state leads to violence. Therefore, he preferred democratic socialism. Ambedkar argued that equality can be brought in through constitutional measures and by democratic process political democracy rests on four premises. They are: (1) The individual is an end in himself. (2) The individual has certain inalieanable rights which must be guaranteed to him by the Constitution. (3) The individual shall not be required to relinquish any of his constitutional rights as a condition precedent to the receipt of a privilege. (4) The State shall not delegate powers to private persons to govern others. Here, Ambedkar had a philosophical problem of how to establish State socialism without sacrificing individual liberty. The solution he has offered is by the law of the Constitution. But he has realised after the implementation of the Indian Constitution which is substantially different from his original draft that democratic process is the means through which socialism can be achieved without much violence. Therefore, he had electoral alliances with the Praja Socialist Party in 1951. As Ambedkar is a great libertarian, he had asserted that 'equality will be of no value without fraternity or liberty'.[4] It is left to us now to evaluate his views in terms of the contemporary situation.

Notes

1. Vasant Moon, *Dr. Babasaheb Ambedkar: Writings and Speeches*, Vol. 3, Government of Maharashtra, Bombay, 1987.
2. Ibid.
3. Vasant Moon, op. cit., Vol. 3.
4. Ibid.

18

Caste and Patriarchy

Ambedkar's Insight into the Status of Indian Women

M. Nalini

Ambedkar evinced a keen interest in women's problems. His views and efforts to improve the condition of women, in the various capacities that he served as a member of the Bombay Legislature, as the law and labour member of the Viceroy's Executive Council, as the chairman of the drafting committee of the Constituent Assembly of India and as the Union Cabinet Minister for Law in the first ministry of independent India are noted and well-known.[1] Particular mention is due to the Hindu Code Bill which he had drafted and was persistently anxious to be enacted into law for it would revolutionise women's socio-economic conditions. But on being hampered and disallowed to enact it into law, he even resigned from his Cabinet position.[2]

Yet, his contribution to the analysis of the position of women in India is not known widely. He has dealt with the issue in detail in specific works like 'The Rise and Fall of Hindu Woman', and in his unpublished writings under 'Revolution and Counter Revolution in Ancient India: Women and the Counter Revolution.' Further, he has touched on the subject of women's status in his work 'Caste in India' and 'Annihilation of Caste' and also under

'Riddles in Hinduism'.[3] His analysis of the history of the rise and fall in the status of the Hindu women is thought-provoking. Gerda Lemer in her *The Creation of Patriarchy*, explains how the process of evolution of patriarchy 'was manifested in changes in kinship organization and economic relations, in the establishment of religious and state bureaucracies and in the shifts in cosmogonies expressing the ascendancy of male god figures'.[4] It is interesting to note that Ambedkar touches all these issues though often in different contexts and from a different perspective. But he does offer new insights into the process by which patriarchy becomes established and institutionalised in the Indian context.

I

This section briefly recapitulates Ambedkar's depiction of the changing status of Indian woman and his analysis about the decline in her position. Quoting extensively from various sources, he shows women were well respected in the Vedic period. They had all the opportunities to pursue education, including study of *Vedas*; and were even eligible for the Upanayanam.[5] Post-puberty marriage (i.e. adult marriage) was the norm for girls and they could have a say in the choice of partner. They could end a marriage and remarry and even widows remarried. According to Ambedkar, even during Kautilya's time, women lived with dignity.[6]

But with the Manu Dharma Sastra age, there was a steep deterioration in the status of women. Manu denounced women as licentious seducers and characterised them as evil incarnate. Having painted them thus, he condemns them and follows up by formulating tyrannical laws to deprive women of all freedom and dignity and to control her fully. Accordingly, woman should always be under the charge of her male kinfolk, she should not study *Vedas* and so cannot participate in the religious services. Thereby, she was doomed to sinful existence perpetually. For women, marriage was a permanent and sacramental union, but men had divorce rights. Worse still, most monstrously, woman though sold, deserted or divorced by husband, was still bound by the marriage bond. Husband could legally inflict corporal punishment on wife and killing a woman was seen as a minor crime 'upapataka'.[7]

Ambedkar also notes that the emergence of cruelly evil practices like child marriage for girls, ban on widow remarriage, severe rules of widowhood and *sati*, occurred during this Manu Sastra era.[8]

Ambedkar hypothesises that such a decline in woman's status occurred due to many reasons. Manu Dharma Sastra, the embodiment of Brahmanism, follows a great revolutionary phase, that of Buddhism. Buddhism offered more opportunities for liberty and equality to all including women. Naturally, a large number of those who felt deprived or stiffed under Vedic religion turned their backs on it to follow Buddhism, i.e. mainly women and Sudras. This led to an increasing number of inter-caste marriages, according to Ambedkar, striking at the roots of caste system.[9] Since this threatened, the very structure which ensured superiority and privileges to Brahmins, the latter sought to impose restrictions on women (and Sudras). To achieve these objectives they also sought the crystallise and make the caste system rigid.

Ambedkar argues that to maintain the caste system, endogamy had to be ensured. Therefore, Brahminism imposed strict and total control over women's sexuality. Out of these compulsions, the Brahmin caste set up an enclosure over itself and then arose girl child marriages, ban on widow remarriage, miserable rules of widowhood and even sati (which were soon followed by the other upper castes). Such practices, according to Ambedkar, arose out of the need to maintain parity among males and females of marriageable age within the endogamous groups.[10] Otherwise exogamy cannot be avoided and exogamy would end caste system and with it the advantages that secured to Brahmins. He bolsters his argument by citing the new laws prohibiting *Varna* inter-marriages. He particularly calls attention to the prohibition on a high caste woman from marrying a low caste man. But a high caste man had access to women of lower castes with no responsibility towards the offspring. This was made possible by the new rule of matriliny (*matrusavarna*) to be followed for such high caste men marrying low caste women (*anuloma* marriage). This in effect was the privilege to males of higher caste to lawfully commit prostitution with low caste women and absolve of any further responsibility.[11]

II

A few scholars who have attempted to sketch the history of woman in India, have examined the changes that have occurred over time, and have discussed about the adversities that Indian woman faced since the Vedic period. But none has suggested in connection with the caste system. This is basic and innovative argument put forth by Ambedkar. This section reviews critically Ambedkar's assumption that there is a relation between rise of caste system and the decline in the status of woman.

The first part of the section interweaves the evolution of caste and its consolidation as a caste system as derived at by D.D. Kosambi, R.S. Shama and Romila Thapar;[12] with the history of the gradual deterioration in the status of woman and its crystallisation as a feature of Indian society as portrayed by P. Thomas and A.S. Altekar.[13]

During the early Vedic period, there was no caste or class differentiation within the tribe.[14] Caste emerged during the transition from the semi-nomadic pastoral economy of the early Vedic age into a more settled agrarian economy.[15] In the post-Rig Veda society (1000–800 B.C.), the new problems of food production on a large scale with different techniques of production went beyond the simple tribe, and caste evolved within the tribe.[16] The Brahmanic model of caste was formed around the ninth century B.C. but it was still a fluid arrangement with frequent inter-caste mobility prevailing in general.[17]

With regard to the position of women, Thomas maintains that women were held in high esteem in the pre-Vedic and early Vedic periods. But since Rig Veda, the position of women declined compared to earlier times when marriage was not sacramental, and women had practically unlimited freedom in sexual matters.[18] Altekar also holds that women's position was fairly satisfactory up to 1500 B.C. and that very gradually changes crept in since then reflected in the slump in women's education, and a concomitant curtailment of women's religious rights and role.[19]

Thus, in the early Vedic period, there exists neither caste nor woman's degradation. It is strikingly obvious that the emergence of caste stratification and the signs of beginning of decline in women's status coincide in the later Vedic period.

By the pre-Mauryan period, the caste system became rigid. This did not proceed unchallenged. Buddhism as a movement spearheaded the mood of the era which questioned and attacked this rigidity of the caste system, the stronghold of the Brahmins and the efficacy of their rituals and ceremonies. But the rebellions were not successful, they only prompted Brahminism to cover up its loopholes and continue its juggernaut like March. By the fourth century, Brahmanism gained a decisive upper-hand, the caste system was crystallised and the priorities and privileges of Brahmins were established.[20]

Altekar refers to the gradual decline in female education, the gentle easing out of women from religious privileges and functions, though still post-puberty marriages were observed and divorce was allowed.[21] But Altekar accepts that since sixth century, the deterioration in the status of women was rapid and marked. Women were no more educated, and were unfit for religious roles.[22] Early marriages became the norm; and marriage became a religious sacrament that should not be broken. Public opinion was ranged against remarriage of widows.

Thomas also notes the yet another descent down the rungs of the ladder regarding women. He assumes that development of eschatological notions about a son's competence to redeem parents from hell led to this further downside in status of women. As per the *grihyasutras* of the period, women were excluded from religious roles, there was a reduction in age of marriage and he points out that prostitution had become rampant by the Mauryan period.[23]

Thus, we find that around the Buddhist period the evolution of caste as a system reached a mcre fixed and rigid form and under Brahmanism withstood rebellion onslaughts, while the devolution in the status of women continued unabated to a more dismal level.

In the post-Buddhist period, the triumphant Brahmanist forces held fast to their position.[24] Manu Dharma Sastra codified the Brahmanic norms as the religious rules and caste system became a sanctified institution. It also acquired the status of the law of the State and by second century A.D. the force of the ossified caste system was invincible.

The era of *Manusmriti* is notorious also for the indignities it heaped on women. According to Altekar, the disastrous consequences of discontinuation of Upanayanam, neglection of education and lowering of marriage age for girls[25] engendered the theory of perpetual tutelage of women by fourth century B.C. As per the Samhitas, a man's debts are liquidated only through a son and thus birth of son became a religious necessity,[26] and a daughter was unwanted. Marriage became an irrevocable union specifically for wife, even if husband discarded her. Widow remarriage was prohibited and *sati* encouraged.[27]

Thomas echoes these ideas when he points to the codes striving to establish the abject dependence of women on men, conceding to husbands the right of physical correction of wives, banning widow remarriages, demanding child marriage and even encouraging *sati*.[28] Thus, between 200 B.C. to 300 A.D., Indian women were pushed down to abysmal depths. This degradation was sanctified as religious norm and law of the state by *Manusmriti*.

Thus, on the one hand, caste system became rooted in Indian society and on the other hand women's subordination and degradation became embedded in Indian culture.

III

This recounting corroborates the coincidence of rise of caste system and the downfall in woman's status. But there are a few vague and confusing ideas about a woman's status in Ambedkar's assessment. He claims women were equal and free prior to Mann,[29] and were so even during Kautilya's time.[30] It is surprising that he does not explicitly recognise and denounce women's subordination and degradation where it exists to Manu, though at the same time he notes that Manu's contribution was to codify sanctify existing norms as religious laws. It has to be acknowledged that subordination of women was a fact, and degradation was a continuous process arising much earlier than *Manusmriti*. Perhaps, in his fervour to condemn *Manusmriti*, he cites the earlier conditions of women in a more favourable light.

Ambedkar's another contention is that *Manusmriti*, the epitome of Brahmanism, was a counter, revolution on the assumption that Buddhism was a revolution, radically altering women's status. But historically, the decline in the status of woman was only a continuous process begun during the Vedic age and carried to its logical end by the *Manusmriti*. Once again, if it is conceded patriarchy emerged before *Manusmriti* then the latter cannot be the cause of women's downfall and therefore is not a 'counter revolution', but a more a continuation. Buddhism offered an alternative scheme to an extent, but being weak and ineffective on the whole, only served to prompt Brahminism to rectify its loopholes and clamp down the already rigid norms of caste system and rules of degraded womanhood under the guise of secular and religious codes.

Ambedkar's assumption that the atrocious evils like female child marriages, ban on widow remarriage, widowhood, and sati are the results of the endogamous nature of caste system requiring male-female parity within the caste group, is also questionable. While on the one hand, widowhood and even *sati* were practised by women (supposedly to maintain parity), on the other hand men continued to practise polygamy and were also allowed exogamy (a higher caste male could marry lower caste women). This state of things disproves the assumption that widowhood and *sati* arose out of the need for maintaining male-female parity within a caste group. This is not to deny that under an endogamous caste system, permeated by notions of purity and pollution, women as procreators have an extra premium attached to the purity of their sexuality, which goes beyond ordinary 'patriarchy'. Still the institutions of widowhood and *sati* are inexplicable within these formulae.

Ambedkar assumes that it was the endogamous nature of caste system which led to subordination and degradation of women. But this feature—of men controlling women, their sexuality, procreativity and labour known as patriarchy—prevails even in societies where there is no caste. Elsewhere too 'women's sexual subordination was institutionalised in the early law codes and enforced by the full power of the state'.[31]

When we look for the factors generally inducing the rise of patriarchy, it is acknowledged that women's subordination is linked with the emergence of class divisions in society. 'The first class antagonism which appears in history coincides with the development of the antagonism between man and woman in monogamous marriage, and the first class oppression with that of the female sex by the male'.[32] In India 'caste' is recognised 'as class on a primitive level of production.'[33] Therefore, it is no surprise (seeing patriarchy's correlation to class society) that the misfortune of Indian women became linked to the rise of the early caste system 'which corresponded to the progressive development of class society'.[34] Indeed the contours of changing status of Indian women through history, are but an echo of the more or less similar worldwide process. In Engel's terms, 'women occupied not only a free but also a highly respected position among all savages and all barbarians of the lower and middle stages and partly even of upper state'.[35] This serves as an apt description of status of women in pre-Vedic, early Vedic and even to an extent of later Vedic period in India—a period of primitive tribal economy, intermingled with semi-nomadic pastoral economy. But to continue Engel's idea, 'with the overthrow of mother right, women were degraded, enthralled, became the slave of man's lust, a mere instrument for breeding children.'[36] This equally matches the decline in women's position following the transition to an agrarian economy in the later Vedic and post-Vedic periods.

Thus, to discover the actual process and details of the decline in the status of women in India, it is necessary to follow the lead provided by Ambedkar, recombining his ideas within Engel's framework to unravel further 'the connection between structural changes in kinship relations and changes in division of labour on the one hand, and women's position in society on the other'.[37]

Notes

1. Mallik, Basant Kumar, 'Ambedkar on Women's Progress', *Mainstream*, Vol. XXV, No. 3, 11 April 1987, pp. 7–10; Ahir, D.C., 'For the Sake of Women', in *The Legacy of Dr. Ambedkar*, Delhi: B.R. Publishing Corporation, 1990, p. 129.
2. Das, B. (Ed.), 'On the Eve of Resignation from Cabinet', in *Thus Spoke Ambedkar*, Vol. I, Punjab: Bheem Patrika Publications, 1963, p. 99.

3. Ambedkar, B.R., *The Rise and Fall of Hindu Woman*, Jalandhar: Bheem Patrika Publications, 1980; *Castes in India: Their Mechanism, Genesis and Development*, Jalandhar: Bheem Patrika Publications, 1977; Education Department, Government of Maharashtra, *Dr. Babasaheb Ambedkar's Writings and Speeches,* Vol. 3: The Triumph of Brahminism, pp. 266–331; and *Woman a Counter Revolution*, pp. 429–440.
4. Lerner, Gerda, Women and History, Vol. I: *The Creation of Patriarchy*, New York: Oxford University Press, 1986, p. 7.
5. Ambedkar, B.R., *The Rise and Fall of Hindu Woman*, op. cit., p. 21.
6. Education Department, Government of Maharashtra, *Dr. Babasaheb Ambedkar's Writings and Speeches*, Vol. 3, pp. 433–434.
7. Ambedkar, B.R., *The Rise and Fall of Hindu Woman*, op. cit., pp. 22–27.
8. Education Department, Government of Maharashtra, *Dr. Babasaheb Ambedskar's Writings and Speeches*, Vol. 3, p. 301.
9. Ambedkar, B.R., *Rise and Fall of Hindu Woman*, op. cit., pp. 27–29.
10. Education Department, Government of Maharashtra, *Dr. Babasaheb Ambedkar's Writings and Speeches*, Vol. 3, p. 296.
11. Ibid., p. 307.
12. Kosambi, D.D., *The Culture and Civilisation of Ancient India in Historical Outline*, New Delhi: Vikas Publishing House, 1977; Sharma, R.S., *Sudras in Ancient India*, Delhi: Motilal Banarsidass, 1958; Thapar, Romila, *Asoka and the Decline of Mauryas*, Delhi, Oxford University Press, 1982; Thapar, Romila, 'Social Mobility in Ancient India', in R.S. Sharma (Ed.), *Indian Society: Historical Probings*, New Delhi: People Publishing House, 1974, p. 97.
13. Thomas, P., *Indian Women Through the Ages*, Calcutta: Asia Publishing House, 1964; Altekar, A.S., *The Position of Women in Hindu Civilisation*, Delhi: Motilal Banarsidass, 1978.
14. Kosambi, D.D., *The Culture and Civilisation of Ancient India in Historical Outline*, op. cit., p. 80.
15. Thapar, Romila, *Asoka and the Decline of Mauryas*, op. cit., p. 4.
16. Kosambi, D.D., *The Culture and Civilisation of Ancient India in Historical Outline*, op. cit., p. 85.
17. Thapar, Romila, *Asoka and the Decline of Mauryas*, op. cit., p. 56.
18. Thomas, P., *Indian Women Through the Ages*, op. cit., p. 54.
19. Altekar, A.S., *The Position of Women in Hindu Civilisation*, op. cit., p. 54.

20. Thapar, Romila, *Asoka and the Decline of Mauryas*, op. cit., p. 4 and p. 56; Sharma, R.S., *Sudras in Ancient India*, op. cit., p. 280.
21. Altekar, A.S., *The Position of Women in Hindu Civilisation*, op. cit., p. 340.
22. Ibid., p. 344.
23. Thomas, P., *Indian Women Through the Ages*, op. cit.
24. Thapar, Romila, *Asoka and the Decline of Mauryas*, op. cit., p. 57.
25. Altekar, A.S., *The Position of Women in Hindu Civilisation*, op. cit., p. 348.
26. Ibid., p. 326.
27. Ibid., p. 347.
28. Thomas, P., *Indian Women Through the Ages*, op. cit., pp. 220–224.
29. Education Department, Government of Maharashtra, *Dr. Babasaheb Ambedkar's Speeches and Writings*, Vol. 3, p. 437.
30. Ibid., pp. 433–437.
31. Lerner, Gerda, *The Creation of Patriarchy*, op. cit., p. 9.
32. Engels, F., *The Origin of the Family, Private Property and the State*, Moscow: Progress Publishers, 1977.
33. Kosambi, D.D., *The Culture and Civilisation*, op. cit., p. 50. He also notes that 'the development of caste foreshadowed a general class society beyond the exclusiveness of a tribe', p. 86.
34. Kosambi, D.D., 'Early Stages of Caste System in Northern India', *Journal of the Bombay Brunch of the Royal Asiatic Society*, October 1947, p. 50.
35. Engels, F., *The Origin of the Family, Private Property and the State*, op. cit., p. 49.
36. Ibid.
37. Lerner, Gerda, *The Creation of Patriarchy*, op. cit., p. 23.

19

Ambedkar's Views on the Indian Caste System

V. Subrahamanyam

The paper is aimed to explain Ambedkar's views on the Indian caste system. He has focused his attention on the problem of caste in the Indian society, and also contributed to the sociological literature of modern India. Ambedkar's works on *Caste in India*, *Annihilation of Caste*, *Who Were the Sudras*, and *The Untouchables* have shown the way for anthropological thinking in India. These works have a historical orientation and throw a critical light on the problem of the caste as the inhibitory and controlling element in the social organisation and structure. Ambedkar has critically examined the problem of caste in our society in the light of historical evidence and explained how it became the fundamental criterion of social action.

A paper on 'Castes in India: Their Mechanism, Genesis and Development', presented by Ambedkar at a seminar in the Columbia University, New York, reveals his critical analysis of the presence of caste institution in the Indian society. In the paper, he stated that 'in my opinion a student of ethnology, in one sense at least, is much like the guide. Like his prototype, he holds up the social institutions to view, with all the objectiveness humanly possible, and inquires into their origin and function'. Further, he pointed out that 'the caste problem is a vast one, both theoretically and practically. Practically, it is an institution that portends tremendous consequences. It is a local problem, but one capable of much wider mischief, for as long as caste in India does exist, the Hindus will hardly inter-marry or have any social intercourse with outsiders; and if Hindus migrate to other regions on earth, Indian caste would become a world problem'. This statement clearly envisages about the intensity of caste problem in modem India. He critically examined the ethonologists' views on the origin of castes in India and suggested that the amalgamation of the various stocks was not the sole criterion of homogeneity. Ethnically, all people are heterogeneous. It is the unity of culture that is the basis of homogeneity. But it is because of this homogeneity that caste becomes a problem so difficult to be explained.

He reviewed Senart's, Nesfield's, Risely's and Ketkar's definition of caste, and commented by saying that 'the definitions of three westerners include too much or too little: none is complete or correct by itself and all have missed the central point in the mechanism of the caste system. Their mistake lies in trying to define caste as an isolated unit by itself and not as a group within and with definite relations to the system of caste as a Whole'.[1] Senart draws attention to the 'idea of pollution' as a characteristic of caste with regard to this point it may be safely said that it does not mean a peculiarity of caste as such. It usually originates in priestly ceremonialism and is a particular case of the general belief in purity consequently its necessary connection with caste may be completely defined without damaging the working of caste. The idea of pollution has been attached to the institution of caste, only because the caste that enjoys the highest rank is the priestly caste; while we know that the idea of pollution is a characteristic of caste only in so far as caste has a religious flavour. Nesfield, in his analysis, dwells on the absence of taking food with those outside the caste as one of its characteristics. In spite of the newness of the point, we must say that Nesfield has mistaken the effect for the cause. Caste, being a self-enclosed unit, naturally limits social intercourse, including messing, etc. to members within it. Consequently, this absence of messing with outsiders is not due to positive prohibition, but is a natural result of caste, i.e. exclusiveness. No doubt, this absence of messing originally due to exclusiveness, acquired the prohibitory character of a religious injunction, but it may be regarded as a later growth. Risely makes no new point which deserves special attention.

Ketkar has done much for the elucidation of the subject. Not only is he a native, but has also brought a critical acumen and an open mind to bear on his study of caste. His definition merits consideration, for he has defined caste in its relation to a system of castes and has concentrated his attention only on those characteristics which are absolutely necessary for the existence of a caste within a system, rightly excluding all others as being secondary or derivative in character. With respect to his definition, it must, however, be said that in it there is a slight confusion of thought, lucid and clear as otherwise it is. He speaks of prohibition of inter-marriage and membership by autogamy as the two characteristics of caste. I submit that these are two aspects of one and the same thing, and not two different things as Ketkar supposed them to be. If you prohibit inter-marriage, the result is that you limit membership to those born within the group. Thus, the two are the obverse and the reverse sides of the same medal.

In regard to caste system in India, Ambedkar pointed out that people of India form a homogeneous whole. The various races occupying definite territories have more or less fused into one another and possess cultural unity, which is the only criterion of homogeneous population. Given this homogeneity as a basis, caste becomes a problem altogether new in character and wholly absent in the situation constituted by the mere propinquity of endogamous social or tribal groups. Caste in India means an artificial chopping off of the population into fixed and definite units, each one prevented from using into another through the custom of endogamy. He emphasised that 'endogamy is the only characteristic that is peculiar to caste'. He also mentioned the observance of the custom of exogamy at clan or *gotra* level. The prevalence of exogamy in the primitive societies is a fact too well known to need any explanation with the growth of history, however, exogamy has lost its efficacy, and excepting the nearest blood-kins, there is usually no social bar restricting the field of marriage. But regarding the people of India, the law of exogamy is positive injunction even today. Indian society still savours of the clan system, even though there are no clans, and this can be easily seen from the law of matrimony which centres round the principle of exogamy, for it is not that *sapinders* (blood-kins) cannot marry, but a marriage even between *sagotras* of the same class is regarded as a sacrilege. The various *gotras* of India are and have been exogamous; so are the other groups with totemic organisation. He stated that with exogamy as the rule there could be no caste, for exogamy means fusion. But we have castes, consequently in the final analysis creation of castes, so far as India is concerned, means the superimposition of endogamy on exogamy. Thus, the superimposition of endogamy on exogamy means the creation of caste. Such an analytical definition was given by Ambedkar in regard to the caste. He has given anthropological illustrations for his definition of the caste.

It is appropriate here to mention about Sedguik view in regard to the observance of the custom of endogamy at caste level and exogamy at *gotra* level by the Indian people. He pointed out that the Indian caste system with its endogamous castes and its exogamous *gotras* is a perfect method of preserving what is called in genetics the 'pure line'. The endogamy prevents extern hybridisation, while the (internal) exogamy prevents the possibility of a fresh pure line arising within the old one by the isolation of any character not common to the whole line.

Dr Ambedkar mentioned that the problem of caste ultimately resolves itself into one of the repairing the disparity between the marriageable units of the two sexes within it. Both the surplus man and surplus woman constitute a menace to the caste, if not taken care of, for not finding suitable partners inside their prescribed circle, very likely they will transgress the boundary, marry outside and import offspring that is foreign to the caste. He discussed the problem of widow remarriage and enforced widowhood, which he considered the reason for surplus woman. He also suggested that the problem of surplus man (widower) is much more important and much more difficult than that of the surplus woman in a group that desires to make itself into a caste. He has pointed out that no scientific reasons prevails for the customs of *sati*, enforced widowhood and girls marriage. We have plenty of philosophy to tell us why these customs were honoured, but nothing to tell us the causes of their origin and existence. He said that 'a caste is an enclosed class'.

Ambedkar criticised Manu and said that Manu did not give the law of caste and could not ordain the present order of Hindu society. His work ended with the codification of existing caste rules and the preaching of caste *dharma*. The spread and growth of the caste system is too gigantic a task to be achieved by the power or cunning of an individual or of a class. Similar in argument is the theory that the Brahmins created the caste. Ambedkar pointed out that 'there is a strong belief in the mind of orthodox Hindus that the Hindu society was somehow molded into the framework of the caste system and that it is an organisation consciously created by the *Shastras*'.[2] He explained that the whole process of caste-formation in India is a process of imitation of the higher by the lower. His study of the caste problem mainly reveals four main points: (1) that in spite of the composite make-up of the Hindu population there is deep cultural unity, (2) that caste is a parceling into bits of a larger cultural unit, (3) that there was once caste to start with, and (4) that classes have become castes through imitation and ex-communication.

A great deal of controversy exists on the caste origin in India. Different theories have been proposed by different Indian and western scholars about the origin of castes.[3] In our society, the most popular theories are *varna* theory, *varna* hypergamy and hypogamy (*anuloma* and *pratiloma*), occupational theory, racial theory, ecological and geographical factors and the political condition of the ancient India. In regard to caste, Ambedkar has also given certain explanations for its origin. He states that the history of India is a tally of events of caste discrimination, preached and practised in the name of God. It is due to the role of religion in the early laws that the priest became the most potent instrument of the stability and status quo. He interpreted the concept of struggle for existence like, 'desires whenever acute because of the limited goods of existence, out of which they can be satisfied, disturbs this balance.' In order to maintain the balance, men have relied upon religion and upon reasons. For the Indian historical content

Ambedkar shows how the desire of monopoly of social control made the priest the most powerful factor in social control.

In regard to the problem of caste in India, Ambedkar clearly pointed out that caste is barrier to social progress and individual advancement of freedom. And also he informed that the control of minds of men by some powerful individuals is bad as such it retards any progressive movement. The peculiar characteristic feature of the Indian caste system is the social inequality, which we see in the caste hierarchy. The caste hierarchy represents the social position of each and every caste, the Brahmins stand at the top and the Harijans lies at the bottom. Not only the social inequality but also economic and political inequality is found in between the highest and the lowest *jatis*. At present, the power struggle between different dominant castes and in between the highest and the lowest castes are very common, which led to caste conflicts. The so-called dominant or highest castes are not allowing the lowest castes to reach up to their levels. Especially in the rural villages the caste is so rigid when compared with that of the urban areas. In the rural villages the lowest castes are still economically depending on the dominant peasant castes. The position of the downtrodden communities in the rural villages seems to be very low and they lag behind in many spheres. Ambedkar has rightly pointed out this problem in the year 1916 and done much scholarly work on it. So far no solution has come out for the resolution of the problem. Therefore, serious and in-depth research studies are necessary to find out the solutions to this problem. It is the responsibility of the educators, scholars and thinkers to focus their attention on this problem taking the radical thinking of Ambedkar as a beacon light.

Notes

1. Vasant Moon (Ed.), 'Annihilation of Caste', in *Dr. Babasaheb Ambedkar's Writings and Speeches*, Vol. 1 and 7, Education Department, Government of Maharashtra, Bombay, 1979 and 1990.
2. Op. cit.
3. J.H. Hutton, *Caste in India*, Bombay: Oxford University Press, 1946.

Part III

Ambedkar as Constitution-maker and Institutions Breaker

20

Ambedkar

A Creative Iconoclast

V.R. Krishna Iyer

Few persons in India in this century have come so near to a combination of constitutional statesman and creative iconoclast as Babasaheb Ambedkar. When a suppressive past holds the present generation prisoner, a freer future for the successor generation demands the twin faculties to destruct and construct. Feudal colonial India could not win independence or build a just Republic without deliberately liquidating the hard layers of caste injustices keeping millions of depressed humans suffocating. A catalystic process of socio-political oxygenation was a necessity if Bharat were to be revived. The ghastly scenario of social and economic deprivations and sub-human inflictions in the midst of which Ambedkar was born made this Promethean humanist a passionate rebel whose mission was a social democracy. Bakunin has observed that the urge for destruction is also a creative urge. The fire of anger to burn down caste injustice, build up egalite in society and compassion in human relations made Ambedkar a firebrand futurist against feudal casteism and dehumanisation in life, and found in him a furious founding father of brave new Bharat. Rightly did Jawaharlal Nehru, in his tribute to this noble soul, observe: 'The way he will be remembered most will be as a symbol of the revolt against all the oppressive features of ...

society. We rebelled against something against which all ought to rebel.' Indeed, Ambedkar was the practical, political, intellectual and spiritual leader of the destruction of a removing which the construction of a democratic secular socialist republic would have been moonshine. It is in this dialectical dimension we have to measure the greatness of one who was born 'Untouchable', but rose to heights unapproachable to many who claim to be leaders in politics.

Human dignity, equality of opportunity and social justice in an unequal society area the *sine qua non* of authentic fraternity. As the architect of our Constitution, Ambedkar strove to concretise this profound ideology born out of a conviction that 'democracy means a form and method of government whereby revolutionary changes in the economic and social life of the people are brought about without bloodshed'.

It is strange but true despite the despair of the depressed classes for whose upgradation he battled all his life, Ambedkar opposed lawlessness, even in the shape of civil disobedience and sanction for political purposes, as *grammar* of anarchy and insisted on the contrary that the rule of law, dynamic, democratic and humanist must be made a reality if the Republic were to reach its destination and redeem its tryst with destiny. It has been remarked about this great critic of the *status qua* that he was a parliamentarian par excellence.

He spared no effort in criticising the government on policy matters whenever he felt that the later was following a wrong path. His thought-provoking suggestions and succinct summaries used to evoke admiration of the entire House. While speaking on the floor of the House, he used to touch on issues like a true statesman and firmly placed the interest of the nation above everything else. As an eminent parliamentarian, he was genuinely concerned about the role of the Parliament in ameliorating the lot of the people, particularly the underprivileged. On the floor of the Rajya Sabha, he had declared that unless Parliament took care of the welfare of the people within a reasonable time, it would be treated with utter contempt by the public.

'His respect for the chair was unquestionable not being swayed by the heat and passion of the moment, he used to follow strictly the time-tested rules and conventions'.[1]

To abide by the law never means support for the vested interests constituting the dominant forces in the society. On the contrary, lawlessness may led to chaos and may be used as a pretext for violent suppression of the weaker sections. Ambedkar, every inch of him, was a courageous challenge to the cult of caste and the myriad indignities inflicted on the lowliest masses. Indeed, he had the daring to disagree with Gandhiji on the fundamentals of Hinduism and yet was sensitive in his soul to save his life by signing the Poona pact, giving in somewhat. Ambedkar demanded annihilation of caste without which Hinduism deserved to perish. Gandhiji opposed untouchability and other Hindu vices, but did not advocate abolition of the caste system. Again, Ambedkar was convinced that land for the landless was a condition for Indian liberation, otherwise *swaraj* would only mean rule by the brown saheb, in the place of the White. Gandhiji stood for trusteeship and faith in the properties classes to behave with compassion. Way back in 1930, Ambedkar argued:

> We hold that the problem of the depressed classes will never be solved unless they get political power in their own hands.
>
> The idea of *swaraj* recalls to the mind of many of us the tyrannies, oppressions and injustices practised upon us in the past and the fear of their recurrence under *swaraj*.

In a speech ringing with logic Ambedkar complained:

> It is one which is midway between that of the self and the slave, and which may, for convenience, be called servile—with this difference, that the serf and the slave were permitted to have physical contact. From which the depressed classes are debarred … .
>
> It must be recognised that Indian society is a gradation of castes forming an ascending scale of reverence and a descending scale of contempt—a system which gives no scope for the growth of that sentiment of equality and fraternity so essential for a democratic form of government.

Even at the Round Table Conference, Ambedkar said:

> Untouchables were treated as slaves because (1) they were so socialized as never to complain of their low state; (2) they never dreamed of trying to improve their lot, by forcing the

> other classes to treat them with the common respect; (3) the idea that they had been born to their lot, was so ingrained in their mind that it never occurred to them to think that their fate was anything so irrevocable; and (4) nothing would ever persuade them that men are all made of the same clay, or that they have the right to insist on better treatment than that meted out to them.

The militant *mahar* that he was, Ambedkar must be seen as a larger leader of oppressed people and defender of gender justice and human rights. 'Tell the slave that he is a slave and he will revolt against his slavery' was the Ambedkar hope. He told his fellow men:[2]

> My heart breaks to see the pitiable sight of your faces and to hear your sad voices. You have been groaning from immemorial and yet you are not ashamed to hug your helplessness as an inevitability. Why did you not perish in the prenatal stage instead? Why do you worsen and sadden the picture of the sorrows, poverty, slavery and burdens of the world with your deplorable, despicable, detestable, and miserable life? You had better died and relieved this world if you could not rejuvenate yourself. As a matter of fact, it is your birthright to get food, shelter and clothing in equal proportion with every individual, high or low. If you believe in living a respectable life you should believe in self-help which is the best help.

Again he even referred to French and American instances and urged:[3]

> We are demanding equal rights which are the common possession of the entire humanity but due to inhibitions created by the Shastras we have been denied these human rights. I am telling you that wherever human rights were snatched away, there, battles and bloodshed and wars were fought and bloodshed was witnessed. In case of France when the nobles denied the human rights to the lower class people, they massacred the enables until they finally won the battle. The battle was continued for more than ten years. In America too, the American people fought the civil war, in order to emancipate the Negroes from slavery. In the civil war, those who died did so after doing certain noble deeds. Those who

> remained alive enjoyed the happiness of free men. Such a kind of battle was required in order to restitute the lost human rights. But, I do not understand how our people, even thought they were put to injustice, mortification, and insults, still, how they could tolerate them like a humanity, and like a submissive cow. We never feel sorry, we never get annoyed and we never realise and insults. Even though they were put to injustice, mortification, and insults, still, how they could tolerate them like a dumb lot of humanity, and like a submissive cow. We never feel sorry, we never get annoyed and we never realise the insults.
>
> We are self-satisfied, even though we have been kicked by the caste Hindu people. What are the reasons which made dead in mentality and spirit? I find we do not have sufficient knowledge and wisdom, and secondly, we do not have economic, social and physical strength. whoever, has knowledge, wisdom and strength is capable of tyrannizing those who do not have either of them. Therefore, the particular code of conduct was assigned to us by those who had knowledge, wisdom and strength. I am very sorry to say because of the ignorance, gullibility and utter submissiveness, we are suffering these injustices. As we are not conscious of the heritage acquired by the humanity we made our position deplorable, helpless, and hapless and therefore, we are facing the difficulties of food, cloth and the place of shelter even though India is a country which is called a golden country. In the midst of plenty, we are poverty-stricken. I, therefore, given you the clarion call not to be satisfied, that you should not be satisfied, self-complacent and be the worshipper of the old value. I do not want, whatever the ancestral deeds, we should do the same thing. We have to change the present situation. When we change the present situation I am sure, the code of conduct forced on us will also change. If you do not change, then it will be quite impossible for us to fight against the odd circumstances. Don't believe in time. Don't believe in accidents and coincidence. Believe that man is the creator of history, and he can come out successful, not withstanding the odd circumstances.

His passion for liberation of Indian women persuaded him to change the Hindu law comprehensively and emancipate Hindu womanhood. He drafted the comprehensive Code, but orthodox opposition mounted and Nehru faltered, leading to Ambedkar's resignation. He wrote:[4]

> For a long time I have been thinking of resigning my seat from the Cabinet. The only thing that had held me back from giving effect to my intention was the hope that it would be possible to give effect to the Hindu code bill before the life of the present Parliament came to an end. I even agreed to break up the bill and restricted it to Marriage and Divorce in the fond hope that at least this much of our labour may bear fruit. But even that part of the bill has been killed. I see no purpose in my continuing to be a member of your Cabinet.

Ambedkar's concluding speech in the Constituent Assembly unfolds the constructive edifice of thought built on the foundation of eradication of inequality:[5]

> These downtrodden classes are tired of being governed. They are impatient to govern themselves. This urge for self-realisation in the downtrodden classes must not be allowed to devolve into a class struggle or class war. It would lead to a division of the house that would indeed be a day of disaster. For, as has been well said by Abraham Lincoln, a house divided against itself cannot stand very long. Therefore, the sooner room is made for the realisation of their aspiration, the better for the few, the better for the country, the better for the maintenance of its independence and the better for the continuance of its democratic structure. This can only be done by the establishment of equality and fraternity in all spheres of life. That is why I have laid so much stress on them.

Even on the political side, he opposed the cult of personality and upheld the positive side of equal status for each in democracy. The following is his eloquence in the Constituent Assembly:

> The second thing we must do is to observe the caution which John Staurt Mill has given to all who are interested in the maintenance of democracy, namely, not to lay their liberties at the feet of even a great man, or to trust him with powers which enable him to subvert their institutions. There is nothing wrong in being grateful to great men who have rendered life-long services to the country. But there are limits to gratefulness. As has been well said by the Irish patriot Daniel O'Connell, no man can be grateful at the cost of his honour, no woman can be grateful at the cost of her chastity and no nation can be grateful

at the cost of its liberty. This caution is far more necessary in the case of India than in the case of any other country. For in India, *bhakti* or what may be called the path of devotion or hero-worship plays a part it plays in the politics unequal in magnitude by the part it plays in the politics of any other country in the world. *Bhakti* in religion may be a road to toe salvation of the soul. But in politics, Bhakti or hero-worship is a sure road to degradation and to eventual dictatorship.

For him, humanity was the centre even more importantly than nation, a position he explained in the Constituent Assembly:[6]

> I remember the days when politically minded Indians resented the expression 'the people of India'. They preferred the expression 'the Indian nation'. I am of opinion that in believing that we are a nation, we are cherishing a great delusion. How can people divided into several thousands of castes be a nation? The sooner we realise that we are not as yet a nation in the social and psychological sense of the word, the better for us. For then only we shall realize the necessity of becoming a nation and seriously think of ways and means of realising the goal. The realisation of this goal is going to be very difficult-far more difficult that it has been in the United States. The United States has no caste problem. In India there are castes. These castes are anti-national: in the first place because they bring about separation in social life. They are anti-national also because they generate jealousy and antipathy between caste and caste. But we must overcome all these difficulties if we wish to become a nation in reality. For fraternity can be a fact only when there is a nation. Without fraternity, equality and liberty will be no deeper than coats of paint.

How true are these far-sighted observations even today! If you realise the import of his point, you will understand the disintegrative crisis of our country in its current phase:[7]

> It was due to the reason that, a patriot and a nationalist in India is one who sees with open eyes his fellowmen treated as being less than men. But his humanity does not rise in protest. He knows that men and women for no cause are denied their human rights. But it does not prick his civic sense to helpful action. He finds whole classes of people shut out from public

> employment. But it does not rouse his sense of justice and fair-play. Hundreds of evil practices that injure man and society are perceived by him. But they do not sicken him with disgust. The patriot's one cry is power for him and for his class. I am glad I do not belong to that class of which takes its stand on democracy and which seeks to destroy monopoly in every shape and form. Our aim is to realize in practice our ideal of one man, one value in all walks of life-political, economic and social.

All these ideas, destructive and constructive, but complementary and holistic, find meaningful expression in the Constitution. Nevertheless, the SC/ST community, with its more than hundred members in Parliament, are too meek, too weak, too politically genuflective and cringe for crumbs of corrupt power to radicalise the socio-economic structure. For instance, the land question in most states excludes the landless. Why are they? The SC/ST by and large. Ambedkar had insisted on destructive a justice vis-a-vis land. But the self-seeking in these communities cash in on Ambedkar, but do not resist the terrible and traumatic infliction on their brethren. The Dalit's future is still dark and dubious because their parliamentary surrogates make noises but obey the high-caste parties when it comes to action. The *varna dharma* is still a fact of life in India and no political Dalit has yet threatened to fight or quit when their girls are molested or sold, their boys are made to serve as serfs and their hamlets are burned to ashes. Ambedkar will not forgive the Dalit MPs for not heeding his simple logic.

Can it be said that the proletariat of India, poor as it is, recognise no distinction except that of rich and poor, can it be said that the poor in India recognise no such distinction as caste or creed, high or low?

Ambedkar further speaks:

> No intellectual class has prostituted its intelligence to invent a philosophy to keep its uneducated countrymen in a perceptual states of ignorance and poverty as have done in India.

In sum, a realistic appraisal of Ambedkar comes from Nehru:

> Dr Ambedkar will be remembered as a symbol of revolt against the oppressive features of the Hindu society. His virulent

opposition to these oppressive features and kept peoples mind awake. Although he was highly controversial figure, yet he played a very constructive role in making of the Constitution of India and Hindu Law Reform.

Gandhiji called him 'a patriot of sterling worth'. I regard him as a current version of the Buddha's trinity of values—*pragna* (disceming rejection of superstition), *karuna* (dynamic compassion), and *samata* (egalite). Let me quote Ambedkar himself:

> Negatively, I reject the Hindu Social Philosophy propounded in the *Bhagavat Geeta* based as it is, on the *triguna* of the Sankhya philosophy which is in my judgment a cruel perversion of the philosophy of Kapila and had made the caste system and the system of graded inequality the law of Hindu social life. Positively, my social philosophy may be said to be enshrined in three words: liberty, equality and fraternity. Let no one however say that I have borrowed my philosophy from the French Revolution. I have not, my philosophy has roots in religion and not in political science. I have derived them from the teachings of my master—the Buddha.

He substantially agreed with the Marxist creed except for violence, dictatorship of the proletariat, and godlessness, perhaps. He observed:

> Buddhism is a true religion and I will lead a life guided by the three principles of knowledge, right path and compassion. Buddhism teaches *prajna* (understanding against superstition and supernaturalism), *karuna* (love) and *samata* (equality). This is what man wants for good and happy life. Neither God nor soul can save the society.

Humanism and Buddhism, liberty and fraternity, materialism divinised by spiritualism, if imbibed by society, that social order will be the finest tribute to Ambedkar. Alas, his centenary celebrations by hypocrites, high caste Hindus and publicity-hunting ministers are phony. Indeed, Ambedkar centenary is administered as the opium of the Dalits. Arise, awake, unite and battle, regardless of party policies, for that militant humanism in action, which is the banner of revolt and reconstruction, Ambedkar held.

His destructive-constructive war for rehumanisation, on a systematic basis, is best expressed in his off quoted words sublime:

> My final words of advice to you is educate, agitate and organise, have faith in yourself. With justice on our side, I do not see how we can lose our battle. The battle to me is a matter of joy. The battle is in the fullest sense spiritual. There is nothing material or social in it. For ours is a battle not for wealth or for power. It is a battle for freedom. It is a battle for the reclamation of the human personality.

Notes

1. Sudarshan Agarwal, Secretary-General, Rajya Sabha in the preface to the book *Dr. B.R. Ambedkar: The Man and His Message*.
2. Lokhande, G.S., *Dr. B.R. Ambedkar: A Study in Social Democracy*, New Delhi: Sterling Publishers, 1982, p. 171.
3. Ibid., pp. 171–172.
4. Ibid., p. 207.
5. Concluding speech of Dr. Ambedkar in the Constituent Assembly on 25 November 1949.
6. Ibid.
7. Speech before the Round Table Conference, pp. 438–441.

21

Ambedkar

An Architect of Indian Constitution

Rega Jaganmohana Rao

The Indian Constitution is the supreme law of the land that has provided us a Sovereign Democratic Republic, committed to the concept of a welfare state based on egalitarian values in which people are the masters through their representatives in the Parliament responsible for democratic governance in the country. The draft Constitution was the result of the collective efforts of a galaxy of great leaders, legal scholars and luminaries in the Constituent Assembly such as Jawaharlal Nehru, Rajendra Prasad, Sardar Patel, B.R. Ambedkar, Sir Alladi Krishnaswamy Ayyar etc. who successfully enacted the document under the stewardship of Ambedkar as the chairman of the Drafting Committee. The law of the land was finally adopted on 26 November 1949 and came into force on 26 January 1950 which marked the beginning of a new era in the history of India. Handing over the historic document, Ambedkar said: 'If we wish to maintain democracy not merely in form, but also in fact what we must do?... . We must ... hold fast to constitutional methods of achieving our socio-economic objectives where constitutional methods are open, there can be no justification for unconstitutional methods. These methods are nothing but the grammar of anarchy, and the sooner we abandon the better for us'.

While assessing the towering personality of Ambedkar, A.M. Rajashekaraiah said:

> Dr Ambedkar's contribution to the evolution of free India lies in his striving for secularising Indian politics, state and society; and his struggle for making out justice—political, social and economic—to one and all as a humanist. He breathed the spirit of liberalism and nationalism into the lives of not only untouchables, but of all Indians... . He was a nationalist, democrat and a patriot par excellence. He proved to be a great statesman... . His courage and conviction was something astounding, which would not bend him down to compromising his principles even for the sake of his people ... . In his capacity as the chairman of the Drafting Committee, he hammered out a comprehensive workable Constitution into which he incorporated some of his views, 'though not all of them. He gave free India its legal frame, and the people, the basis of their freedom. To this end his contribution was significant, substantial and spectacular'.[1]

The above passage reflects the relevance and significance of Ambedkarism in the making of the Constitution of India in the process of which Ambedkar played the key-role as the chairman of the Drafting Committee with the help and assistance of the other great stalwarts, such as Pt. Nehru, B.N. Rao, Sir Alladi, etc. whose contribution was no less significant in the making of the Indian Constitution and building up a comprehensive legal frame for free India.

The purpose of this paper is to examine mainly the question as to how far the philosophy of Ambedkarism (Ambedkar's socio-economic and constitutional philosophy etc.) is reflected in the Indian Constitution. Apart from highlighting the significant role played by Ambedkar in making the Constitution of India which is described as a Sovereign, Democratic, Secular and Socialist Republic, an attempt is made to examine how the Government of India is committed to the establishment of an egalitarian social order based on the famous 'trinity' of principles—liberty, equality, fraternity on the foundations of which Ambedkar's social (economic) democracy is sought to be built up.

The commendable service rendered by Ambedkar in piloting the draft Constitution passing through the very rough and tough weather of the Constituent Assembly sessions, was universally acclaimed and acknowledged by all sections of India and in which he exhibited great erudition and skill in constitutional law and other related disciplines such as history, economics, sociology and anthropology. His concern for the enrichment of the principles of liberty, equality, fraternity and social justice would be manifested in his statement that, 'to have inequality between class and class, between sex and sex, which is the soul of Hindu society untouched and to go on passing legislations relating to socio-economic problem is to make farce of our Constitution'.

The Constitution of India provides for a sovereign, secular, democratic socialist republican form of government committed to establish an egalitarian social order based on the principles of equality (socio-economic and political) and liberty (of thought and expression). It provides for a legal mandate in the form of fundamental rights and directive principles of State policy with a view to promote respect for fundamental human rights, such as freedom of speech, right to equality, right to life and liberty and to preserve and protect the interests of the Scheduled Castes and Scheduled Tribes in order to ameliorate the conditions of the neglected sections in the Indian society.

The very Preamble of the Constitution echoes the egalitarian principles of social justice, equality, liberty and fraternity on the foundations of which the so-called parliamentary democracy and welfare state are built up. And the V and VI Schedules and Part XVI of the Constitution contain the provisions for the promotion of welfare and well-being of the Scheduled Tribes.

Federalism

The Constitution provides for federal structure and parliamentary form of government on the lines of the Government of India Act, 1935. Ambedkar was a strong advocate of federal structure of the union and states and staunch supporter of parliamentary democracy based on the principles of strong centre and independent states. Ambedkar's social democracy comprises politicians, political parties with high standards of political morality, honesty and integrity, and strong and highly responsible opposition party or parties committed to the cause of the downtrodden and the depressed classes. Ambedkar also did great service to the nation by proposing the institution of unified judicial system (single judiciary) starting from down court to high court and high courts to the apex court—the Supreme Court of India, uniformity in laws, and common All India Services with a view to strengthen the national unity and integrity.

Pleading in support of a strong Centre, Ambedkar said: 'The basic principle of federalism is that the legislative and executive authority is partitioned between the Centre and the states not by any law to be made but by the Constitution itself. The states are in no way dependent upon the Centre for their legislation or executive authority. The states and the Centre are co-equal in this regard.' It was his strong belief that federalism would rest on a balance between the Centre and the federal units. What is needed is neither complete independence nor total dependence, but inter dependence that creates harmony, orderly progress and prosperity. Unity while allowing diversity, oneness while providing for diversion, is the outstanding characteristic of modem federalism.[2]

Ambedkar firmly believed that a federal state is an institutional means for the solution of human affairs. The federalism means an ideal polity with the union at the Centre and states at the periphery. It does not mean a league of small states united in a loose relationship nor the agencies of the Union Government deriving powers form it. Both the union and the state governments derive authority from the Constitution.

The Indian Constitution has accordingly adopted a mid-way between centralisation and decentralisation of power for the reason that (1) there is a clear demarcation of governmental powers between the Centre and the states; (2) each government is independent of the other in its own field; and (3) the Constitution has provided for an independent judiciary for settling disputes between the union and the states in respect of division of powers. Ambedkar's concept of federalism is that the state is a federation in normal times and turns into unitary type in emergency. According to him, the term 'Indian Union' means that the Indian Federation is not the result of an agreement by the units, and that the component units have no freedom to secede from it and the union should be strong, stable, capable of holding together irrespective of state loyalties and thereby such a union of states lead to national unity and integrity.

Parliamentary Democracy

Ambedkar was a strong advocate of parliamentary form of government right from the inception of Government of India Act of 1935. He believed in the peaceful democratic methods of legislation, persuasion, discussion, consensus, etc. as the most appropriate means for achieving socio-economic change. He firmly believed that the parliamentary system of government alone can usher in an egalitarian society through the application of principles of social democracy, such as socio-economic justice and equality amongst the people.

Ambedkar was of the view that the essential pillars for the successful functioning of parliamentary system of government are:

1. For the successful functioning of the democracy, active, functional opposition is required. Responsible and complete opposition party is the key to free political life. No democracy can function successfully without such an opposition party.
2. The second pillar of parliamentary democracy is free and fair elections.

In the absence of these two pillars of democracy or in the absence of any one of these, democracy degenerates into mobocracy and dictatorship in the name of democratic form of government.

The Preamble of our Constitution echoes the principles of parliamentary democracy. It reads:

We, THE PEOPLE OF INDIA, having solemnly resolved to constitute India into a SOVEREIGN (SOCIALIST SECULAR)[3] DEMOCRATIC REPUBLIC and to secure to all its citizens:

JUSTICE, social, economic and political;

LIBERTY of thought, expression, belief, faith and worship;

EQUALITY of status and of opportunity; and to promote among them all;

FRATERNITY assuring the dignity of the individual and the unity (and integrity)[4] of the nation.

Pandit Jawaharlal Nehru, our first Prime Minister, emphasised the above principles while presenting a resolution on the aims and objectives of the newly adopted draft Constitution, before the Constituent Assembly. He further urged the House to adopt the resolution without any protest or amendment.

Ambedkar, though conscious of the inherent defects of parliamentary democracy, preferred it as the best model suitable to conditions in India. The major weakness of this system is that essential changes like the realisation of social and economic justice and equality cannot be expedited and promises made could be fulfilled only at a slow pace. This naturally leads to the discontentment and unrest among the people who may in turn revolt against the system and result in violent methods. Therefore, watchful, vigilant public opinion, and effective implementation of laws and responsible executive, committed legislature, and impartial judiciary are very much essential to the success of parliamentary democracy. Hence, Ambedkar sounded a note of warning many a time that if parliamentary democracy fails to bring socio-economic justice, the result would be anarchy, rebellion and bloodshed.[5] In particular, the plight of the weaker sections—the poorest of the poor, will have to be immediately attended to. Then only the fruits of democracy can be realised. Thus, Ambedkar was very much against dictatorship and all forms of force and coercion. He would only welcome democratic form of government despite its drawbacks.

Ambedkar, after pointing out the pitfalls of democracy, made certain positive suggestions for its successful working. These are:

1. Every democratic form of government aiming at the welfare of all people must not allow dynastic rule or hereditary authoritarian, autocratic rule to grow under its umbrella of welfare and well-being of the people. The government should always struggle for the common good of all its citizens of the country irrespective of caste, creed, religion or region.
2. The presence of a responsible and equally committed opposition party to act as a check on the excessive, authoritarian, autocratic tendencies of an otherwise well formulated democratic form of government.

3. The adoption of the principle of quality, equal treatment in administrative, legislative matters and equal protection of laws must be the heart and soul of any successful government.
4. He strongly believed that democracy, whether the parliamentary or presidential form, federal or unitary type, or both mixed up together, would only survive when healthy conventions based on moral principles are evolved. No democratic form of government shall survive, without observing the principles of constitutional morality, such as fair method of election, with honesty and integrity, etc.

The constitutional morality would also mean an effective coordination between conflicting interests of different people and the administrative cooperation to resolve them amicably without any confrontation amongst the various groups working for the realisation of their ends at any cost. For Ambedkar, moral fabric of the society, governed as well as the governance must be strong. In other words, public conscience, moral order and constitutional morality, ethics of politicians, that constitute the core of policy-making, must be very sound and strong if democracy is to survive for long period of progress and prosperity for the common people.

Fundamental Rights

The third part of the Indian Constitution guarantees the fundamental rights to the citizens/persons against the State. The novel feature of this part is:

1. These are the rights against the Central government, Parliament, State government and state legislature local and other authorities within the territory of India (Article 12).
2. Some of the rights contained in Articles 15(2), 17, 23 and 24 are also enforceable against the individuals as they are very significant rights relating to the prohibition of 'discrimination on grounds of religions, race, caste, sex or place or birth, forced labour and employment, etc.'.

The national leaders like Mahatma Gandhi, Jawaharlal Nehru and B.R. Ambedkar, being influenced by western ideals of 'equality and egalitarianism' of Rousseau and John Stuart Mill, rejected the basis of Hindu orthodoxy and preached the gospel of equality in national movement.[6] Ambedkar espousing the cause of

Backward Classes declared that caste inequality is man-made rather than ordained by God. It was mainly because of his dramatisation of the cause of the depressed classes the Constitution included the policy of compensatory discrimination. Explaining the significance of including Article 16(4), he said:

> The drafting committee has taken (all) the care to safeguard the principles of equality of opportunity, and at the same time to satisfy the demand of communities which have not been represented in the service under the state.[7]

During the deliberation on the passage of part III of the Constitution, Ambedkar said:

> ... the most criticised part of the constitution is that which relates to fundamental rights. It is said that Article 13 (now Article 19) which deals with fundamental freedoms, is riddled with so many expositions that the exceptions have eaten up the rights altogether. It is condemned as a kind of deception. In the opinion of critics fundamental rights are fundamental unless they are also absolute rights in the 'American Bill of Rights' as real because they are not subjected to limitation or exceptions. l am sorry to say that the whole criticism is based on misconception. It is incorrect to say that the fundamental rights are absolute. The real distinction between the two is that non-fundamental rights are the gift of the law, and the fundamental rights are the gift of the constitution which has got every authority, interest of the state or its people to qualify them.[8]

The most significant feature of the fundamental rights is that these rights are made 'justifiable'. The right to move the Supreme Court for enforcement of fundamental rights under Article 32 is itself a fundamental right. Article 32 authorises the Supreme Court to not only issue directions, orders or writs in the nature of habeas corpus, mandamus, certioraris, etc. or any other appropriate remedy as the case may be for the enforcement of fundamental rights guaranteed by the Constitution. These Constitutional remedies are similar to those suggested by Ambedkar in Clause I of Section II. Without Article 32, the insertion of fundamental rights in the Constitution would have become meaningless as rights are real only if they are accompanied by remedies.[9] Explaining the importance of Article 32, he observed:

> ... I am very glad that the majority of those who spoke on this Article have realised the importance and significance of this Article ... without which Article, the constitution would be a nullity ... . It is the very heart of it and I am glad that the house has realised its importance.[10]

Directive Principles

One of the distinctive features of the Indian Constitution is the enunciation of directive principles of State policy. Ambedkar explained the scope of directive principles as follows:

> The directive principles are like the instruments of instructions which were issued to the Governor General and the Governors of Colonies, and those of India, by the British Government under the Government of India Act, 1935. What is called 'directive principles' is merely another name for the instruments of instructions to the legislature and the executive. Whoever captures power will not be free to do what he likes with it. In the exercise of it he will have to respect these instruments of instructions which are called directive principles.[11]

Refuting the criticism, that whatever be the ethical or political value of the directive principles, they have no place in the Constitution because they are only pious declarations, Ambedkar observed that:

> ... the directive principles of State policy may not be enforceable in a court of law, but the principles laid down therein are the essence of egalitarianism, and hence are equally fundamental as the Centre and the state are directed to apply them in the actual governance of the country in order to usher in the new social and economic order in India.[12]

According to Ambedkar, the directive principles have a great value for they lay down that our ideal is economic democracy.[13] Because we do not want merely a parliamentary form of government, though the mechanism provided in the Constitution, without any direction as what our social order ought to be, we deliberately included the directive principles in our Constitution. Our object in framing this Constitution is really two-fold:

1. to lay down the form of political democracy, and
2. to lay down that our ideal is economic democracy and also to prescribe that every government what ever it is in power, shall strive to bring about economic democracy.

Position of the President

Dealing with the question what the position of the president under the Indian Constitution is, Ambedkar said that:

> ... the President of India occupies the same position as the king under the English Constitution. He is the head of the state but not of the executive. He represents the nation, but does not rule the nation.[14]

These words of the founding father of the Constitution make it clear that the president is the titular head and the prime minister is the real head who really rules the country in the sense of the term. What he means is that the president is only the constitutional head of the State, and the prime minister is the *de facto* head of not only the Council of Ministers, but also of the entire country. The real power, therefore, rests in the prime minister.

The Constitutional Mandate

The real contribution of Ambedkar is reflected in the protective discrimination scheme or the reservation policy of the government envisaged under some provisions of part III (fundamental rights), and many of part IV provisions dealing with the constitutional mandate to ameliorate the conditions of the so-called Scheduled Castes and Scheduled Tribes and the other Backward Classes. Provisions like Article 17 prohibiting untouchability, Article 30 dealing with the protection of minorities, Article 32 guaranteeing the citizens constitutional-right to enforce the fundamental rights in courts of law etc. are some of the notable examples.

Articles 15(4) and 16(4) of part III and part XI, and Schedules V and VI dealing with the upliftment of Scheduled Castes and Scheduled Tribes speak clearly about the substantial and significant contribution of Ambedkar for the development of the unfortunate Untouchables who continue to suffer under the clutches of caste imperialists and religious fundamentalists of modem India.

Thus, these significant contributions of Ambedkar, the illustrious son of India and the unquestioned leader of the downtrodden depressed classes of people in India, one can very easily discern the impact of western political philosophy and culture on the personality of Ambedkar which he imbibed during his stay mostly in USA and England. And therefore, the original contribution of Ambedkar we find in his life mission, the abhorrent and inhuman practice of untouchability developed. Undoubtedly, the unique contribution of Ambedkar could be seen from the relentless battle he fought like 'Bhima of Mahabharat' against the social leprosy in the form of casteism, untouchability and Hindu religious fundamentalism manifested in the abominal practice of 'Chatur Varna' or 'Vanrasrama Dharma' placing the three high castes—Brahmins, Kshatriyas and Vaisyas—on the higher pedestal relegating the Hindu religious minorities, such as the unfortunate Untouchables to the inferior positions of inhuman professions like sweeping, scavenging and thus cleaning the dirt and filth of the villages and towns. Therefore, he made it his life mission to uplift the Untouchables and the other downtrodden masses from the unequal position of inferiority to that of unequal position of parity in socio-economic status with other high caste Hindus. It was for achieving this goal the reservation policy or the scheme of protective discrimination was advocated and achieved by him for 10 years at least to ameliorate the conditions of the various depressed and downtrodden sections of Hindu society. It would be a matter of great interest to note here that Ambedkar was against the policy of perpetual reservation system for the simple reason that it would perpetuate inferiority amongst the reserved categories who should develop themselves on the basis of self-reliance and self-help by developing self-confidence but not on the charity of somebody else. Reservation policy is not a matter of charity but a legal obligation on the part of the government to improve the lot of the innocent neglected sections of Indian population. Being a great humanist, he always stood for very high standard of human values, dignity of human persons or individual. However, his struggle for fundamental human freedom and the socio-economic emancipation of Untouchables, his dream about the creation of an egalitarian social order still remains an unfulfilled wishful thinking despite the extended period of reservations for SCs and STs for another four decades and the same was extended to 50 years in January 1990 by 62nd Amendment to the Constitution of India. And hence, the plea for retention of reservations for SC and ST so long as untouchability continues. It is also argued by legal scholars like Justice Krishna Iyer that the required change and development amongst Untouchables and other backward sections, and the cherished goal of egalitarian social order cannot be achieved unless and until the forward among backward and the elitist groups amongst SCs and STs are eliminated and the constitutional mandate is strictly carried out with commitment seriousness and sincerity by the executive entrusted with the onerous task of implementation of the scheme.

The Constitution of India has sustained all these years and passed through critical and turbulent periods in the history of our nation. The Constitution is not bad and unworkable, it is the men who are incharge of it that matters.[15]

Notes

1. Rajasekharaiah, A.M., *Dr. Ambedkar and the Politics of Emancipation*, Bombay: Sindhu Publications, 1971, pp. 326–327.
2. Pylee, M.V., *Constitutional Government in India*, New Delhi: S. Chand & Company Ltd., 1984, p. 269.
3. The Constitution (42nd Amendment) Act of 1976 added the words 'Socialist and Secular'.
4. Similarly, for the words 'Unity of the Nation', the words 'Unity and Integrity of the Nation' were substituted.
5. This reminds us about the recent revolutionary changes that have taken place in the various countries in Eastern Europe. In Romania and Poland there is mass upsurge leading to liberation of political set-up and ending up of the party rule. Similarly, East and West Germany united to become one Germany State.
6. Singh, Paramanand, *Equality, Reservations and Discrimination*, New Delhi: Deep & Deep Publications, p. 10, 1982.
7. Constituent Assembly Debates, Vol. VII, pp. 707–712.
8. Ibid., pp. 40–41.

9. Ahir, D.C., *Dr. Ambedkar and the Indian Constitution*, Buddha Vihara, Lucknow, 1973, p. 93.
10. Constitution Assembly Debates, Vol. VII, p. 953.
11. Ibid., pp. 41–42.
12. Ibid.
13. Ahir, D.C., *Dr. Ambedkar and the Indian Constitution*, op. cit., pp. 101–102. See also Constituent Assembly Debates, Vol. VII, pp. 494–495.
14. Ibid., p. 39.
15. Ibid., p. 61.

22

Sixty-Five Years of Indian Constitution

A Prolegomenon of Social Justice

K.S. Chalam

The NDA I government was in a crisis in getting some of their bills passed as they did not have sufficient numbers in Rajya Sabha (they have secured the numbers in 2014). Therefore they were thinking of calling for a joint session to muster the numbers. But, the Constituent Assembly was very clear in getting this provision in the Constitution saying that the Rajya Sabha, being an elders house and permanent, should consider issues of durable significance for the future of the nation and not to meet the petty interests of some self-centred groups or individuals. It is time to review some of the salient features of the Constitution particularly with reference to social justice on the eve of the completion of 65 years of its presence in guiding the destiny of the nation.

The Indian sub-continent was considered during the first half of the twentieth century as the most dynamic and politically volatile part of the world. It was not only due to the post-war conditions and anti-colonial struggles of the people, but also due to the emergence of leadership from among the subaltern. It is destiny that made the sub-continent to become India and Pakistan. It is in the process of nation-building that the two countries have embarked upon constitution-making as the first step. It is ironical that both the countries have elected the Scheduled Castes leaders as the chairmen of the Drafting Committee of the Constitution. Dr B.R. Ambedkar was elected as chairman of the Drafting committee of India and Dr Jogendranath Mandal was made chairman of the Constituent Assembly of Pakistan and the 1st Law Minister. In fact, both of them were elected from Bengal and the *namasudras* have played an important role in their election. The history of the sub-continent was crueller to Jogendranath Mandal than any one of his contemporaries as his name is not even remembered by the Dalits themselves. Pakistan Dalits remember him for the concessions he got from Jinnah. However, the two Dalit leaders emerging as the Constitution-makers of two important countries of Asia have something fundamental and common. This may be kept in mind while evaluating the achievements and failures of the constitutional law in India and Pakistan.

Amendments to the Constitution

The Constitution of India was amended 108 times by 2003. The Constitution was amended three times within 5 years of its adoption. Therefore, Dr B.R. Ambedkar in his parliamentary debates in the Rajya Sabha on 15 September 1954 has said that, 'I do not know of any Constitution in the world which has been amended so rapidly and if, I may say so rashly, by the government in office … . Is the Constitution not different in any sense from an ordinary law? Is it merely a scrap paper to be amended at whim of anybody? I have been noticing the great contempt or the low regard or respect which the government has for the Constitution'. Thus, the chairman of the drafting committee himself was disillusioned with the attitude of the elected representatives of the ruling class and also the legislative wing of the government, but even the judiciary seems to have the same attitude towards the provisions of the Constitution, particularly with reference to the economic and social clauses. Therefore, one need not wonder that the onslaught on the Constitution will remain perpetual and eternal. Let us look at the history of the process of erosion of the constitutional morality and the context in order to understand the reasons for the amendments.

Increasing Needs of the State

It is necessary to take into consideration the growing needs of the modern state in its attempt to amend a written Constitution. But that does not mean that the state can rush for a Constitution amendment without exhausting first the available alternative means to achieve an economic or social objective. In fact, it is alleged by scholars that the elected governments are slowly becoming agents of interest groups or representatives of class interests rather than demonstrating the vision of an enlightened society. The contradictions were present even during the framing of the Constitution particularly with reference to the Right to Property. Before the Article 31 was dumped in 1978 through the 44th amendment, there was great debate in the constituent Assembly. Dr Ambedkar has noted that there were three groups within the Congress party to use the article to their advantage. It was Jawaharlal Nehru who was against compensation. But Pant was interested in the Zamindar Abolition and Sardar Patel was arguing for full compensation. Therefore, Dr Ambedkar himself was interested in the first amendment to the Constitution to facilitate land reforms. But, the landed interests seem to have entered the mindset of the judiciary and created problems for the effective implementation of economic programmes that led the Indira Gandhi government to amend the Constitution to bring Article 300A and drop Article 31. This was necessitated due to the needs of the emerging society. In fact Dr Ambedkar had agreed with the idea of an evolving nation of Thomas Jefferson and quoted him n his parliamentary debates. It is said that 'each generation as a distinct nation, with a right, by the will of the majority to bind themselves ... each generation has a right to determine the law under which it lives'. Here one must underline the difference between the will of the majority and the whims of the major lobbies that in general came from the propertied classes. A cursory analysis of the judicial pronouncements and the comments made by legal experts clearly indicate the flaws in some of the judgments. In this context, we can quote what learned Shiv Shankar, former Minister of Law and Justice, had said about it. In a very thought provoking article, Rakesh Sukla in the 2 September 2006 issue of *Economic and Political Weekly* quoted Shiva Shankar to point out the feudal mindset of some of our honourable judges. It is noted that 'Mathadipatis like Keshvananda and Zamindars like Gorak Nath evoked a sympathetic cord nowhere in the whole country except in the Supreme Court of India. And the bank magnates, the representatives of the elitist culture of this country, ably supported by industrialists, the beneficiaries of independence, got higher compensation by the intervention of the Supreme Court in Cooper case. Antisocial elements, i.e. FERA violators, bride burners and a whole lot of reactionaries have found their haven in the Supreme Court'. This comment by a legal luminary and a former Minister of Law of the country indicate the position of our judiciary vis-à-vis the Constitution. Recently, I had an opportunity to share the dais with Ram Jeth Malani, former Law Minister, at the golden jubilee celebrations of the Department of Law at Mumbai University on 24 April 2010. He was quoting judgement after judgement in his presentation to substantiate his argument that how the judicial pronouncements helped to plunder the common property resources of the country, particularly in the tribal areas of India. In fact, he has vindicated what Shiva Shankar had said long ago.

Concept of Private Property

In this context, we may find how Dr Ambedkar as a visionary realised the limitations of constitutional provisions and anticipated the contradictions in our social and economic life. Therefore he gave a social and economic agenda in his 'States and Minorities' as he thought that some of his ideas could not be brought under the Constitution due to the competing groups in the constituent assembly. He wanted agricultural land to be nationalised and the commanding heights of the economy to be placed under the control of the public sector. Perhaps he was expecting that some of his dreams would be realised through the implementation of the provisions of the Constitution. But, the executive and the judiciary, the two important pillars of Indian democracy, delegated with the responsibility of translating the provisions of the Constitution into reality seem to have failed. It is a well-known fact that the special bench of the Supreme Court in the case of Bank Nationalisation Act 1969 struck down the Act on the grounds that it did not have certain principles of adequate compensation. It is not only in the case of Bank nationalisation but even in the area of other economic issues; the Supreme Court seems to have remained always with the property classes. It is strange that neither the courts nor the intelligentsia have ever looked at the concept of private property in India. They have simply adopted the principles as observed in the Anglo-Saxon countries particularly the USA where the conditions are different. India never had the concept of private property before the permanent settlement. The laws in USA are alien to India as they were framed by the settlers to get legal sanction of grabbing property of the natives without the moral authority. The native Indians who were basically the *Adivasis* and Dalits kept outside the purview of land settlement during the British regime both in the princely states as well as in the British India government. Even the land held by these sections obtained through the alienation proceedings are now being taken away by the government using the principles of 'eminent domain'. The compensation paid to the displaced persons is based on the colonial Land Acquisition Act 1894. Even in the calculation of valuation of compensation to the owner of the property, the economic principles of law of diminishing marginal utility is not considered and the value of the property of a zamindar, a rich peasant or a small farmer are considered as similar. This is a great flaw in the Indian legal system. Further, the value of the property is now converted into liquid form in stocks and shares. The intensity of this kind of conversion and their transfer to other countries has increased several folds after 1991. The judiciary seems to have not commented much on these issues except in the recent judgment of K.G. Balakrishnan wherein he endorsed the right of the State to natural resources. The issue of compensation and Right to Life are becoming serious issues in the process of rapid economic development. The State is increasingly considered as an agency of a class or caste is considered by activist scholars, would be seized of limited vision about the future of the victims. The Dalits and *Adivasis* are now left with limited opportunities in a growing private sector and their displacement from the existing sources of livelihood such as land, traditional skills and other sources (with an agenda of capitalist expansion) will be double marginalised. It is in this context, the provisions of the Constitution need to be ingeniously and effectively interpreted by the judiciary to protect the common man in general and the Dalits and *Adivasis* in particular. In are era of judge made law verdict based on precedent replacing constitutional wisdom, the ingenuity and enlightened outlook of the judiciary is the last resort for the victims. Otherwise, the dominant groups and the propertied classes who are increasingly getting into the legislature will make and unmake constitutional amendments to suit their self or class interests. This may be kept in mind in pronouncing judgments on constitutional issues so as to restrict the vested interests and not to mend or amend constitutional wisdom.

Social Justice and the Constitution

The socially and educationally deprived sections of the society have reposed greatest confidence in the Constitution with the belief that it will come to their rescue in times of impingement. Therefore, the evaluation of the process of constitutional support to the poor and underprivileged and socially and historically marginalised groups can be attempted in terms of the judicial activism in social laws. It is in this context, the Supreme Court judgement pronounced by Chief Justice Y.K. Sabharwal and 4 other hon'ble judges evoked wide publicity and discussion in the media. However, some of the observers and intellectuals have been saying that once the State has accepted and executed the lopsided judgement delivered in the case of Mandal Commission, it is inevitable to expect a judgement of this kind for SCs and STs also. Some scholars of social jurisprudence have commented that our judiciary has remained by and large a Hindu feudal institution and there is no surprise if they adhere to those values. It is said that the same is abundantly reflected in the majority of cases where upper caste orthodox Hindus deliver the controversial judgements on social issues. The Supreme Court has so far not represented the people of India or the democratic principles for which the Constitution stands for and in its shadow it survives. It is ironical that none of the judgements relating to social jurisprudence contain an element of basic principles of justice nor a reference is made about the developments that are taking place in the world of knowledge in legal profession. Most of the time they represent simply a few statements devoid of any intellectual vision generally expected in an subject of this kind.

It is generally expected that a constitutional Bench sitting on a judgement will shape the destiny of millions of people and will be guided by principles of justice. The basic tenet of justice is 'fairness'. It is also true that the learned judges cannot take shelter behind 'the veil of ignorance'. They are all learned and experienced judges and they know the dynamics of the Indian society. They are also aware of the fact that scholars like John Rawls who has maintained that the background 'conditions of justice' need to be taken into consideration while making an analysis of a case. But, unfortunately in most of the cases including the recent judgment on creamy layer, there is no profound scrutiny of the issues involved or any intellectual inputs are put in coming to terms with the reality of the Indian society. It is very strange that the learned judges have often not seriously read the provisions of the Constitution and are guided by the popular opinion of the educated elite who constitute a minority in the Indian society. It is clear from the judgement, which speaks of constitutional requirements as backwardness, inadequacy of representation and overall administrative efficiency in Article 16 of the Constitution. But Article 16, including 16 (4A) and 16(4B), are unconditional provisions to provide equality of opportunity to majority of the population of the country who have been denied opportunities because of the operation of the Dharam Shastras (which were upheld by traditional priesthood). It is found that in the Mandal Commission judgment and also in some landmark judgements like Golaknath etc. the judiciary has been protecting the *dharmadhipatis* and their traditional roles. They have created precedents. They are all judges who have made legal provisions but have never gone through the scrutiny of the democratic legislative process. Like many traditional religious institutions, the Supreme Court is upholding those precedents as tenets of law as they are convenient both to the judiciary and to the ruling classes.

The flaw in the legal process of the apex court is inherent as the Supreme Court is considered as above board and is not publicly accountable. In most of the cases, it is believed that the learned judges are not even accountable to their conscience as some of their pronouncements are deliberately done without reference to the facts of the cases and actual constitutional position. It is clear from the Indra Sawhney case that a deliberate quantitative restriction of 50 per cent reservation is imposed while Article 335 speaks about the maintenance of efficiency of administration while considering the claims of members of Scheduled Castes and Scheduled Tribes who constitute 22 per cent of the population, and how can a 50 per cent ceiling be imposed on the reservation for 22 per cent population? Article 335 is not related to the reservation of other Backward Classes. The case of Backward Classes arises at a separate Article only after the appointment of a Commission to investigate the conditions of Backward Classes under Article 340. Therefore, the Mandal judgement appears to be a misreading or one can allege that it is a deliberate attempt to distort the constitutional provisions relating to caste-based reservations.

In the judgment relating to creamy layer, the Hon'ble Chief Justice and the other Members of the Bench, it is alleged, have been citing their own judgements as set of guidelines of law to substantiate their arguments. This is definitely a bad tradition or fraud on Constitution, devoid of any ethical or theoretical substance. It seems there is a growing quantity of literature relating to precedents and their limitations.

The founding fathers of the Constitution knew the background conditions of social justice in India while making Article 15 and Article 16. These two Articles are fundamental in protecting the interest of the socially and educationally Backward Classes of citizens and/or Scheduled Castes and Scheduled Tribes. One must see the historical conditions under which the first amendment to the Constitution was made to incorporate Article 15 (4). This Article mentioned about two distinct groups of Backward Classes of citizens. It is elementary knowledge that we cannot read Article 14 and 15 together. Article 14 relates to any person and this person can be a citizen or a non-citizen, a child or any one. Article 15 and also Article 16 speak about citizens in a group. Therefore, the learned judges should have considered the distinction between an independent person and a citizen in a group. The rights of a person are individual in nature whereas the special provisions conferred on a citizen under Article 15 and Article 16 relate to the entire group. If, one is inclined to read more in Article 15(4), it is clear that it is an open-ended category as far as Backward Classes of citizens are concerned. It is the duty of the Backward Classes Commission to study, scrutinize and classify any person in a group as Backward Classes. There is no restriction. That is the reason why in certain states Brahmins and so-called upper castes are also classified as Backward Classes, based on the yardsticks used to classify them as Backward Classes. But in the case of Scheduled Castes and Scheduled Tribes, it is a closed ended category as the classifications of Scheduled Castes and Scheduled Tribes were made before the Constitution came into existence. There is a long history about the classification of the Scheduled Castes and Scheduled Tribes. There is one single test which is very significant in classifying Scheduled Castes as a separate category i.e. untouchability. Apart from other 10 classifying tests none of them is applicable for other social categories like Backward Classes. Scheduled Castes is only a unique category. Similarly, Scheduled Tribes both in the schedule V and VI areas are those who are isolated from the mainstream society. They cannot be grouped with any other category. It is strange that the learned judges have not considered this unique nature of the constitutional categories of people as separate entities and have put them together as one erroneously to arrive at a 50 per cent quantitative limitation for reservations. There is no legal or theoretical justification in lumping SC, ST and OBC together. Even if one considers 50 per cent as a quantitative restriction to ensure efficiency, it is possible to argue that the efficiency levels of open category candidates which ranges above 50 per cent efficiency will be more than the efficiency levels of the below 50 per cent reserved category. In other words, if the total efficiency levels of all the open category candidates are aggregated, there will be still enough places for the below category candidates to extend it to even 70 per cent as the elite believe that the open category of 10 per cent are so efficient. This will take care of the efficiency of administration. In fact the reverse is happening in administration as the reserved categories are carrying the brunt of work while the open category officers boss over. Further, the creamy layer is applied only to the disadvantaged groups and similar creamy layer is not applied to open category candidates in employment that creates a blatant discrimination against them. This is nothing but *varna dharma* of feudal era values which the learned judges of apex court appears to uphold. This was not the intention of the founding fathers of the Constitution. It is strange to find that the learned judges defend their action in creating or self-appointing judges as *swayambhus* through collegium system, not seen elsewhere in the civilised world. As the number of judges from the socially marginalised is zero or near zero, the collegium remains, it is alleged, as an upper caste clique.

It is instructive to find from the legal history of advanced societies that when judgements on social issues are pronounced, a lot of discussion, thinking and expert advice is taken as it has far reaching implications for the society at large. It is the intellectual competence and the willingness of the learned judges that makes them to be broad based and visionary in outlook to foresee the future of a country. An incapability, and to use the language of the Constitution, the incapacity of a judge to see the large implications of the constitutional provisions makes the judgement trivial. It is always found in the legal literature that the legal luminaries have been dynamic in their pronouncements to help the society progress by providing enough scope and opportunities for the majority of the oppressed to advance, even by creatively interpreting some of the static provisions of a written Constitution. Unfortunately, in most of the judgements, particularly during the last two decades, the judgements delivered by the learned judges of the Supreme Court of India appear to be narrow and backward bending to uphold the traditional feudal values. This is a very dangerous trend as the prestigious institution owes its existence to the majority will of the people and if the majority of the people do not repose confidence in the institution, the institution will collapse, but not the Constitution. As the Constitution is a gift of the democratic process and a social contract, it shall always prevail.

23

Ambedkar's Contribution to the Demolition of Tradition in India

K.S. Chalam

Ambedkar has been eulogised as the saviour of the Untouchables in India in several writings and research publications. Though it is true to a certain extent, the stigma attached to the great son of India as a leader of the Untouchables is really not a tribute. Because Ambedkar like Gandhiji and other national leaders fought for the emancipation of the masses who have been oppressed under the yoke of Brahmin imperialism. It is foolish to relate the caste of Gandhiji to that of Vaisya and Ambedkar to that of Untouchables though they were accidentally born in a community and have been influenced by their circumstances. Ambedkar is perhaps the first educated proletariat in modem India who took up the cause of the downtrodden that included the Untouchables. He has taken up the challenges of the times and defended the rights of his people. Therefore, any systematic attempt in assessing the contribution of a great personality like Ambedkar must take into consideration the total perspective and the gains accrued to the majority of the people through the struggles and mass movements took up by him and not by reducing him to the caste to which he belongs. It is with this intention that an attempt is made here to assess the contribution of Ambedkar to the demolition of the dominant tradition which is responsible for the low status of women and Sudras. It is our view that the intellectual contributions, political struggles and the policy decisions in which Ambedkar was involved had far-reaching implications benefitting majority of the Indian population, notably women and Sudras.

In the pantheon of Indian reformers who have worked for the development of women, Ambedkar's name figures significantly well after Buddha. Several reformers and intellectuals of high repute have done yeomen service to regain the lost glory of Hindu women. But these movements appeared to have helped only a section of the society as most of the movements are elite-oriented. People generally quote Raja Ram Mohan Roy who was instrumental in getting the inhuman *sati* abolished. But *sati* as a ritual was in vogue only among the upper castes. Though the contribution of Raja Ram Mohan Roy could not be underestimated, it is however to be remembered that women belonging to the majority of the population have remained untouched by this. It was Ambedkar, who for the first time, discussed about the 'rise and fall of Hindu women' and made a scathing criticism against the scriptures, particularly the Manu's code, which was responsible for the enslavement of women in India. In his unpublished writings on Revolution and Counter *Revolution, Riddles in Hinduism* and through his magnum opus Hindu Code Bill, he has brought out clearly that Hindu women had a high position in the society in Vedic times and prior to Manu's code and the degradation has only started with Manu. Ambedkar has quoted extensively from the scriptures to prove that the ancient Indian society was matriarchal and slowly with the advent of the caste system, women were reduced to that of slaves. Ambedkar mentions that Manu made marriage as a sacrament, making the woman attached to a man without any right to separate or divorce. But, Manu allowed that man can remain free. It was necessary according to Ambedkar to introduce such stringent laws to protect the caste system. The endogamy had been introduced into the social intercourse to set up an enclosure round the Brahmins so that caste barriers would not be crossed. It is found that the fall of Hindu woman started with the spread of caste system in India. Therefore, Ambedkar had decided to break the shackles of the

Hindu woman by creating legal opportunities to make her equal to man in all spheres of life. In his draft Constitution, Ambedkar has incorporated Article 15 which says that State shall not discriminate people on grounds of caste, religion, sex and birth. Not being satisfied with providing constitutional safeguards, Ambedkar had brought in a historical document in the Parliament in the form of Hindu Code Bill. The introduction of Hindu Code Bill in the Parliament was a historical event which had ushered in the development of women in India. Though it was withdrawn and Ambedkar had to resign in protest, it is definitely a landmark in the women's struggles in India. Unfortunately, this has not been recognised visibly in any of the elitist women's liberation movements in India today. Through the process of the introduction of this Bill, Ambedkar had raised an issue for the first time in Indian history for discussion. He wanted that woman should be an equal partner of man. She should be given the right to divorce; own and inherit property and be independent of her own. These pronouncements along with the legislative measures that he undertook as the labour member of the legislative assembly are pieces of his profound concern for the development of women. Ambedkar had also introduced the Mines Maternity Benefit Bill in 1943 to provide working women an entitlement of leave on pay for eight weeks at the rate of eight annas per day. He had declared that it is 'unlawful and criminal for her to work' during pregnancy.[1] It is through these provisions and other structural reforms in the department of the status of women, Ambedkar hit a nail on the centuries old traditions.

Apart from the incorporation of specific legislations and Articles in the Constitution, Ambedkar had developed a broad framework for the development of the masses in the country. It is also necessary to look into the various liberation struggles which he led for the development of the depressed classes in India which were to have far-reaching consequences and influences on the development of women in India.

Development of Sudras

Perhaps it was Ambedkar who had written a treatise on the history and development of Sudras in India for the first time. Though his spiritual *guru* Mahatma Phuley started the historical analysis on the evolution of the concept of Sudras and Ati-Sudras in India in the 19th century, it was left to Ambedkar to extend the argument further. Therefore, it is not true to accept that Ambedkar has worked for the Scheduled Castes and Scheduled Tribes alone. His contribution for the development of the masses included Sudras also.

As a scholar Ambedkar gathered material mostly from the literary sources to establish first who were the Sudras and then to tell them about their present position so that they can fight for their lost glory. Ambedkar was very clear from the very beginning that he was attempting to unravel the mystery of the present low status of the Sudras because of the fact that they constitute 75 to 80 per cent of the population and the issue was therefore not a trivial one.[2] But the book is written for the ignorant and the uninformed Sudras, who do not know how they came to be what they are ... when one remembers that it is the Sudras, who have largely been instrumental in sustaining the infamous system of *chaturvarna*, though it has been the primary cause of their degradation and that only Sudras can destroy the *Chaturvarna* ... the necessity of education and thereby preparing the Sudra fully for such a sacred task to outweigh all other considerations.[3] Further, he has added that the status of the Sudras and the Untouchables in the Hindu society has remained just what it has been. This shows the strategy of Ambedkar in preparing these oppressed Indians together to fight against their greatest common enemy. This has been realised after 45 years of Ambedkar's dream in the form of Mandal Commission now.

The Sudras, according to Ambedkar, constitute a part of the Aryan society. In his appendix tables to the book on Sudras, Ambedkar has provided quantitative data from *Vedas* and other Hindu scriptures to show the frequency of how many times the word 'Arya', occurred in Hindu scriptures. His major conclusions about the Sudras constitute the following:[4]

1. The Sudras were one of the Aryan communities of the solar race.
2. The Sudras ranked as the Kshatriya *varna* in the Indo-Aryan society.
3. There was a time when the Aryan society recognised only three *varnas*, namely, Brahmins, Kshatriyas and Vaishyas.

The Sudras were not a separate *varna* but a part of the Kshatriya *varna*.

4. There was a continuous feud between the Sudra kings and the Brahmins, in which the Brahmins were subjected to many tyrannies and indignities.
5. As a result of the hatred towards the Sudras due to their tyrannies and oppressions, the Brahmins refused to invest Sudra with the sacred thread.
6. Owing to the loss of the sacred thread, the Sudras became socially degraded, fell below the rank of the Vaishyas and came to form the fourth *varna*.

After making the above tentative statements about the status of the Sudras, Ambedkar lists out the riddles so that they can themselves question these and fight for their position. It is interesting to see that Ambedkar has written about the history of the Sudras, before writing about his own Untouchables. This shows his secular and broadmindedness in approaching the real problem. Of course, he has written *The Untouchables* in 1948 as a sequel to his treatise on the Sudras.[5] These two books, Ambedkar hoped, would enlighten the so-called 'depressed classes' consisting of some of the Sudras, Untouchables and tribes. He has provided a practical approach suggesting that the development of a community or group depends upon the building of the fight against the tyranny of established culture known as Brahminism in India. Though the two treatises on caste are based on literary sources and therefore contained some inconsistencies and contradictions, they have however provided ammunition to act like 'atomic bombs on the dogmas of the Arya *Samajis*' under whose influence the country still persists.

Economic Concessions

Ambedkar was not satisfied with the ammunition supplied to these oppressed communities in the form of literature to fight against the imperialists, but he had also made some concrete contributions in the form of legislation, constitutional provisions, etc. It was Ambedkar who for the first time brought in the abolition of *watandari* system in Maharashtra wherein Untouchables were attached to land as slaves. But, this legislation has provided impetus to bring in such laws later in different parts of the country where lower Sudras like the service castes were liberated from bonded labour. His thesis that the definition of an economic holding should contain in itself a provision for the capitalisation on land and its productivity has enabled many a marginal farmers who in general are Sudras to come out of the definition of 'viable farmer'.

Apart from the theoretical arguments in bringing home the need for the provision of economic benefits to the Sudras, Ambedkar had passed legislations like Factories Amendment Bill, 1944, in which he made provisions for washing places and fire escapes for the factory workers. As most of the workers are from the lower communities, these facilities helped them to develop their status as independent labourers. He was instrumental in getting the Indian Trade Unions Bill, 1943 to be introduced in the legislative assembly to provide legal sanction for the organisation of trade unions in India. In his draft memorandum on the safeguards of Scheduled Castes prepared to submit before the Constituent Assembly, Ambedkar had laid down clearly that 'all citizens are equal before the law and possess equal civic rights'. He had further strengthened the fundamental rights by providing remedies in case of invasion of fundamental rights. It is here that the profound statesmanship of Ambedkar is exhibited by making provisions for economic safeguards for the poor by bringing a modified version of 'state socialism' as a part of the Constitution. Though he could not put in all these provisions in the Indian Constitution, a major thrust of the Indian Constitution has remained to be socialistic and welfare-oriented. Besides, it is to largely benefit the Sudras and Untouchables in India. The present Mandal Commission recommendations which are a boon for many backward classes who in general are Sudras is a classic contribution of Ambedkar for the welfare of Sudras. He has, thus, laid strong foundations for the demolition of the *varna dharma* and other Hindu reactionary principles.

Ambedkar has successfully used the economic sociology which was prevalent at the time of his education in Europe and America. Therefore, one can see its influence even in his PhD dissertation on the 'Evolution of Provincial Finance in India'. The last sentence of this treatise contains: 'Thus, in India, the political problem is essentially a social problem, and a postponement of its solution virtually postpones the day when India can have a free government subject to the mandate of none but her own people'.[6] This wonderful piece of scholarship written prior to the Independence of India is still valid. It is now left to us to evaluate whether we have succeeded in completing the tasks which Ambedkar had initiated.

Notes

1. Government of Maharashtra, *Collected Works of Dr. Babasaheb Ambedkar*, Vol. 10, 1991, p. 87.
2. Ibid., Vol. 7, 1990, p. 9.
3. Ibid., p. 18.
4. Ibid., p. 204.
5. Ibid., p. 239.
6. Ibid., Vol. 6, 1989, p. 308.

24

Practicability of Ambedkar's Views on Annihilation of Caste

K.E. Rajpramukh

Very rarely, we witness emergence of an extraordinary individual on the intellectual horizon and Ambedkar was one such versatile scholar whose writings include topics related to politics, economics, history, philosophy, religion, culture and anthropology. In his writings on 'Caste in India', he has adopted an anthropological approach in the treatment of the subject matter. In fact, it was a paper presented before an anthropological seminar at Columbia University in 1916. The method employed in the paper was ethno-historical and it was the result of the prevailing evolutionary school of thought in those times. The problem with this method is that it is fraught with difficulties and the arguments could be anything but conclusive and convincing. In the last years, since 1920s, there was a gradual shift from evolutionary perspective to structural-functional analysis and the literature on caste since then increased multifold. It is surprising to find that Ambedkar's views on caste were not taken seriously by the later day scholars probably because his dialectical approach was not relished by those western scholars whose view Joan

Moencher (1974) has called 'from the top down'. In the words of Berreman (1971), it is 'the Brahminical view of caste'.

Ambedkar's radical views on caste were a direct result of his realisation of being a member of a social system with inherent structural inequalities founded on the institution of caste. It was also inevitable that with his exposition to the western ideals of liberty, equality and fraternity, he could visualise how 'exploitation' as a mechanism operates to the advantage of some of those who placed themselves high in the hierarchy. It is worth mentioning here that most of the social reformers including the political leaders and freedom fighters, had some kind of exposure to the West and brought with them alien notions like, equality, socialism and democracy to India.

Some 20 years later, after his elaborate exposition on caste, in 1935, he finally returned to the question of 'annihilation of caste'. He was to give his speech at the 1936 annual conference of Jat-Pat-Todak Mandal of Lahore but did not deliver it owing to the cancellation of the conference by the reception committee on the ground that the views exposed in the speech would be unbearable to the conference. He later published it in the same year on his own and the contents of his writings drew severe criticism from Mahatma Gandhi. Ambedkar did not relent but gave a fitting reply answering threadbare every point raised by Mahatma Gandhi. The most astounding feature of this debate was the forceful and authentic manner in which Ambedkar articulated his views. Such as his scholarship, his courage of conviction and impressive style were the hallmarks of all his writings. In short, I would say, he was a genius.

Let us now look into his views on annihilation of caste. I would like to point out at the outset what Kamble remarked about his inability to incorporate measures to abolish caste in the Indian Constitution. In his words: 'Why could not Dr Ambedkar, the principal architect of the Constitution, who had always spearheaded the movement for the annihilation of caste, prevail upon the Constituent Assembly for the abolition of caste, the tree that bears the fruits of untouchability?' Kamble himself answers the question, that it could be due to unpreparedness of the vast majority of its members. But the fundamental question remains: Is it practicable at all to abolish caste?

Ambedkar's main arguments in his 'annihilation of caste' centre round these following observations:

1. According to the scriptures a 'Brahmin' alone could be a teacher and an intellectual, and such a situation inevitably hinders any reform.
2. The caste system as a whole generates only 'inefficiency' at every level.
3. That property alone is not the source of 'power' as held by socialists but also religion and social status.
4. Caste system is not merely a division of labour but it is also a 'division of labourers' which rules out social mobility.
5. Caste system cannot be said to have evolved from a eugenic arrangement of maintaining purity of blood within the groups.
6. Caste has completely disorganised and demoralised the Hindus.
7. There is an inherent anti-social spirit in the caste system.
8. Caste system generates selfish and narrow attitude about one's own caste.
9. Once caste system grew, Hindu religion ceased to be a missionary religion because the problem arises as to which caste the new convert should be assigned.
10. Unity is hard to achieve in caste system because of tremendous in-built inequalities.
11. Caste has killed public spirit.
12. Caste has destroyed the sense of public charity and made public opinion impossible. A Hindu public is his caste.
13. Both caste and *varna* are pernicious.
14. There is no place for 'reason' in Hinduism.

Having, thus, set out his case for the desirability of the abolition of caste after establishing its pernicious nature, Ambedkar lays down his concrete propositions to annihilate caste. After examining at length the question of abolition of sub-castes he realised the futility of such an exercise and asserts that it does not ultimately annihilate caste. As regards inter-caste marriages, which many held as the real solution to the problem of caste, he did not sound very optimistic but lauded the efforts of social reformers. He was then left with the following cardinal propositions:

1. There should be one and only one standard book of Hindu religion, acceptable to all Hindus and recognised by all Hindus. This of course means that all other books of Hindu religion such as the *Vedas*, the *Shastras* and the *Puranas*, which are treated as sacred and authoritative, must by law cease to be so and the preaching of any doctrine, religious or social contained in these books should be penalised.
2. It should be better if priesthood among Hindus was abolished. But as this seems to be impossible, the priesthood must at least cease to be hereditary. Every person who professes to be a Hindu must be eligible for being appointed as a priest. It should be provided by law that no Hindu shall be entitled to be a priest unless he has passed an examination prescribed by the State and holds a *sanad* from the State permitting him to practise.
3. No ceremony performed by a priest who does not hold a *sanad* shall be deemed to be valid in law and it should be made penal for a person who has no *sanad* to officiate as priest.
4. A priest should be the servant of the State and should be subject to the disciplinary action by the State in the matter of his morals, beliefs and worship, in addition to his being subject along with other citizens to the ordinary law of the land.
5. The number of priests should be limited by law according to the requirements of the state as is done in the case of the ICS.

Ambedkar, thus, sums up his views on annihilation of caste, which are directed against the very foundation of Hindu religion. The basic question again comes up here. Are his views practicable? While forwarding his above propositions, he was evidently seeking the state to enforce its authority to realise them. These propositions sound too wild for the simple reason that a typical Hindu's life is thoroughly entwined in religious notions. We have to keep in mind that 'religion' is such a potent and powerful institution that some one went to the extent of describing it as the opium of the masses. At the end of his address, Ambedkar seems to have realised the impossibility and impracticability of the solutions he offered and goes on to exhort the Hindus to see reason in his argument and discard their past and seek a new social order based on equality, liberty and fraternity.

Apart from the exchange of views between Ambedkar and Mahatma Gandhi, on the question, a change which is desirable and inevitable, it is also worthwhile to examine the factors hindering that change. As we all know that more than half of Indian population is still illiterate and it is easy to arouse religious sentiments among them because of their inability to apply 'reason' to different spheres of life and much more so to religious life. Even among the educated, 'reason' has no place in religious life. So long as this tendency continues, it becomes well nigh impossible to break the barriers of religion to bring about a new social order. I do not intend to sound too pessimistic but only point out the difficulties involved in the realisation of Ambedkar's views. Perhaps he himself knew about it for when he was given an opportunity to incorporate his views in the Indian Constitution, he could not do it. The reasons for not doing so may be different but he contended himself treading on the specialists path, whom he deprecated earlier for relegating religion and social status, though they are equally, if not more powerful instruments of change, than economic factors. Many safeguards have been incorporated to ameliorate the conditions of the weaker sections in the Indian Constitution.

To conclude, I would only say, irrespective of whether his views are practicable or not, Ambedkar was the first to articulate his scholarly radical views on caste and he was undoubtedly the first who systematically brought out the many evils and the pernicious nature of caste. He was in fact the first to question in public the very foundations and fundamentals of caste and was responsible in mobilising public opinion against such a monster called 'caste'. That is where exactly Ambedkar's greatness remains for ever. So also, his exhortation to dominant Hindus to unlearn the *Shastras*, the *Vedas* and other scriptural texts.

References

Berreman, G., 'The Brahminical View of Caste', *Contributions to Indian Sociology*, 5, 1971, pp. 16–23.

——, *Caste and Other Inequities*, Meerut: Folklore Institute, 1979.

Beteille, Andre, *Inequality and Social Change*, New Delhi: Oxford University Press, 1972.

Kamble, N.D., *The Scheduled Castes*, New Delhi: Ashish, 1982.

Mencher, Joan, 'The Caste System Upside Down, or the Not So Mysterious Caste', *Current Anthropology*, 15, 1974, 469–493.

Moon, Vasant (Ed.), 'Annihilation of Caste', in *Dr. Babasaheb Ambedkar's Writings and Speeches*, Vol. 1, Education Department, Government of Maharashtra, Bombay, 1979.

25

Sudras in the *Vedas*

A Critical Exposition by Ambedkar

R.K. Chauhan

If at all there is something left that is not understood properly by mankind, it is about his own creation and that of the universe. Therefore, each religion has its own story to offer. The science has its own theory. Within the same religion,[1] there are different versions. The mankind has explored all myths. But, the religion which was created by mankind allowed the human creation to remain a myth for ever for the personal gain of a particular sect. The reality observed by a few saints and seers were ignored by the majority, instead, what has been said in religious text had been given contrary meaning and definition since it favoured particular class of the society.

Everybody knows that the Sudras formed the fourth *varna* of the society. But very few have cared to inquire who were these Sudras and how they have been made fourth *varna*.[2] To understand it, it is necessary to trace out briefly from where and in what context it is said. It is a universal belief that the *Vedas* are the religious texts of the Hindu religion. What is the meaning of the word *Veda* and from where it came? *Veda* is a *sruti*, a rhythm not composed by the intellect but heard, a divine word that came vibrating out of the infinite to the inner audience of the man who had previously made himself fit for the impersonal knowledge.[3] *Sruti*, in turn, means revealed scripture.[4] The belief that *sruti* is nothing but what is heard from sages and seers arising from their spiritual experience is widely accepted.[5] Darsanas, on whose authority the systems are based, the *Vedas* have no author at all.[6] Therefore, it lacks authority, a view held by Sankara, against contrary view taken by Ramanuja and Madhava.

Although, a study on *Vedas* itself is revealing as well as interesting, we confine this study to what has been said in *Vedas* about Sudras as perceived by Ambedkar. It is a well known fact that *Vedas* are grouped into four categories: (1) *Rig Veda*, (2) *Yajur Veda*, (3) *Sama Veda*, and (4) *Atharva Veda*. According to *Vishnu Purana*, all the (four) *Vedas* came from the (four) mouths of Lord Brahma (the four faced God).[7] The *Rig Veda* came from the eastern mouth of Brahma. From his southern mouth he created the *Yajur Veda*. *Sama Veda* came from this western mouth. And the Atharva came from his northern mouth.[8]

Creation of Universe

It is spelt out in *Rig Veda*,[9] and popularly known by the name of *Purusha Sukta*. It starts saying that *purusha*, who created the universe, had thousand heads and thousand feet. Another altogether cosmogony is also found in *Rig Veda*.[10] It contains how trees, earth, and sun came into existence. In addition the creation of universe is also found in *Yajur Veda* and *Atharva Veda*, which are, however, not familiar versions. Contrary to the above, the old testament contains only one version which appears not only believable but also contains an order or creation.[11]

Creation of *Varna* System

Verses 11 and 12 of *Purusha Sukta* explain how the four classes, namely Brahmins or priests, Kshatriyas or soldiers, Vaishyas or traders and Sudras or menials arose from the body of creator.[12] The latter developed Sutras, such as Apustamba Dharma Sutra and Vasistha Dharma Sutra injected a graded society based on extraneous considerations. Whereas the former made one caste superior by birth to the next in the order, the latter denied—the Sudras—the right to receive the sacraments (recital of *Vedas*).[13]

Injuries Inflicted on Sudras by Sutras, Smritis and Shastras

The worst crime committed on Sudras was by the religious texts such as *Manu Smriti, Vishnu Smriti, Gautama Dharma Sutra* and *Brihaspati's Dharma Shastra* in addition to the above mentioned two *Sutras*. These *Sutras* and *Smritis* prescribed dangerous penal punishment for the innocent acts of Sudras. Such punishments prescribed ranges from cutting out the tongues of Sudras on uttering the words of *Vedas* and filling the ears with lack or tin if he listens to *Vedas*.[14]

As stated earlier, verses 11 and 12 of the Purusha Sukta contains the Constitution of society—into four classes. But these verses are not being understood properly.[15] Instead, they are treated as mandatory injunction from God (the creator) that he created the *varna* system.[16] Not only that, the infliction of infirmities on Sudras as contained in the latter developed *Sutras* and *Smritis* are also treated as commandments from God. This misunderstanding or lack of knowledge led to the degradation of Sudras from the very beginning from the creation of mankind till today and even shall continue to survive as long as mankind will survive. The reasons for such an apathy are many. The objective behind the Constitution of society into four classes was something unique and every one ought to know it. Aurobindo has explained it beautifully in a lucid manner.[17]

Aurobindo's Commentary on *Varna* System/Caste System

The ancient Indian idea was that man falls by his nature into four types.[18]

The economic order of society was cast in the form and gradation of four types. The Indian idea in its purity fixed the status of a man in this order not by his birth, but by his capacities and this inner nature, and, if this rule had been strictly observed that would have been a very clear mark of distinctness, a superiority of a unique kind. But, in practice, we find that birth became the basis of the *varna*. Further, according to Aurobindo, the Brahmins had not a monopoly either of sacred learning or of the highest spiritual knowledge and opportunities. However, the

Brahmins, by virtue of their full occupation of time and energy to the study of sacred writings secured a predominance. Ultimately, the study of the *Vedas* and the *Upanishads* passed mainly into their hands, although always open to the three highest orders, it was denied in theory to the Sudras. This laid the foundation for water-tight compartmentalisation of different caste sub-caste.[19]

Reasons for the degradation of Sudras in the Hindu religious system according to Ambedkar are as follows.[20]

1. That the Sudra was to take the last place in the social order.
2. That the Sudra was impure and therefore no sacred act should be done within his sight and within his hearing.
3. That the Sudra is not to be respected in the same way as the other classes.
4. That the life of a Sudra is of no value and anybody may kill him without having to pay compensation and if at all of small value as compared with that of the Brahmin, Kshatriya and Vaishya.
5. That the Sudra must not acquire knowledge and it is a sin and a crime to give him education.
6. That a Sudra must not acquire property. A Brahmin can take his property at his pleasure.
7. That a Sudra cannot hold office under the state.
8. That the duty and salvation of the Sudra lies in his serving the higher classes.
9. That the higher classes must not inter-marry with the Sudra. They can, however, keep a Sudra woman as a concubine. But if the Sudra touches a woman of the higher classes he will be liable to dire punishment.
10. That the Sudra is born is servility and must be kept in servility forever.

The above reasons are evident even today. In a preface to his book on *Who were the Sudras*, Ambedkar had narrated his own personal experience as how the other caste people gone even to the extent of threatening to take his own life for his attempt to write on the status of Sudras as given in the *Vedas*. To put it in his own words:

> I received a shower of letters from angry Hindus, who because quite unbalanced by my speech on the subject delivered in

> Madras. The letters were full of filthy abuse, unmentionable and unprintable, and full of dire threats to my life. Last time they treated me as first offender and let me off with mere threats. I do not know what they will do this time. For I know very well that they are a base crew who, professing to defend their religion, have made religion a matter of trade. They are more selfish than any other set of beings in the world, and are prostituting their intelligence to support the vested interests of their class.
>
> It is a matter of no small surprise that when the mad dogs of orthodoxy are let loose against a person who has the courage to raise his voice against the so-called sacred books of the Hindus, eminent Hindus occupying lofty places, claiming themselves to be highly educated and who could be expected to have no interest and to have a free and open mind became partisans and join the outcry.
>
> Even Hindu judges of high courts and Hindu chief ministers of Indian states did not hesitate to join their kind. This very book is an illustration in point. It contains an exposure of the real character of the conspiracy against the Sudras, which no Brahmin scholar could have had the courage to present.

Conclusion

It is now evident to conclude that the *varnas* found in the *Vedas* are determined not on the basis of birth, but on the basis of their discharge of broadly classified duties and functions. As the *Vedas* do not have author(s), since it meant what is heard, it is quite possible to have distortions in the process when it is passed from one ear to another ear, it is more so since such passing took place from one generation to another generation of the same family (in the beginning of the era).

Mankind were not aware of the process of creation and nature in the beginning. In view of this, they had decided to attribute anything and everything. The reason being, people placed unquestioned faith on God and on account of mysticism. In addition to such attributes, these beliefs remained beyond scrutiny of mankind. In other words, they developed a tendency to attribute a particular thing in the name of god in order to avoid further controversy and social unrest. It is, in this manner, the creation of universe, mankind and *varna* system and subsequent development of caste system etc. were considered as the creation of God. Due to the passage of time, it remained unquestioned, however, some deviations either way were allowed if it benefitted the few. This is how we are having thousands of castes and sub-castes today, although only four categories were mentioned in the *Vedas*. Actually, caste system is the off-shoot of *varna* system only.

In this way, the Sudras had been debarred from learning, listening, and recitation of the *Vedas* through the process of serious punishment to such people other than Brahmins. Thus, Ambedkar is the first Indian to expose the Vedic literature and *Dharma Sutras* which have supported the obnoxious caste system in India.

Notes

1. Hindu religion. The *Rig Veda* contains two entirely different versions about creation. One in 90th hymn and another in 72nd hymn of the 10th Mandala of *Rig Veda*. In addition to the creation is also found in *Yajur Veda* and *Atharvana Veda*. For the details of creation, refer *Dr. Babasaheb Ambedkar's Writings and Speeches*, Vol. 7, referred as 'Ambedkar, Vol. 7'.
2. Ambedkar, Vol. 7, p. 21.
3. Sri Aurobindo, *The Secret of Veda*, Sri Aurobindo Ashram, Pondicherry, 1985, p. 9.
4. Sri Aurobindo, *Hymns to the Mystic Fire*, Sri Aurobindo Ashram, Pondicherry, 1952.
5. Nagaraja Rao, P., 'The Wisdom of Vedas', in *Essays in Indian Philosophy and Religion*, Bombay: Lalvani Publishing House, 1971, p. 92.
6. *Aprapte Sastram Pramanam-Jaimini's Sutra*, p. 92.
7. Ibid., p. 93.
8. Quoted by Dr. Ambedkar in his book *Who Were the Sudras?*
9. One version is given in 90th hymn of the 10th Mandala of *Rig Veda*.
10. Seventy-second hymn of the 10th Mandala of *Rig Veda*. For details, see Ambedkar, Vol. 7, p. 27.
11. The Old Testament, Good News Size, Society of St. Paul India, 1979.

12. Ambedkar, Vol. 7, p. 23.
13. Ibid., p. 24.
14. See *Dr. B.R. Ambedkar's Writings and Speeches*, Vol. 7. This paper is based mostly on this volume.
15. Ibid., p. 23.
16. Ibid.
17. Sri Aurobindo, *The Foundation of Indian Culture and the Renaissance in India*, Sri Aurobindo Ashram, Pondicherry, 1971. See Dr. Ambedkar, Vol. 7 also.
18. Ibid. There are, first and highest, the man of learning and thoughts and knowledge; next the man of power and action, ruler, warrior, leader, administrator; third in the scale, the economic man, producer and wealth getter, the merchant, artisan, cultivator: these were twice-born, who receive initiation, Brahmin, Kshatriya, Vaishya. Last came the more undeveloped human type, not yet fit for these steps of the scale, unintellectual, without force, incapable of creation or intelligent production, the man fit only for unskilled labour and menial service, the Sudra.
19. The Brahmin class was called upon to give the community its priests, thinkers, men of letters, legislators, scholars, religious leaders and guides. The Kshatriya class gave it its kinds, warriors, governors and administrator. The Vaishya order supplied it with its producers, agriculturists, craftsmen, artisans, merchants and traders. The Sudras class ministered to its need of menials and servants. As far as this went, there was nothing peculiar in the system except its extraordinary durability and, perhaps the supreme position given to religion, thought and learning not only at the top of the scale—for that can be parallelled from one or two other civilizations—but as the dominant power.
20. Ambedkar, Vol. 7.

Part IV

Perspectives of Research on Ambedkar

26

Perspectives of Research on Ambedkar's Socio-Economic Philosophy

A. Somasekhar

Ambedkar was an erudite and versatile person and one of the greatest builders of modern India. The Columbia University hailed him as one of India's leading citizens, a great social reformer and a valiant upholder of human rights. He has been regarded as more than an institution—a social reformer, a redeemer, the law marker and what not. His socio-economic philosophy, his views on religion, economics and politics and his sermons are very much relevant to present and future times.

The excellent academic record of Ambedkar was a testimony to his intellectual brilliance. He was not only an intellectual, but a critical thinker and analyst. This is the right time for all of us to read, think and comprehend what this intellectual giant stood for in this civilised world. An attempt is made hereunder to visualise the perspectives of research on the basis of Ambedkar's socio-economic philosophy.

Research Contributions

Ambedkar was a prolific writer and authored a large number of books. These included *Caste in India, The Problem of the Rupee, Evolution of Provincial Finance in British India, Thoughts on Pakistan, Ranade, Gandhi and Jinnah, Thoughts on Linguistic States,* etc. Ambedkar's contribution to public finance is an outstanding one. In his hook *The Problem of the Rupee,* Ambedkar attempted an exposition of the vents leading to the establishment of the exchange standard and an examination of its theoretical basis. He brought out clearly how this settlement of exchange rates obviously affected the lives of Indian masses. He won laurels by this exceedingly thought provoking book. In his another book *The Evolution of Provincial Finance in British India,* he exposed the way the vested interests at home collude with the European occupiers. Seligman praised this book as 'the objective recitation of the facts and impartial analysis' of the centre-state financial relations in British India. It is worth noting that the underlying principles stated in his book have guided the reports of successive Finance Commissions in independent India.

Ambedkar's thoughts on current Indian problems, such as land reforms, landless labourers small holdings, collective fanning, land revenue, etc. are more relevant even today. According to him, the fundamental cause of India's economy was the cornerstone of his economic ideas. There should be no landlord, no tenant and no landless labourer. He stood for the progressive transformation of the society, removing glaring social and economic inequalities that were due to the capital system. Besides writing on economic and political topics, Ambedkar also contributed to the discussion on the social problems.[1]

Tributes were paid to Ambedkar for his jealous and arduous task of piloting the Constitution of free India in the Constituent Assembly. He was described as 'The Modem Manu'. His contribution dispelled all doubts and fears and he was considered to be one of the great patriots of this country. Thus, Ambedkar's dynamic and national character is reflected in the part played by him at the Indian Round Table Conference, political and social and economic philosophies, the verdict on Hinduism, as a leader, fighter, law-maker, etc. His deep thoughts and penetrating and acute analysis covered from caste and untouchability to land reforms and foreign policy of India. He demonstrated tremendous analytical power to explain social, economic and political issues which is a unique inter-disciplinary framework.

Socio-Economic Philosophy

As an economist, while agreeing with the Marxian view about the existence of exploitation in the world, Ambedkar did not support the Marxian strategy for economic development. He opined that in Indian context political or religious exploitation is no less oppressive than economic exploitation. He was against communism since it stands for revolution and not for transformation. He advocated the concept of 'State socialism' based on three basic tenets:

1. State ownership of agricultural lands and key industries to meet the demands of poor strata of society.
2. Maintenance of productive resources by the state.
3. Just distribution of produce among people without distinction of caste or creed.

Ambedkar always stood for casteless and classless society but not stateless society. According to him, a good state is that which guarantees protection against prosecution of one community by another and also against internal disturbances, violence and disorder in any part of its territory. Ambedkar regarded rights as 'natural' and 'inherent' in the individual. To him the state existed only to prevent injustice, tyranny and oppression. Rights are protected not by law but by the social and moral conscience of society. If the social conscience is such that it is prepared to recognise the rights which law chooses to enact, rights will be safe and secure. But if the fundamental rights are opposed by the community, no law, no Parliament, no judiciary can guarantee them in the real sense of the word. He tried to seek harmony between the people and legal powers of the state.

The concept of economic development, according to Ambedkar, means eradication of poverty, elimination of inequalities of income and means of production and to save the masses from exploitation.

Agriculture

As regards land reforms, Ambedkar in his paper on 'Small Holdings in India and Their Remedies' stated that consolidation of holdings would obviate the evils of scattered holdings provided these are economic holdings. He opined that the remedy for the evils of agriculture in India does not lie in the enlargement of holdings but in the matter of increasing capital and capital goods. He regarded agriculture as an industry and favoured cooperative collective farming. He insisted on capital intensive agriculture.

Industrialisation

Ambedkar remarked that the industrialisation was necessary for India and maintained that 'industrialisation facilities consolidation. It lessens the premium of land. It must precede consolidation. It is a barrier against future subdivision and consolidation'.[2] He was aware that surplus agricultural labour could be accommodated in industry and solve the problems of unemployment. He preferred industrialisation within the framework of mixed economy, where State management and state ownership of industry were necessary. He advocated for nationalisation of industries, life insurance and road transport.

Social Humanism

Religious awakening and social reform became the touchstones of his whole thinking process. He urged collective aspects of human life and opined that a developing society could not flourish without a balance between material and spiritual awakening. His social humanism aims at securing an integrated human personality as well as an emotionally integrated human society; and implies to regard every human being as an end in himself with a right to his own development in his own way. Ambedkar's programme of humanism is mainly concerned with the emancipation of the poor, the fallen and the weak.

Issues for Development Research

While writing on Indian economy, particularly planned economic development, Ambedkar highlighted the weakness of Indian inequitable socio-economic structure. He advocated that the state should plan the economic life of the people in such a way that it should lead to the highest point of productivity without hampering the growth of private enterprise but ensuring an equitable distribution of wealth. In the context of Ambedkar's philosophy and its relevance to present times, several issues emerge to improve the quality of life of Scheduled Castes (SCs) which are briefly discussed below:

1. Ambedkar is the father of human development and architect of social democracy. The goal of welfare state cannot be attained without human development either in developed countries or in developing countries. The concept of Human Development Index (HDI) which was introduced by United Nations Development Programme (UNDP) in May 1990, takes into account three basic elements of human well-being-longevity (life expectancy), knowledge (education), and the access to resources (in terms of real per capita income). The provision of facilities for education, nutrition and health to weaker sections will go a long way in the promotion of human development. Scientific assessment of HDI of SCs has to be made in comparison to general population.
2. The approaches and strategies adopted by state and central governments through planned development have been in tune with Ambedkar's strategy of economic development with a thrust on eradication of poverty, elimination of exploitation of the masses and ending of inequalities. The performance of planning era reveals that a noticeable impact is found in the implementation of constitutional safeguards. Beneficiary-oriented schemes have been under implementation for the development of SCs. It is evident from the recent studies that most of the development benefits are grabbed by advanced groups resulting in denial of social justice. As such analytical studies are to be undertaken to reconsider/re-examine Ambedkar's economic ideas to meet the present day needs of SCs.
3. In the present-day society, social scientists and intellectuals have to play a vital role in solving the social tensions. Past history reveals that the revolutionary movements initiated by pioneers like Sant Kabir, Ravidas, Guru Nanak, and Mahatma Phuley and culminated by Mahatma Gandhi and Ambedkar instilled a new sense of awareness among SCs by and large

under the influence of these movements, it is observed that the SCs refused to accept the status as ordained by the caste system since many centuries. This statement needs a thorough probe calling for the vital role of intellectual community in solving social tensions.

4. In order to achieve social justice, the governments have taken up several measures, such as land reforms, distribution of land to weaker sections, tenancy legislation, etc. These measures resulted in strengthening the inner strength and resistance power of weaker sections especially SCs and STs since 1960s and correspondingly the frequency and brutal ferocity of atrocities has grown apace. Demand for better wages in rural areas is another trigger of atrocities. The recent incidents in Tsundur in Andhra, Pinth Deshmukh in Maharashtra and Kumher in Rajasthan indicate the assertion of social equality in the day-to-day interactions with other caste people by educated SC youth inspired by Ambedkar's ideology. It is observed that the depressed classes are peaceful and Ambedkar taught them the lesson of peaceful and lawful rebellion. On account of this, exploitation should not take place and the state should not be complacent. These situations require diagnostic studies by emeritus professors.
5. The present situation demands the extension of certain legislations and regulations, such as PCR Act, SCs/STs (Prevention of Atrocities) Act, 1989 to the Christians of Scheduled Caste origin since they are also subjected to atrocities by upper caste Hindus and Christians of upper caste origin. It may not be out of context to quote that 'untouchability which was condemned by missionaries as a social curse still continues in one or the other form within the framework of Christianity.'[3] Further, certain common atrocities, such as social boycott, economic boycott, social blackmail and economic blackmail, etc. are not covered by these Acts. As such, operational research studies are necessary to plug the loopholes in the implementation of these Acts.
6. According to National Convention of SC/ST Parliamentarians and Legislators held in June 1992, the planning era since

independence did not take into account the subjugation and bondage of SCs and STs and could not ensure liberation and equality. It is noticed that the mechanisms of SCP and TSP are not allowed as powerful instruments as originally envisaged but these were through the passage of years, routinised and trivialised. This situation needs to be rectified and a meaningful, comprehensive and powerful processes of planned development incorporating the vital and lost dimension of liberation and equality for SCs/STs has to be initiated. Research-oriented plans are to be formulated for the development of SCs and STs.

7. Macro-economic policies are relevant to SCs and STs. The New Economic Policy is based on 'market friendliness'. The National Convention observed that 'private industry and private business have always cruelly ignored their needs of advancement and development.'[4] Narasimham Committee report has recommended the reduction of priority sector lending form 40 per cent to 10 per cent without taking into account the needs of SCB and STs. Further, the bankers, the Reserve Bank and the Ministry of Finance have been opposing the differential rate of interest scheme of a mere 1 per cent lending to the poor with a sub-target for SCs and STs. The New Economic Policy keeping in view of Article 38 and the directive principles enshrined in the Constitution needs to be re-examined to achieve a just national economy based on socialist principles, equal society and a fair democratic policy as visualised by Ambedkar.
8. The Government of India Act of 1919 provided for special representatives through mixed electorates. Ambedkar pleaded for special representation for SCs in 1919 as well as in the Round Table Conferences. Every historian knows that how the communal award of 1932 was opposed by Gandhi. The Poona pact negated the communal award. The scope of reservation was discussed during the Constituent Assembly debates. Reservation was treated as a form of distributive justice to help members of weaker sections. Ambedkar suggested that more than 50 per cent would seem to be unreasonable.

The rule of reservation has been under strict implementation in our state and special recruitment drive is also taken up to fill up the backlog vacancies. The National Convention felt that the policy of reservation has to be revitalised by removing all obstacles and obstructions and by extending it to the newly emergent public sector enterprises. The percentage of reservation has to be revised in accordance with the percentage of SC and ST population in 1991 Census and it should be retained as legally enforceable stipulation whenever any public sector enterprise ceases to be a public sector enterprise. Legislation has to be brought about for reservation of SCs and STs with adequate penal provisions.

9. Since Independence, the government has taken up several measures, such as abolition of intermediary tenures, confirmation of ownership rights to tenants, imposition of land ceilings, distribution of surplus lands, land assignment, etc. besides providing a productive assets base for poor SCs and removed to considerable extent the institutional and motivational obstacles for modernisation of agriculture and establishment of a more egalitarian social structure. In spite of various achievements and policy initiatives the poverty appears to be the basic problem especially among the disadvantaged sections of the society. It is a fact that development gap exists between SCs and general population. It is observed that 'though SCs have been living in the midst of Hindus and in spite of best opportunities provided to them, they are not able to lead the life on par with general population.'[5] This situation needs the attention of social scientists for thorough study with multi-dimensional approach.

Research Panorama

The issues are innumerable in number which need careful study for taking any policy decision. It is needles to emphasise that studies on SCs have assumed greater significance in the field of social sciences research for the last few decades due to changing socio-economic status. Scientific surveys and studies are necessary at micro and macro levels to reveal the truth of multi-dimensional situations. Adequate number of micro level as well as macro level, topical as well as areawise, comprehensive as well as in-depth studies focusing attention on a scientific analysis of the impact of planned programmes on the life of SCs is the need of the hour.

Sufficient literature is not built up on SCs when compared to STs. Three decades ago, the census department has conducted ethnographic studies on various castes of Andhra Pradesh but there is a need for conducting ethnographic studies for SCs in particular in order to know the levels of social development of various communities and sub castes among SCs including the specially vulnerable groups, so that appropriate remedial measures can be taken. The SCs of Andhra Pradesh are spread over all the districts of the state and they are at various levels of development. The common feature of all the sub-castes is poverty, exploitation, illiteracy and social disabilities. In view of the situation, the nature and type of research to be applied should be, action and problem-oriented. The need is to develop applicable and testable generalisations on the basis of careful painstaking and imaginative research. While conducting micro level studies, the researcher takes into account the macro social processes and provides an added accent on prime movers and pace setters of change. On the basis of Ambedkar's socio-economic philosophy, the research panorama covers from small micro level studies of specific field problems to large scale holistic monographic studies besides undertaking benchmark surveys and evaluation of development programmes.

Ambedkar opined that economic emancipation is the very foundation for the social progress of SCs. A group of economists and sociologists specially Prof. K. Sachidananda (1971), A.L. Srivastava, H.S. Varma and J.V. Raghavendhra Rao (1970), E.V.S. Patrudu (1971), R.N. Kulahalli and A. Bope Gomagi (1962) and Khan Mumtaz Ali (1980) opined that the SCs have to change a lot still to acquire social and economic equality with the rest of the Indian society. The economic policy has to shift its emphasis from quantity to quality with new technologies and techniques, low cost, improved management and high efficiency. In the context of Ambedkar's social philosophy, the programme and policies for the development of SCs are to be moulded to aim at integrated human society.

Ambedkar was essentially a pragmatist. Action research has to be given due place to realise the aspirations of Ambedkar. Further, to commemorate the memory of Ambedkar, the intellectual community may earnestly take up certain programmes, such as promotion of inter-disciplinary research, Constitution of a task force for policy making, creation of a chair in economics/politics/sociology/law departments of university besides prescribing syllabus on Ambedkar in post-graduate studies.

Notes

1. Ambedkar, B.R., 'State and Minorities', quoted by N. Jhadav in *Economic and Political Weekly*, 13 April 1991, p. 982.
2. Ambedkar, B.R., 'Small Holdings in India and their Remedies', *Journal of Indian Economic Society*, Vol. 1, 1918, p. 28.
3. Behera, Deepak Kumar, 'Socio-Cultural Problems of the Christians of S.C.', *Man and Life: Journal of the Institute of Social Research and Applied Anthropology*, Vol. 15, Nos. 1 and 2, January–June 1989, p. 64.
4. Resolutions of National Convention of SCs & STs Parliamentarians and Legislators held at New Delhi, 16–17 June 1992.
5. Somasekhar, A., 'Quality of Life of Scheduled Castes: Facts and Issues', paper presented in the Seminar on Relevance of Dr. B.R. Ambedkar for the present times conducted at Hyderabad on 19 April 1992.

27

Post-Ambedkar Scheduled Castes Agitations in Andhra Pradesh

A Critical Evaluation

K.S. Chalam

An Apology

The term 'agitation' is being used in this paper rather than the usual concept of 'movement'. It is also our intention not to use the term 'Dalit' in the context of fractured identities of subversive agitations within the ambit of the term first time in India in this state. The author owes an explanation for not using the traditional terminology, which is popular among Dalit scholars and others working on Dalits.

There is a growing literature on social movements with reference to Dalits in India. But the theory of social movements takes into consideration those agitations which are sustained through institutional structures. In fact, there are several explanations in the use of the term social movement. It is said that it is 'an extra-institutionalised collective political action which strive for or resist social and political change'. It is an illegal public protest,

Reproduced from *Social Action*, July-September 2007.

according to David Baley. But a protest or agitation turns out to be a movement when it is sustained through collective action. Heberle defines movement as 'collective attempts to bring change or create new social order'. Viewing the Scheduled Castes agitations in Andhra Pradesh from the above mentioned framework makes the task difficult as the agitations are sporadic, momentary and issue based. Therefore, we have refrained from using the term 'social movement' to analyse the Dalit agitation in Andhra Pradesh. We have also not used the term Dalit as a collective of all socially deprived groups. There is no social cohesion among the 59 identified Scheduled Castes in Andhra Pradesh. Further, a separate agitation for the identity and share in the benefits has been spearheaded for the last one decade in the state. In fact the colonial identity of the Scheduled Castes or ex-Untouchables is lost long back with protracted battles against the indigenous culture of the native Indians. This has been done deliberately by the settlers both in the past and in recent times. Interestingly the native Indians themselves have played into the hands of their enemies by denying their own cultural identity once they are converted into a different faith. It has almost disappeared in the mainstream Dalit consciousness in Andhra Pradesh except in a few pockets in Telangana and other under developed regions of the state.

Andhra Pradesh was formed as a separate state in 1956, the year in which Babasaheb Ambedkar passed away. Therefore, the Scheduled Castes' agitations in the state need to be viewed as Post-Ambedkar agitations. Though Andhra Pradesh administratively emerged as an independent entity, it in fact consists of four distinguished regions. Each region has its own socio-economic and geographical identity. But, in the mainstream literature the dominant region of coastal Andhra is projected as Andhra Pradesh. This has inhibited the unique nature of Scheduled Caste problems in Telangana, Rayalaseema and North Andhra. The so-called social movements and protest movements of Andhra Pradesh as depicted and explained by scholars relate to coastal Andhra Pradesh only. In fact the region had a unique advantage of conversions by 1931. It was estimated by Forrester D.B. that 20 per cent of the depressed classes in Godavari districts, 32 per cent in Krishna and 57 per cent in Guntur have been converted to Christianity by 1931. It was in this region that Ambedkar movement originated. Except in the studies of Gail Omvedt who has studied Ambedkar movement separately for Telangana (Hyderabad) and coastal Andhra, none of the scholars paid any attention to the diversity in the problems of Scheduled Castes in different parts of the state. The social movements in Telengana region are absorbed in the left and radical left struggles from 1950, before the formation of the state. (Telangana became a separate state in 2014) The Rayalaseema region has a unique problem of factionalism and the Scheduled Castes are the active players in this game. The North Coastal Andhra is the most neglected and marginalised region and therefore the agitations and events have never been brought to the attention of the scholars except as a part of Srikakulam struggle. It is now clear that a study of the agitations of the Scheduled Castes in Andhra Pradesh is expected to pay attention to the different aspects of the struggles unique to each region. A blanket generalisation may not help the scholar to comprehend the problem.

Methodologies

There appears to be no unanimity in the use of a single method to study the agitations, struggles and movements of the Scheduled Castes in Andhra Pradesh in particular and social movements in general. Several approaches have been followed by scholars to study the social movements. There are broadly three approaches that are popular in the study of Dalit movements.

1. The revised historical materialism wherein the dialectical nature of the caste, identified as class caste is followed by Gail Omvedt in her study on Dalits and the Democratic Revolution. She has analysed the ideology and organisation of a movement as an anti-caste and class struggle with its interactions with freedom struggle. She has used the Marxist categories of class, dialectics and ideology of base and super structure in her analysis.
2. The institutional process of M.S. Gore who has developed a theory of social context to place Ambedkar and his movement in an ideological perspective.

3. Relative deprivation or social exclusion approach as a new theory of social development in the context of globalisation. This is a revised theory of capability approach developed by Amartya Sen mostly bringing economic categories for analysis rather than the social classes of castes in India. But it can be productively be used to study the Dalit situation in the global context.

Struggles in Andhra Pradesh

It is observed that the approaches used by scholars to study the social movements or struggle of Dalits are not uniform. Further, most of the studies undertaken on Scheduled Castes or Dalits in Andhra Pradesh are related to the Ambedkar period, prior to 1956 before the formation of the state. Therefore, the studies do not focus on the process of change and the issues that are generated from struggles to resolve those problems. Most of the studies concentrate on Ambedkar movement as an extended ideology of all India character without considering the specific nature of each state and region. As a result, they have failed to bring out the shortcomings of the movements to provide insights into the problems.

The following important events are identified here around which the Scheduled Castes agitations in Andhra Pradesh are concentrated.

1.	1962	Sanjivaiah became the first Dalit Chief Minister of Andhra Pradesh
2.	1969	Kanchikacherla Kotesu was burnt alive in Krishna District
3.	1983	Burning of 4 persons in Padiri Kuppam in Chittor district
4.	1985	The Karamchedu massacre took place on 17 July in Prakasam district resulting in the formation of Dalit Mahasabha
5.	1991	Chunduru carnage took place on 6 August in Guntur district. The breaking of Dalit Mahasabha
6.	1992	Dalit writers, artists and intellectuals collective formed in Hyderabad
7.	1995	Madiga Dandora was formed in coastal districts of Andhra Pradesh
8.	1998	Vempenta incident in Kurnool district where Dalits were brutally killed through the alleged involvement of Naxlite groups
9.	2001	Dalit human rights organisation as an NGO initiative formed to represent the Dalit issue at WCAR at Durban
10.	2003	The Scheduled Castes reservations were categorised by the government as ABC and D

The Context of the Struggles

The 10 important events identified in the history of Scheduled Castes struggles in Andhra Pradesh took place over a period of four decades. This covers the major part of the period after the formation of the state in 1956. In all the events, the significant factor of dispute appears to be social exploitation and the protest against caste discrimination. It is further noticed that the first events in the beginning of the agitations has shown the Dalit upsurge, symbolically resulting in the capture of the post of chief minister of a state first time in the country. The major content of the protest movements, which are an extension of the anti-Brahmin struggles from the combined Madras Presidency appear to have social equality as its agenda. This has facilitated the emergence of the leadership of Dr Sanjivaiah, a scholar politician.

The Kanchikacharla Kotesu case became a landmark in the history of Dalit struggles in Andhra Pradesh. This incident helped the ruling castes to become conscious of their hegemony over the Dalits in the advanced districts of Andhra Pradesh. The Padiri Kuppam case is the beginning of a new political regime based on anti-Brahmin struggle and consolidation of caste power of a Sudra caste in Andhra Pradesh. Caste is always seen in India in its practice, otherwise it has no meaning. Therefore, when a particular caste becomes strong, it tries to show its power in relation to another caste, mostly the deprived castes like Scheduled Castes. This is what has happened in Padiri Kuppam and in Karamchedu. The Karamchedu massacre was so brutal that two Dalit minor girls were raped and their private parts mutilated. The brutal massacre gave a conscious development of an organisation to protest against the incident. The formation of the Dalitha Mahasabha was a long felt need of the Dalits in the state, as the mainstream Dalit struggles in the state were confined to job reservation by the organised few till the incident happened in Karamchedu. Within five years after the Karamchedu incident, the Chunduru incident took place in the neighbouring district of Guntur. But, the usual daliting, i.e. breaking into pieces has taken place within the Dalit mahasabha when the Chunduru issue came up for agitation. However, these two important events moved the intellectuals and writers belonging to the Scheduled Castes and some backward castes to form into an organisation to reflect on the woes of Dalits in Andhra Pradesh.

The madigas of Andhra Pradesh, the victims of Karamchedu became conscious of their conditions and rights. They perceived that injustice is done to them by *malas* within the Dalit group and therefore wanted a separate identity for their group. This helped to form a separate organisation called 'Madiga Dandora'. The *malas* protested against this and formed a separate organisation called 'Mala Mahanadu'. The ghastly incident in Vempenta where about half a dozen Dalits were killed passed out without any significant attention in the melee of internal bickerings. Keeping the world conference against racism, the NGO sector reacted positively to take the Dalit issue to the international forum through the formation of Dalit human rights group. The government of Andhra Pradesh has passed a government order dividing the Scheduled Castes reservations into ABCD groups in 2003. The *malas* challenged it in the Supreme Court and it was struck down by Supreme Court as unconstitutional. Interestingly all the struggles in the state moved around the above issues and took place in the advanced districts of coastal Andhra Pradesh.

An Evaluation of the Struggles

We have presented the incidents and data on the scheduled castes struggles, which are basically caste related issues in Andhra Pradesh. It is now difficult to evaluate the struggles in terms of any of the methodologies that have been used by scholars. We have not been able to develop a political economy of Dalit movements in India. The Marxist scholars have used the European categories to study Indian caste and have not been totally succeeded in evaluating the struggles and movements. But, we can evaluate the struggles in terms of the empirical data in relation to other major events in the Andhra Society, so as to get some meaningful conclusions. We are trying to relate the incidents and events in the context of the overall change and development in Andhra society here. If the events are not related to the overall development in the state, they become autonomous without any substantial meaning in it. In fact, a situation has already set in Andhra Pradesh where the Dalit struggles and agitations are viewed as independent and autonomous without any active participation or relation with other contemporary struggles. In a way it is an alienation of the Dalits from the mainstream. Does it really help the Dalits? How are the Dalits trying to build up their movements or agitations in an era of economic globalisation where events are inter-dependant?

An attempt is made here to evaluate the Scheduled Castes struggles in relation to other developments in Andhra Pradesh. It is very significant to find that all major events in the Scheduled Castes struggles took place in the developed coastal Andhra Pradesh. Social scientists have identified these districts as beneficiaries of green revolution with new inputs both from government and other institutional structures. This green revolution has brought in new social relations in these districts which the social scientists have recorded and analysed as a part of general development model. No attention is paid by the scholars on the issues of caste relations in the process of agrarian change. Some scholars have analysed the events as a part of class struggle or agrarian class conflicts with some attention on caste conflicts. But this may not help Dalit activist to arrive at meaningful conclusions for the continuation of his work with people. It is our view that so far the Scheduled Castes struggles were burdened with social and psychological issues without paying much attention to the economic issues, which perhaps are responsible for the events that we have identified already. This does not mean there is a base-super structure relationship here. Gail Omvedt and others have employed those categories and are now disappointed. Therefore, without going into the methodological questions, we present here the three phases of the agitations/struggles in Andhra Pradesh after the formation of the state.

Self-Respect Movement: Phase I

The Telugu speaking people of Andhra region have inherited the self-respect movement of Madras Presidency when a separate state was formed in 1956. The Adi Dravida and Adi Andhra movement initiated in Hyderabad state by Bhagyareddy Varma had also its impact on the coastal districts of Andhra. Dr Ambedkar had also toured the districts in the early 1940s and enthused the Dalit masses. All these have culminated in the self-respect and anti-untouchability struggles in Andhra Pradesh.

The Scheduled Castes were slowly consolidating themselves as a cohesive group. The leaders among the scheduled castes have started management hostels for the educational development of the Scheduled Castes with state aid. This has given opportunities to some of the ex-Untouchables to enter higher educational institutions and civil service. A separate 'Harijan elite' started emerging in Andhra Pradesh.

Social Equality Struggles: Phase II

The emergence of a few educated Dalits in the civil society as a pressure group helped the educated Dalits to enter public sector jobs. The jobholders have started organising Scheduled Caste Welfare Organisations when they started facing discrimination, humiliation and punishment in their places of work. In order to protect their self-respect and constitutional rights in the area of promotion, transfer and appointments of their kin, these groups have slowly formed Ambedkar organisations to incorporate the support of the local Dalits. The formation of the Ambedkar associations at the district headquarters along with the employees' organisations helped to form a network of Dalits in the state. This helped the Dalit organisations to put forward certain demands before the government. The government has to yield to these demands and allocate funds in the plan budgets of social welfare departments. Most of the demands relate to the enhancement of scholarships, opening up of new residential schools and soon. By the end of the second term of NTR, the government seemed to have realised that it is expensive to meet the demands of the organised Dalits. In fact, the poverty levels among the Dalits in the 1970s was 65 per cent and has remained at 45 per cent even by 1990. They are much higher than OBCs and other castes. But, the demands of the Dalit organisations have accordingly contained issues relating to the amelioration of poverty, abolition of untouchability, etc. We have not made any content analysis of the demands here. But, a cursory look at the protest literature created during the period contains mostly social issues. And most of the issues are addressed to the government for solution.

The literacy levels of the people of Andhra Pradesh are one of the lowest in the country and that of the Scheduled Castes much lower than the national average. In the latest NSS Report

(1999–2000), it is reported that out of every 1,000 households in the age group of 15 years and above, 522 among males and 772 among females are illiterate among Scheduled Castes in Andhra Pradesh. Though Ambedkar and Dalit organisations are very active, the attention paid by these groups on the development of literacy among the Dalits in rural areas is negligible.

It seems there is no relationship between the levels of literacy and crimes against Dalits in India. It is found that Kerala comes as number four in rank in terms of atrocities on Dalits per lakh of population in 1998 while Andhra comes sixth. We have made a study on the atrocities against Scheduled Castes in Andhra Pradesh and developed a composite index of discrimination. The data are presented in Table 1.

Determinants of Caste Discrimination

Caste system in India ascribes different values to different castes. This can be found across all castes. Some castes are discriminated in private sphere, some are in public life and Dalits are discriminated every where. This is because of the low value attributed to the life of a Dalit. This discrimination is practiced in several ways. But in a civilised society certain minimum human relations are expected to be exchanged between individuals who are equal in physical terms. But this is found to be not valid in India. The Dalits are discriminated even in simple human gestures such as giving drinking water, treating all human beings as equal before God, etc. In order to find out how the Dalits are discriminated on the basis of their birth, a statistical estimate is made on the basis of the data culled out from Punnayya Commission report. As the number of cases in each item of discrimination is not uniform and the severity of injury varies from one incidence of discrimination to another, we thought of estimating a composite index of discrimination. Out of the four events of discrimination reported in the Report, we have taken two important events, temple entry and two glasses system to represent discrimination across districts. These two events are reported in all the districts in the State. We have assigned two-third weight to temple entry and one-third weight to two glasses system to estimate the composite index. The indices are presented in Table 1 along with the illiteracy rates and incidence of general poverty and agriculture labourers among Dalits in each district. The value of composite index shows the magnitude of discrimination. It is found that the composite index is not uniform across the districts. It may be related to the economic status of the people represented by their poverty and economic calling. Therefore, we have run the following regression to test the determinants of discrimination.

Table 1

Composite Index of Caste Discrimination

S. No.	*District*	*Composite Index of Discrimination*	*SC Illiterate (%)*	*General Poverty (%)*	*SC Ag. Lab (%)*
1.	Adilabad	11.33	75.74	77.00	23.51
2.	Anantapur	211.33	74.32	62.00	35.43
3.	Chittoor	209.33	64.72	62.40	35.97
4.	Cuddapah	23.33	67.65	54.00	37.87
5.	East Godavari	23.67	60.11	51.00	35.44
6.	Guntur	143.33	62.51	56.60	42.14
7.	Karimnagar	6.33	75.10	53.00	36.17
8.	Khammam	66.33	68.39	58.00	35.47
9.	Krishna	5.00	59.84	47.00	40.43
10.	Kurnool	290.67	71.92	50.50	37.23
11.	Mahbubnagar	754.00	85.49	65.00	47.97
12.	Medak	74.33	82.73	58.00	25.72
13.	Nalgonda	165.00	75.40	58.50	37.65
14.	Nellore	43.00	64.94	48.00	37.54
15.	Nizamabad	15.67	80.46	42.00	32.98
16.	Prakasam	81.33	68.61	53.00	43.36
17.	Ranga Reddy	244.67	69.94	58.00	26.01
18.	Srikakulam	65.33	68.99	60.00	34.85
19.	Visakhapatnam	61.00	55.27	58.80	19.37
20.	Vizianagaram	61.33	71.46	55.00	31.81
21.	Warangal	41.00	72.74	48.50	25.85
22.	West Godavari	15.33	59.26	46.90	42.57

Source: Chalam, K.S., 'Offences and Atrocities against Scheduled Castes in Andhra Pradesh: An Empirical Investigation', *Social Action*, January-March 2004.

The determinants of discrimination

$$CID = \beta_0 + \beta_1 \text{ ilt.} + \beta_2 \text{ Pov} + \beta_3 \text{ Aglab}$$

Where CID = Composite index of caste discrimination
ilt. = Rate of illiteracy among SCs
Pov = Per cent of population below poverty line
Aglab = Per cent of agriculture labour among SCs
β_1, β_2, β_3 are coefficients to be estimated

We have obtained the following results.

$$CID = \beta_0 + \underset{(1.82)}{0.331\, \beta_1} + \underset{(2.14)}{0.440\, \beta_2} + \underset{(2.46)}{0.445\, \beta_3} \quad r^{-2} = 0.45$$

Figures in brackets are t values. They are statistically found significant.

The above results show that the model is statistically significant as it is explaining 45 per cent of the variations. Out of the three variables, poverty among the people and incidence of agricultural labourers among Dalits are found to explain strongly the prevalence of caste discrimination than illiteracy. They are also found to be statistically significant. It is interesting to observe from these results that economic factors are still contributing for the prevalence of caste discrimination in Andhra Pradesh. We have also estimated correlation coefficients between CID and the percentage of Christian population as a stimulant for discrimination. We found that there is no relation between the two. The correlation coefficient between CID and the percentage of SC population in a district is found to be 0.52. Therefore, we are of the opinion that the above model of regression is valid in explaining the determinants of caste discrimination.

Social Exclusion and Alienation: The Present Situation

The data on land holdings, levels of poverty among the Dalits clearly indicate that there is a relationship between the overall development of the state and the development of the Dalits. The caste related development index developed by the author and presented in Table 2 show the index development achieved by the scheduled castes in Andhra Pradesh. Though the rate of growth of the CDI among the Scheduled Castes is lower than the HDI between 1971 and 1991, it is found that it is increasing over a period of time. As pointed out earlier, the development of the

Scheduled Castes is related to the overall development of the State. Interestingly, it is observed by several commentators that Dalits are socially excluded in all developmental activities today. It is because of the economic globalisation process, which is structurally exclusive in nature, scholars like Amartya Sen are emphasising on the phenomenon of social exclusion as a dangerous trend that will lead to deprivation and capability failure.

Table 2

Caste Related Development Index for Andhra Pradesh

	1971	*1981*	*1991*
Life expectancy index	0.367	0.500	0.583
Educational attainment index	0.177	0.341	0.521
Income index	0.046	0.108	0.145
CDI	0.197	0.316	0.416
AP HDI	—	0.466	0.592

Source: Andhra Pradesh HDI, Chalam, K.S., *Human Development in South India*, Anmol, 2002.

The social exclusion as a new phenomenon is a part of the globalisation process. It consists of inequalities, labour market, gender market and food market exclusion. This exclusion will further accentuate the misery of the Scheduled Castes who are already structurally excluded from the mainstream society. The society does not care for these groups as long as they are raising issues of discrimination, without bringing issues with which others are equally interested. An interesting phenomenon of social exclusion of Dalits has already taken place in Andhra Pradesh in terms of urbanisation.

It is found that the Scheduled Castes urban population is declining compared to the overall increase in the proportion of people who are living in urban areas. In Table 3, the SC urban population for the year 1991 and 2001 is presented. It is clear that the population has declined from 17.31 per cent in 1991 to 17.18 per cent in 2001. Except in the districts of Adilabad, Ranga Reddy, Vizianagaram, Anantapur and Chittor where a marginal increase is found, in all the remaining districts Scheduled Castes urban population has declined. It is generally believed that the opportunities of employment, income and power are concentrated in urban centres. But the data suggest that Scheduled Castes in

Andhra Pradesh are excluded from the trend. This is expected from the globalisation process where Scheduled Castes are not considered as a category at all. The Scheduled Caste organisations have also failed to prepare the Dalits for these opportunities or even to fight against such discrimination and exclusion. Already the educated employees have formed into a separate group as a federation without considering serious economic issues of the Dalits in general. The elite organisations are trying to perpetuate and bargain perks and power for the few families that they represent. This phenomenon is also responsible for social exclusion of the majority of the Dalits who are poor, ignorant and unorganised.

Table 3

Scheduled Castes Urban Population to Total in Andhra Pradesh (%)

Districts	*Year*	
	1991	*2001*
Andhra Pradesh	17.31	17.18
Adilabad	19.20	23.45
Nizamabad	10.88	9.34
Karimnagar	13.11	12.87
Medak	8.25	8.20
Ranga Reddy	32.36	35.19
Mahabubnagar	5.51	4.84
Nalgonda	7.37	8.64
Warangal	14.74	14.55
Khammam	16.44	16.98
Srikakulam	12.03	10.47
Vizianagaram	18.46	20.54
Visakhapatnam	45.94	43.54
East Godavari	15.99	15.36
West Godavari	11.73	11.84
Krishna	18.90	15.72
Guntur	18.39	17.28
Prakasam	8.48	8.22
Nellore	13.00	12.31
Cuddapah	13.62	12,41
Kurnoool	19.76	18.60
Anantapur	14.56	15.33
Chittor	9.79	11.77

The Unfinished Agenda

The Scheduled Castes of Andhra Pradesh were one of the earliest groups to participate in the Ambedkar movement. Though Ambedkar movement was confined to the awakened coastal districts due to mass conversions by 1931, it became a state level upsurge by the 1970s. Ambedkar movement was taken up in Andhra as a social upliftment and anti-untouchability struggle as a part of the missionary agenda. In fact, the ruling castes have been very sensitive to the demands of the organised scheduled castes and introduced several schemes and programmes such as IRDP, Food for work etc, as a part of the development agenda to coopt the Dalits. Though Babasaheb Ambedkar realised the lacunae in his struggles after independence and brought the states and minorities as an economic agenda, majority of the Dalit organisations have not taken up economic issues including privatisation seriously. Now Dalits are excluded and alienated from the mainstream. Some critics say that there is only one movement which is permanent and strong, it is conversion as seen from the massive gatherings in all important towns and cities in Andhra Pradesh. But this process has alienated the Dalits from the mainstream society which is now globally integrated. Unless the scheduled castes start organising for reform within each group through self-help and other means to strengthen their solidarity, the social exclusion with which they are suffering now will become permanent in future.

References

Balagopal, K., *Probings in the Political Economy of Agrarian Classes and Conflicts*, Hyderabad: Perspectives, 1998.

Chalam, K.S., 'Economic Development of Scheduled Castes in Andhra Pradesh 1956–2001', *South India Journal of Social Sciences*, June 2004.

——, *Human Development in South India: The Dravidian Marvel*, New Delhi: Anmol, 2002.

——, *Relevance of Ambedkarism in India*, Jaipur: Rawat Publications, 1993.

Chinna Rao, Y., *Dalits Struggle for Identity*, New Delhi: Kanishka, 2003.

Gore, M.S., *The Social Context of an Ideology*, New Delhi: Sage, 1995.

Omvedt, Gail, *Dalits and the Democratic Revolution: Dr. Ambedkar and the Dalit Movement in Colonial India*, New Delhi: Sage, 1994.

Punnayya, K., Justice Punnayya Commission Report, Vol. I and II, Government of Andhra Pradesh, 2000.

Ramakrishna, V., *Social Reforms in Andhra*, Bombay: Vikas, 1983.

Satyanarayana, A., 'Dalit Identity and Consciousness in Modern Andhra', *Vikalp*, Vol. VI, No. 2, 1999.

Sen, Amartya, *Social Exclusion: Concept, Application and Scrutiny*, Delhi: Critical Quest, 2004.

Bibliography

Ahir, D.C., 'The Buddha and the Future of His Religion', *Maha Bodhi*, Calcutta, 1950.

——, *Dr. Ambedkar and the Indian Constitution*, Buddha Vihara, Lucknow, 1973.

——, *Dr. Ambedkar on Buddhism*, Siddhartha Publications, Bombay, 1982.

Ahluwalia, B.K. and Shashi Ahluwalia, *B.R. Ambedkar and Human Rights*, Manas Publications, New Delhi, 1990.

Altekar, A.S., *The Position of Women in Hindu Civilisation*, Motilal Banarsidass, New Delhi, 1978.

Ambedkar, B.R., *Annihilation of Caste*, Bheem Patrika Publications, Jalandhar, 1936.

——, *The Buddha and His Dhamma*, Siddharth College Publications, Bombay, 1957.

AVARD, *Panchayat Raj as the Basis of Indian Polity: An Exploration into the Proceedings of the Constituent Assembly*, Association of Voluntary Agencies for Rural Development, New Delhi, 1962.

Bailey, L.R., *Ambedkarian Thoughts: Relevance of Ambedkar Mission*, Buddhist Publishing House, Jalandhar, 1977.

Baisantry, D.K., *Ambedkar: The Total Revolutionary*, Segment Book Distributors, New Delhi, 1991.

Behera, Deepak Kumar, 'Socio-Cultural Problems of the Christians of S.C.', *Man and Life: Journal of the Institute of Social Research and Applied Anthropology*, Vol. 15, No. 1 and 2, January-June 1989.

Bernstein, R.J., *John Dewey*, Washington Square Press Inc, New York, 1967.

Berreman, G., 'The Brahminical View of Caste', *Contributions to Indian Sociology*, Vol. 5, 1971.

——, *Caste and Other Inequities*, Folklore Institute, Meerut, 1979.

Beteille, Andre, *Backward Classes in Contemporary India*, Oxford University Press, New Delhi, 1992.

——, *Inequality and Social Change*, Oxford University Press, New Delhi, 1972.

Bharathi, K.S., *Foundations of Ambedkar Thought*, Datt & Sons Publications, Nagpur, 1990.

Biswas, A.R., Manu, Dr. Ambedkar and the Supreme Court (unpublished), 1990.

Bolitho, Hector, *Jinnah: Creator of Pakistan*, John Murray, London, 1954.

Borale, P.T., *Segregation and Desegregation in India*, Manaktalas, Bombay, 1968.

Bose, N.K., 'Class and Caste', in *Culture and Society in India*, Asia Publishing House, New York, 1967.

Chagla, M.C., *Roses in December*, Bharatiya Vidya Bhavan, Bombay, April 1978.

Chalam, K.S., *Education and Weaker Sections*, Inter-India, New Delhi, 1988.

——, *Caste-Based Reservation and Human Development in India*, Sage Publications, New Delhi, 2007.

——, *Economic Reforms and Social Exclusion*, Sage Publications, New Delhi, 2011.

——, *Social Economy of Development in India*, Sage Publications, New Delhi, 2017.

Clutterbuck, Richard, *Guerrillas and Terrorists*, Ohio University Press, London, 1967.

Collins, Larry and Dominique Lapierre, *Freedom at Midnight*, Vikas Publishing House, New Delhi, 1979.

Coupland, Reginald, *The Indian Problem (Parts I, II & III: 1833–1944)*, Oxford University Press, London, 1935.

Davids, Mrs Rhys and F.L. Woodward, *The Book of the Kindred Sayings (Part II: Sanyutta Nikaya)*, Pali Text Society, London. 1907.

Dewey, John, *Ethics* (in collaboration with) John and J.H. Tufts, Henry Holt and Co., New York, 1910.

Diehl, Anita, *Periyar E.V. Ramaswami*, B.I. Publications, New Delhi, 1978.

Durant, Will, *The Story of Philosophy*, Square Press, Washington, 1961.

Eastwood, Granville, *Harold Laski*, Mowbrays, Oxford, 1977.

Falboll, V., *A Collection of Discourses (Suttanipata)*, Motilal Banarsidass, New Delhi, 1968.

Gaekwad, Fatesinghrao, *Sayajirao of Baroda*, Sangam Books, London, 1989.

Gandhi, M.K., *An Autobiography: My Experiments with Truth*, Navajivan Publishing House, Ahmedabad, 1966.

Ginsberg, Morris, 'Social Class', in *Encyclopedia of the Social Sciences*, Vol. III-IV, The Macmillan Co., Bridan, 1959.

Government of Maharashtra, *Dr. Babasaheb Ambedkar: Writings and Speeches*, Vol. 1 to 11, Education Department, Bombay, 1987.

Hanton, Rosalind, *Caste, Conflict and Ideology*, Orient Longman Ltd., Hyderabad, 1985.

Hiro, Dilip, *The Untouchables of India*, The Minority Rights Group Report, London, 1982.

Hutton, J.H., *Caste in India: Its Nature, Function and Origins*, Oxford University Press, Delhi, 1981.

Jahagirdar, Justice R.A., 'Religion, Caste and Politics', *Faith*, 1982.

Jahagirdar, P.J., *Mahadev Govind Ranade*, Publications Division, Government of India, New Delhi, 1971.

Jatava, D.R., *Evolution of Indian Social Thought*, Bohra Publications, Jaipur, 1987.

——, *The Buddha and Karl Marx*, Phoenix Publishing House, Agra, 1968.

——, *The Political Philosophy of Dr. Ambedkar*, Phoenix Publishing Agency, Agra, 1965.

——, *The Social Philosophy of B.R. Ambedkar*, Phoenix Publishing House, Agra, 1965.

Kadam, K.N., 'Buddhism as Rationalism and Humanism and Other Essays on Religion and Rationalism' (unpublished), 1981.

——, 'Currents and Counter Currents in Ancient Indian History' (unpublished), 1985.

——, *Dr. Babasaheb Ambedkar and the Significance of His Movement*, Popular Prakashan, Bombay, 1991.

——, 'Unpublished Writings: Dr. Ambedkar, The Rationalist and Humanist', 1991.

Kamble, J.R., *Pursuit of Equality in Indian History*, National Publishing House, New Delhi, 1985.

Kamble, N.D., *Deprived Classes and Their Struggle for Equality*, Ashish Publishing House, New Delhi, 1983.

——, *The Scheduled Castes*, Ashish Publishing House, Delhi, 1982.

Kamdar, K.H., *History of India: Political and Administrative (1757–1920)*, M.C. Kothari, Baroda, 1924.

Kausalyayan, Anand, *Yadi Baba Na Hote*, Deeksha Batumi Prakashan, Nagpur, 1968.

Keer, Dhananjay, *Dr. Ambedkar: Life and Mission*, Popular Prakashan, Bombay, 1981.

Khabde, Dinkar, *Dr. Ambedkar and Western Thinkers*, Sugava Prakashan, Pune (authors doctoral thesis), 1989.

Kharat, Shankar Rao (Ed.), *Dr. Babasaheb Ambedkar Yanchi Atmakatha* (Marathi), Indrayani Sahitya, Pune, 1987.

Kosambi, D.D., *An Introduction to the Study of Indian History*, Popular Prakashan, Bombay, 1976.

Kosare, H.L., *Vidarbhateel Dalit Chalvalicha Itihas*, Dnyan Pradeep Prakashan, Nagpur, 1984.

Kshirsagar, R.K., *Bharatiya Republican Paksha* (Marathi), Nath Prakashan, Aurangabad, 1979.

Kuber, W.N., *B.R. Ambedkar*, Publications Divisions, Government of India, New Delhi, 1987.

Kunte, B.G. and B.A. Saletore, *Constitutional History of India*, Premier Publishing Co., Delhi, 1950.

Kunte, B.G., *Source Material on Dr. Babasaheb Ambedkar* (Vol. 1), Government of Maharashtra, Bombay, 1982.

Kusuma, D.R., *Abhinava Buddha Ambedkar Suktulu*, Ambedkar Memorial Society, Hyderabad, 1970.

Lederle, M.R., *Philosophical Trends in Modern Maharashtra*, Popular Prakashan, Bombay, 1976.

Ling, Trevor, *Buddhist Revival in India*, The Macmillan Press Ltd., London, 1980.

Lynch, Owen, *The Politics of Untouchability*, Columbia University, New York, 1969.

Mahar, J. Michael, *The Untouchables in Contemporary India*, The University of Arizona Press, Tucson, Arizona, 1972.

Mangudkar, M.P. (Ed.), *Dr. Ambedkar and Parliamentary Democracy*, Mrs Suvarna Mangudkar, Pune, 1976.

Max Muller, F., *A Collection of Verses (the Dhammapada)*, Motilal Banarsidass, Delhi, 1968.

Mencher, Joan, 'The Caste System Upside Down, or the Not-So Mysterious Caste', *Current Anthropology*, Vol. 15, 1974.

Mishra, Vikas, *Hinduism and Economic Growth*, Oxford University Press, New Delhi, 1962.

Moon, Vasant, *Buddha Dhamma Pradeep*, Sugat Prakashan, Nagpur, 1960.

Murti, G.V. Narayan, *Narayan Guru*, Bharat-Bharati Pustaka Sampada, Bangalore, 1974.

Myrdal, Gunnar, *An American Dilemma: The Negro Problem and American Democracy*, Carnegie Corporation, New York, 1944.

Nagaraja Rao, P., 'The Wisdom of Vedas', in *Essays in Indian Philosophy and Religion*, Lalvani Publishing House, Bombay, 1971.

Naipaul, V.S., *India: A Wounded Civilization*, Andre Deutsch, London, 1977.

Nanchariah, G., 'Dr. Ambedkar's Political and Economic Thought', *Journal of Social Development and Justice*, Vol. 1, March 1991.

——, *Land and Caste*, Himalaya Publishing, Bombay, 1988.

Narasu, P. Lakshmi, *The Essence of Buddhism*, Bharatiya Publishing House, Delhi, 1948.

Narayanan, K.R., 'The Rebel', in B.K. Ahluwalia and Shashi Ahluwalia (Eds.), *Human Rights*, Vivek Publishing Company, Delhi, 1981.

Omvedt, Gail, 'Jyoti Rao Phuley and the Ideology of Social Revolution in India', *Economic and Political Weekly*, Annual Number, 1971.

——, *Cultural Revolt in a Colonial Society*, Scientific Trust, Bombay, 1976.

Paranjpye, R.P., *84 Not Out*, National Book Trust, New Delhi, 1961.

Patil, Sharad, *Dasa-Sudra Slavery in Ancient India*, A.D. Bhose, Pune, 1980.

Phadke, Y.D., *Social Reforms of Maharashtra*, Maharashtra Information Centre, Government of Maharashtra, New Delhi, 1985.

Phuley, Jyothi Rao, *Slavery*, Y.D. Phadke (Ed.), Government of Maharashtra, 1990.

Pradhan, G.P. and A.K. Bhagwat, *Lokmanya Tilak*, Jaico Publishers, Bombay, 1985.

Rajagopalachari, C., *Ambedkar Refuted*, Hind Kitabs, Bombay, 1946 (An attempt to reply to Dr. Ambedkar's What Congress and Gandhi have Done to the Untouchables).

Rajasekhariah, A.M., *Dr. Ambedkar and the Politics of Emancipation*, Sindhu Publications, Bombay, 1971.

——, *Dr. B.R. Ambedkar: The Quest for Social Justice*, Uppal Publishing House, New Delhi, 1989.

Rao, Y. Chinna (Ed.), *Prespectives on Economic Development and Social Change,* Rawat Publication, Jaipur, 2009.

Ramasami, Periyar E.V., *Untouchability: History of Vaikom Agitation*, Periyar Self-Respect Propaganda Institution, Madras, 1981.

Ramteke, S.N. and Others, *Nyaya Murti R.R. Bhole*, Mukti Sangram Prakashan, Mahda, 1982.

Rhys Davids, T.W. and C.A.F. Rhys Davids, *Dialogues of the Buddha (Part II: Digha Nikaya)*, Pali Text Society, London, 1921.

Rodrigues, Valerian (Ed.), *The Essential Writings of B.R. Ambedkar*, Oxford University Press, New Delhi, 2004.

Russell, Bertrand, *Principles of Social Reconstruction*, George Allen & Unwin Ltd., London, 1923.

——, *Sceptical Essays*, George Allen & Unwin Ltd., London, 1934.

Sangharakshita, Mahasthavira, *Religion and Secularism*, Dhammamegha Series, No. 11, Pune, 1983.

——, *The Thousand-Petalled Lotus*, Heinemann, London, 1976.

Schneider, Herbert W., *A History of American Philosophy*, Forum Books Inc., New York, 1957.

Setty, N.S., *A Brief Life Sketch of Dr. B.R. Ambedkar*, Dr. Ambedkar Memorial Society, Hyderabad, 1987.

Shah, Ghanshyam, *Politics of Scheduled Castes and Tribes*, Vora & Co., Bombay, 1975.

Sharma, R.S., *Sudras in Ancient India*, Motilal Banarsidass, Delhi, 1958.

Shastri, Shankaranand, *My Memories and Experiences of Babasaheb Dr. B.R. Ambedkar*, Smt. S. Shastri, Ghaziabad, 1989.

Singh, Paramanand, *Equality, Reservations and Discrimination*, Deep & Deep Publications, New Delhi, 1982.

Singh, Sanghasen (Ed.), *Ambedkar on Buddhist Conversion and its Impact*, Eastern Book Linkers, Delhi, 1990.

Sri Aurobindo, *Hymns to the Mystic Fire*, Sri Aurobindo Ashram, Pondicherry, 1952.

——, *The Foundation of Indian Culture and the Renaissance in India*, Sri Aurobindo Ashram, Pondicherry, 1971.

——, *The Secret of Veda*, Sri Aurobindo Ashram, Pondicherry, 1985.

Thapar, Romila, 'Social Mobility in Ancient India', in R.S. Sharma (Ed.), *Indian Society: Historical Probings*, People's Publishing House, New Delhi, 1974.

——, *Asoka and the Decline of Mauryas*, Oxford University Press, Delhi, 1982.

Thomas, Mathew, *Reform or Revolution*, Segment Books, New Delhi, 1991.

Thomas, P., *Indian Women Through the Ages*, Asia Publishing House, Calcutta, 1964.

Tomkins, Stephen, *The Origins of Mankind*, Cambridge University Press, Cambridge, 1984.

Toynbee, Arnold J., *A Study of History*, Oxford University Press, Oxford, 1978.

Wilkinson, T.S. and M.N. Thomas (Eds.), *Ambedkar and the Neo-Buddhist Movement*, Christian Literature Society, Madras, 1972.

Wilson, K., *The Twice Alienated Culture of Dalit Christians*, Book Links, Hyderabad, 1982.

Zelliot, Eleanor, *Ambedkar and the Mahar Movement*, University of Pennsylvania, 1969.

——, *From Untouchable to Dalit: Essays on Ambedkar Movement*, Manohar, New Delhi, 1992.

Index

Abraham, P., 143
Advani, L.K., 64
agricultural economics, 131–132
agriculture, 40, 170, 258
collective system of, 40, 157
as industry, 132
small-scale capitalist, 173
state ownership of, 166, 176
ahimsa, doctrine of, 69
All India Scheduled Castes Federation, 40
Altekar, A.S., 184, 185
Ambedkar, B.R., 15–19, 22, 120, 122, 128, 137, 150–151, 161–162
annihilation of caste, views on, 240–243
as architect of Indian Constitution, 209–220, 223
on Buddha, 52, 53, 67–68, 138, 151, 176–177
caste system, views on, 191–196, 240
conspiracy against, 175–176
conversion to Buddhism, 68, 118, 151
as creative iconoclast, 17, 199–206
description and contribution of, 35
early life of, 114–115
economic ideas, 39–40, 129–132
Hindu religion, view on, 22, 66–67, 117, 153–154
last days, 119–120
model of economic development, 164–167
multi-faceted personality of, 36–39
non-Brahminical enlightenment, 64–65
as policy-maker, 132–133
Ambedkar, B.R. (*cont.*)
professional life, 115
research contributions, 256–257

and secularism, 84–86, 88
small holdings, views on, 170–174
socio-economic ideas, 150–159
struggles, historical background of, 115–119
as theoretician, 128–130
writings of, 35
Ambedkarism, 16–17, 21
Andhra Pradesh, Scheduled Castes' agitations in, 265–278
annihilation of caste, 47, 240–243
Annihilation of Caste (B.R. Ambedkar), 55, 79, 85, 137, 140
anti-caste struggles, 54–55, 62
Aristotle, 42
armchair philosophy, 37
Ayyar, Alladi Krishnaswamy, 209

Backward Classes, classification as, 230
Backward Classes Commission, 230
Bahishkrit Hitakarini Sabha, 100, 116
Balakrishnan, K.G., 226
Baley, David, 266
Bank Nationalisation Act 1969, 225
Bardhan, A.B., 64
Basavapunnaiah, M., 57, 58
Bedekar, Sudhir, 51, 54
beneficiary-oriented schemes, 259
Bharatiya Samaj Seva Sangh, 111
Bhikkuni Sangha, 70
Bhikku Sangha, 70–71
Biswas, A.R., 76
Bole, C.K., 92
Bombay Legislative Assembly, 96, 119, 133, 137, 141
bourgeois democracy, 58, 59
Brahmaism and Brahmanism, distinction between, 23
'a Brahmana', 53
Brahminical enlightenment, 64
Brahminical law, 76–77
Brahminism in India, 236
The Buddha and His Dhamma (B.R. Ambedkar), 52, 78, 86, 118, 137, 140
Buddha Charita, 68
Buddhism, 22, 31–32, 49, 76, 141, 151
Ambedkar's view of, 68–71
Marxism and, 176–177
practising, 71–72
propagation of, 72
and secularism, 82–84
women status under, 70, 183

caste, 123, 184. *See also* caste system
annihilation of, 47, 240–243
Brahmanic model of, 184
and class, 62, 123
conflicts, 196
consciousness, 123
economic implications, 162–163
Marxist class theory of, 61
origin of, 195
process of formation of, 195
caste discrimination, determinants of, 273–275
caste equations, encouragement to, 125
caste hierarchy, 196
caste inequality, 216
caste problem, 52, 53
caste system, 29, 32–34, 36, 42, 62, 118, 162, 183, 247–249, 273
Ambedkar's views on, 191–196, 201
decline in status of women with rise of, 185–188, 233

endogamy and, 152–153, 193
evil effects of, 124
as form of division of labour, 162–163
genesis of, 123
and industrial development, 63
and inequalities, 111, 162
origin of, 123
and social inequality, 196
Chandra, Satish, 61
Chatterjee, Somnath, 64
Chattopadhyaya, Debi Prasad, 52, 55–56
chaturvarna system of Hindus, 41
Christianity, 67
civil obedience, 42
class contradiction, in society, 58
class enlightenment, 63–64
classless society, 56
class methodology, 57
Class Struggle and Caste Conflict in Rural Areas (S.G. Sardesai), 58
Coase, Ronal Harry, 129
colleges, establishment of, 155–156
Columbia University, 39, 42, 94, 95, 115, 129, 239, 255
combination, 54
for Ambedkarism and Marxism, 54–55
compensation, issue of, 226
consolidation
in agriculture, 179
of holdings, 258
Constituent Assembly
criticism of, 119
Draft Constitution in, 120
Constitution of India, 209, 211, 223–223
amendments to, 223, 224, 227
Article 16, 228
Article 31, 224
Article 32, 216–217
Article 15 and Article 16, 229–230
constitutional mandate, 218–220
directive principles of State policy, 217–218
draft Constitution, 209
federalism, 211–213
fundamental rights, 215–217
parliamentary democracy, 213–215
position of president under, 218
role of Ambedkar in making of, 209–211, 223
social justice and, 227–231
Constitutional Law, 147
constitutional morality, 215
constitutional remedies, 216–217
The Creation of Patriarchy (Gerda Lemer), 182
critical Gandhism, 34
critique of tradition, 28
cultural imperialism, 29
curriculum, 111–112

Dalit movement, 28, 34
Dalits, 139
economic development for, 142–144
economic exploitation, protection against, 144–147
future of, 147–148
in Public Sector, opportunities for, 147
social exclusion of, 276–277
upliftment of, 140, 141
Dasa-Sudra Slavery, 60
Dasgupta, S.N., 52
Davids, Rhys, 70

democracy, 95, 110, 162
  and development, 142
  pitfalls of, 214
  suggestions for successful working of, 214–215
  view on, 42–43, 204
Democracy and Education: An Introduction to the Philosophy of Education (John Dewey), 91, 96
democratic revolution, 63
  Ambedkar's strategy, 63
  communist strategy, 63
democratic socialism, 180
democratisation of higher education, 91–92
  colleges, democratic functioning of, 101–106
  university education, Ambedkar on, 97–101
'depressed classes educational society', 109–110
Depressed Classes Mission, 115, 116
depressed class movement, 115–119
development
  Ambedkar's strategy of, 164–167
  democracy for, 142
  economic, 142–144
  philosophy of, 141
Dewey, John, 41, 84, 86, 94–96, 109–110
dhamma of Buddha, 110
dharam nirapekhsh, 80
directive principles of state policy, 142, 176, 217–218
division of labourers, 162
Drafting Committee, Constitution, 209
Drafting Committee of the Constituent Assembly, 39
dukkha, 51, 53, 69, 141
  abolition of, 176
economic concessions, 236–238
economic development, concept of, 257, 259
economic exploitation
  protection against, 144–147
  untouchability and, 163–164
economic holding, 132, 171–172
economic realism, idea of, 158–159
Economic Reform and Social Exclusion, 147
economic theory, 39–40
education, 90–91, 123, 133
  aims of, 111
  Ambedkar contribution to development of, 93–97, 102
  in British India, 93, 102–103, 107, 108
  curriculum, 111–112
  democratic ideal of, 111, 112
  for depressed classes, 96
  economic importance of, 96, 97
  equal opportunities in, 112
  free and compulsory, 93, 103, 113
  higher education, 91, 108, 133
  methodology, 112
  nature of, 110–111
  philosophy of Ambedkar, 109–114
  primary, 113
  science and technology courses, 110, 111
  technical, 110, 112
  as universal right, 93
  university education, 97–101
  for Untouchables, 110
  western concept of, 91
educationally and socially backward classes, concept of, 95

electicism, 54
Elite Pluralism and Class Rule (Jayant Lele), 62
emancipation of mind, 63
eminent domain, principles of, 226
endogamy, 152–153, 183, 233
enlightenment, 63–65
Enlightenment and the Vision of the New Way (B.R. Ambedkar), 137
environmental movement, 28
equality, in society, 180
Essentials of Dr Babasaheb Ambedkar, 86
The Evolution of Provincial Finance in British India (B.R. Ambedkar), 77, 256
exchange rates, 131, 256
exogamy, 193–194

Factories Amendment Bill, 1944, 237
federalism, 211–213
feudal *jati* society, 61
Free and Compulsory Education Bill, 103
fundamentalism, 75–76, 78
  concept of, 79
fundamental rights, 215–217

Gandhi, Indira, 224
Gandhi, Mahatma, 27, 93, 128, 201, 207, 215, 240
Gholap, D.D., 92
Gore, M.S., 94, 267
gotras, exogamous, 194
Government of India Act, 1919, 261
Government of India Act, 1935, 211
Gramsci, Antonio, 52
Gupta, Dipankar, 57

Habib, Mohammad, 61
Harijans, movement for development of, 118–119
highest castes and lowest castes, struggle between, 196
Hind Swaraj, 27
Hindu Code Bill, 78, 85, 120, 154–155, 181, 233
Hindu ethics, 29
Hindu society, 36, 195
  criticism of, 29, 153–154
Hindu temple entry movements, 116, 117
historical materialism, 57
Holyoake, George Jacob, 79
hostels, for Untouchable students, 155
Human Development Index (HDI), 259
human rights, struggles for, 49
humanisation of castes, 48
humanity of person, 48

ideal society, 159
idle labour
  concept of, 172
  economic effects of, 132, 172
Indian society, 36–37
Indian Trade Unions Bill, 1943, 237
'Indian Union', 212–213
individual freedom, 59
individual/individuality, in philosophy, 30–32, 41, 159
individual, western conception of, 30–31
Indra Sawhney case, 229
industrialisation and development, 179
  need of, 258
Industrial Policy Resolution of 1948, 148

inequalities. *See also* caste system
  eradication of, 204
  in Hindu society, 36
institutional economics, 129
institutional reforms, 131, 132
inter-caste marriages, 183, 241
inter-collegiate teaching, 133
inter-disciplinary methodology, to Indian economic studies, 129
Islam, 67
Iyer, Justice Krishna, 220

Jahagirdar, R.A., 87
Jatava, D.R., 77
Jefferson, Thomas, 224
Jeth Malani, Ram, 225
Jevons, H.S., 171
judicial system, unified, 212

Kamble, Shivaram Janaba, 115
Keatings, G.F., 171
Ketkar, V.S., 60
Kosambi, D.D., 184
Kulkarni, Rupa, 64

land for landless, 201
land holdings, 170–173
landlordism, abolition of, 63
land reforms, 131–132, 258
large holdings, 171
law of karma, in Buddhism, 69
leader of thought, 37
leftist parties, 50
Lenin, 55–56
  definition of class by, 56
Lenin the Philosopher (Debi Prasad Chattopadhyaya), 56
Lewis, Arthur, 179
liberal philosophy, 30
'literature of thought', 35
Locke, John, 43
Lohia, Ram Manohar, 28, 33, 64
lower castes, 36
lowest castes, in rural villages, 196

Madiga Dandora, 270
Mala Mahanadu, 270
Mandal Commission judgment, 227–229
Mandal, Jogendranath, 223
Manu, 23, 30, 41, 62, 152
Manu Dharma Sastra, 183, 185
Manusmriti, 117, 186
Marathwada University, 54
Marxism, 28–29, 55–59
  criticism of, 29
  superiority of Buddhism over, 29
  triad of, 55
Marxism and Anthropology (Maurice Bloch), 58
Marxist enlightenment, 64, 65
Marx, Karl, 176
Milind College, 104
Mines Maternity Benefit Bill, 1943, 234
monetary economics, contribution to, 131
moral responsibility, 31
Muslim rule, 77

Naipaul, V.S., 124, 125
Nandy, Ashis, 33
Narayan, Jayaprakash, 94, 128
nationalisation of industries, 158
nationalised insurance, 146
natural resources, 158
Nehru, Jawaharlal, 43, 119, 120, 128, 154–155, 199, 206, 209, 214, 215, 224
New Economic Policy, 261

oligarcy, 57
Omvedt, Gail, 94, 267
The Origin of the Family, Private Property and the State, 57

Panchasila, 176–177
Pandit, Nalini, 54
Pansare, Govind, 65
parliamentary democracy, 167, 211, 213–215
  weakness of, 214
Parulekar, Godavari, 62
Patel, Sardar, 209, 224
patriarchy, 187
peasant movement, 28
Peoples' Education Society, 116, 155
Phadke, T.D., 64
philosopher, criterion of, 51–53
philosophy, 17, 29, 38
  Buddha's, 51–53
  non-Brahminical theistic materialism, 53
socialistic dialectical realihsm, 53
philosophy of Ambedkar, 27–34, 37–39
  concepts of ethical and religious in, 28–29
  development, 137–148
  dharma and Buddhism in, 31–32
  educational, 109–113
  Gandhi's thought and, 32–34
  Hinduism, attack on, 29
  individual in, 30–32, 41, 159
  political and social philosophy, 40–44
  religion in, 29–30
  socio-economic, 257–264
  socio-political, 122–127
  study of, reasons for, 27–28
  utility and justice in, 30
Philosophy of Hinduism, 29
The Philosophy of Hinduism and Riddles in Hinduism, 27
Phuley, Jyoti Rao, 16, 51–53, 59, 93
Plato, 56–57, 112
political democracy, 43, 142, 180
political parties, and caste, 50
political philosophy, 40–44
political power, 43
Poona pact, 201, 261
possessive individualism, 31
post graduate education, object of, 102
poverty, 66, 141, 176
Praja Socialist Party, 180
Prasad, Dr Rajendra, 154, 209
precedents, 228, 229
primary education, 113
prime minister, power in, 218
Prison Notebook, 52
private property, concept of, 225–227
The Problem of the Rupee (B.R. Ambedkar), 256
proletarian dictatorship, 59
public finance, contribution to, 131, 256
Punnayya Commission report, 273

Rajashekaraiah, A.M., 210
Raju, Ganni, 117
Rajwade, V.K., 59
Ranadive, B.T., 55
rathyatra movement, 64
Rawls, John, 228
religion, 67
  Ambedkar on, 79
  concept of, 78–79
  for development of mankind, 67–68. *See also* Buddhism

religious conversions, 68, 118, 120, 151
religious freedom, 156
religious fundamentalism, 76
religious sanction, 123
Republic (Plato), 56
reservation policy of government, 218, 219
Reserve Bank of India, 131
Riddles of Hinduism, 64
Rig Veda, 246
rights, recognition and protection of, 257
round table conferences, 119, 261
rural villages, downtrodden communities in, 196

Sabharwal, Y.K., 227
sacred society, 80
Sankhya philosophy, 137–138
Saraswati, Swamy Dayanand, 91
sati, custom of, 95, 186, 187
Satyashodhak Communist Party, 51
Sceptical Essays (Bertrand Russell), 78
Scheduled Caste Federation, 50
Scheduled Caste girls, reservation for, 111
Scheduled Castes (SCs), 47, 125, 139, 218, 230
  constitutional safeguards for, 130
  economic emancipation for social progress of, 263
  exclusion of, 125
  human rights to, 49
  humanity of, denial of, 47–48
  issues to improve quality of life of, discussion on, 259–262
  political alternatives for, 49–50
  provisions for, in Constitution, 218
  religious conversion, 49
  studies on, 262–264
Scheduled Castes agitations, in Andhra Pradesh, 265–278
  caste discrimination, determinants of, 273–275
  context of struggles, 269–270
  evaluation of struggles, 270–271
  methods to study, 267–268
  self-respect movement, 271–272
  social equality struggles, 272–273
  social exclusion and alienation, 275–277
  struggles in Andhra Pradesh, 268
Scheduled Tribes, 218, 230
secular society, 80
  and sacred society, 80
secular state, 81
secularism, 75
  Ambedkar and, 84–86, 88
  during British period in India, 77–78
  Buddhism and, 82–84
  concept of, 78–82
  definitions of, 79–80
  historical background, 76–78
  in India today, 86–88
  principal characteristics of, 80–81
  as state policy, 81
Sen, Amartya, 142, 268, 276
servile class, emancipation of, 38
Shama, R.S., 184
Shankar, Shiv, 224–225
Shivaji, 65
Siddhartha College, 104
Singh, V.P., 64
slave society, 57
slavery, 164, 202

small holdings
  data on, 170–171
  views on, 170–174
social democracy, 211
social discrimination, 163
  eradication of, 126
social diseases, 78
social endosmosis, 42
social exclusion, 276–277
social exclusion approach, 268
social humanism, 258
social jurisprudence, 227
social movement, 265
social proletariat, 55
Social Scientist, 57
social stratification, 123
social thinker, Ambedkar as, 36
socialism
  analysis of, 176–178
  and communism, 176, 177
  exploitation, abolition of, 179
  scientific, 178
  state, 178
socialist democracy, 58–59
socialistic society, 156
society
  division of labour in, 162
  ideal, 159
  regeneration of, 126
  view on, 41–42, 159, 161
Somavanishya Mitra, 115
Stalin, 58–59
state, in political philosophy, 42
state ownership, 40, 157
state socialism, 43, 142, 144, 146, 157, 164, 237, 257
  and economic processes of human society, 157
  individual liberty and, 157
  with parliamentary democracy, 158
  purpose behind, 157
  for rapid industrialisation, 166
  salient features of, 165–166
  theory of, 40
States and Minorities (B.R. Ambedkar), 86, 131
Studies in Ancient Greek Society (Georgy Thomson), 61
'the Sudra consciousness', 34
Sudras, 245–246
  degradation of, reasons for, 248
  development of, 234–236
  economic benefits to, 236–237
  injuries inflicted on, by religious texts, 247
  theory of origin of, 151–152
Supreme Court, flaw in legal process of, 228–229, 231
synthesis, 54
  Ambedkarism, 59–63
  Marxism, 55–59

technical education, for Scheduled Castes, 110, 112
Telangana, 267
terrorism, 126
Thapar, Romila, 184
'The Modem Manu,' 256
Thomas, P., 184
Thorat, S.K., 143
Toynbee, Arnold, 124
tribal democracy, 59

United Nations Development Programme (UNDP), 259
universe, creation of, 246
university education, 110
  aim and functions of, 100–101
  views on, 97–101
unjust social order, 37

untouchability, 32, 33, 36, 63, 66, 114, 150, 230
caste system and, 152–153, 163
and economic exploitation, 163–164
eradication of, 125
movement against, 115–119
solution to problem of, need of, 125–126
Untouchables
broken men as, 152
education for, 110, 111
social condition of, 150, 163
The Untouchables, 236
Upanishads, philosophy of, 29–30
upper castes, 36
utilitarianism, 30

Varna inter-marriages, 183
varna society, 60, 61
Varna system, 60
creation of, 246
Vasettha-Sutta, 53
Vedas, 245–246
village community, 179
violence in society, 124

watandari system, abolition of, 236
water from tank, drawing of, 117
western philosophy, 28, 30
Who were the Real Enemies of Shivaji's Hindavi Svaraj, Muslims or Brahmins, 65
Who were the Sudras (B.R. Ambedkar), 60, 248
widow remarriage, 185, 186
woman, status of, 233–234. *See also* Hindu Code Bill
caste system and, 185–188, 233
decline in, during Manu Sastra era, 182–183, 185
in early Vedic period, 182, 184
women's movement, 28
Woods Dispatch of 1854, 93
Workers Civil Liberties Suspension Act, 176
World Bank, 130

Yadav, B.N.S., 61

Ziniewicz, Gordon L., 95